Family Therapy Skills and Techniques in Action

Relationships are a resource for healing a range of psychological difficulties. This is the fundamental principle of family therapy, an increasingly influential form of psychotherapy that is building up a strong evidence base in a range of psychological problems across the life cycle. *Family Therapy Skills and Techniques in Action* is both a guide to a variety of family therapy techniques and a review of their history. It provides a thorough explanation of the techniques, explaining their origins and use in contemporary family practice, whilst guiding readers in learning new skills. The authors provide film examples and transcripts of the techniques in action so that readers can develop their skills in a practical way.

The book is divided into sections that describe and demonstrate skills such as:

- Assessing a family;
- Building a therapeutic relationship with multiple family members;
- Enactment;
- Reframing;
- Using circular questions;
- 'Externalising' the problem;
- Using family therapy skills in individual work;
- Understanding and utilising systemic supervision.

Family Therapy Skills and Techniques in Action will be an essential practical manual for a range of family therapy skills which can be used in family work by family practitioners from a variety of backgrounds: counsellors, support workers, social workers, psychologists, generic therapists and nurses.

Mark Rivett is the director of Family and Systemic Psychotherapy training at the University of Exeter and a family therapist in South Wales. He is a past editor of the *Journal of Family Therapy*.

Joanne Buchmüller is a specialist family and systemic psychotherapist in an adolescent inpatient unit in South Wales and a visiting lecturer in Systemic Family Therapy at the Universities of Bristol and Exeter.

Family Therapy Skills and Techniques in Action

Mark Rivett and Joanne Buchmüller
with Karon Oliver

Routledge
Taylor & Francis Group

LONDON AND NEW YORK

First published 2018
by Routledge
2 Park Square, Milton Park, Abingdon, Oxon OX14 4RN

and by Routledge
711 Third Avenue, New York, NY 10017

Routledge is an imprint of the Taylor & Francis Group, an informa business

© 2018 Mark Rivett and Joanne Buchmüller

British Library Cataloguing in Publication Data
A catalogue record for this book is available from the British Library

Library of Congress Cataloging in Publication Data
Names: Rivett, Mark, author. | Buchmüller, Joanne, author. | Oliver, Karon, author.
Title: Family therapy skills and techniques in action / Mark Rivett and Joanne Buchmüller; with Karon Oliver.
Description: Abingdon, Oxon; New York, NY: Routledge, 2018. | Includes bibliographical references and index.
Identifiers: LCCN 2017020756| ISBN 9781138831445
(hardback: alk. paper) | ISBN 9781138831438 (pbk.: alk. paper) |
ISBN 9781315728216 (Master) | ISBN 9781317542254 (Web PDF) |
ISBN 9781317542247 (epub) | ISBN 9781317542230 (mobipocket/kindle)
Subjects: | MESH: Family Therapy–methods Classification:
LCC RC488.53 | NLM WM 430.5.F2 | DDC 616.89/156–dc23
LC record available at https://lccn.loc.gov/2017020756

ISBN: 978-1-138-83144-5 (hbk)
ISBN: 978-1-138-83143-8 (pbk)
ISBN: 978-1-315-72821-6 (ebk)

Typeset in Times New Roman
by Deanta Global Publishing Services, Chennai, India

www.routledgementalhealth.com/9781138831438

To Eddy, a great teacher, mentor and friend, and to Hannah, the best colleague I could ask for. MR

To my supervisors, past and present: thank you for your guidance and inspiration, and to John, Tom and Harry: I am forever grateful for your practical support and enduring patience. We did this! JB

Contents

Acknowledgements

We would like to acknowledge the generosity of many people in the development of this book. First, to Karon Oliver for her efforts, ideas, collaboration and contribution to this work. Second, to all the publishers and family therapists who have given photographs and permission to re-publish their work. We want to give special thanks to Laura Fruggeri, Giuliana Prata and to Matteo Selvini for their contributions in Chapter 7. Third, to the actors and to John Buchmüller and Thomas Bowes without whom this project would never have happened. And finally, to all the families and students who have enriched our practice over the years. This book has been germinated, cultivated and harvested because of you.

Preface

Context makes the mystery of human relationships more understandable. This is one of the primary lessons of family therapy. Therefore, understanding the context of this book may contribute to an ongoing relationship between reader, writer, therapist and family.

Psychological therapies in the UK and Europe are undergoing a renaissance. In the UK, the seeds of past movements that challenged a purely biological understanding of psychological suffering and that championed consumer voices, have matured into pressure to widen access to a growing array of psychological therapies. With this growth comes a need to find new ways of teaching these therapies that takes them out of the exclusive 'institute' and into the everyday world of social workers, counsellors, mental health nurses and support workers. These clinicians want to learn skills and techniques; they need these skills to complement rather than supplant their current skill base; and they require models of learning that accord with contemporary 'YouTube' styles of learning. This book, with its accompanying films, aims to satisfy this new interest specifically in family therapy.

Although this book is a response to a very new demand, it is also a poem to the past. As new generations of clinicians and family workers emerge, the knowledge about where this or that technique comes from fades. It is true that this book is founded on the idea that the application of a technique is as important as its origins. Yet history has its value. Sometimes digging in the past unearths hidden gems. Family therapy, in both its evidence-based and social-constructionist formats, has moved away from this history. We hope therefore that this book will serve as a reminder that demonstrates that many of the techniques that grew from the fertile soil of family therapy are eminently practical and applicable in contemporary family practice.

Chapter 1

Introduction
Setting the scene

Psychotherapy and counselling have always had a private, if not secretive, aura about them. This may be in part because they have some historical connection to the act of religious confession, where only the priest and God know what is divulged. However, in an era of professional accountability, democratic openness and the widening of access to psychological therapies, such secretive patterns seem somewhat outdated. Historically, family therapy has 'bucked' this secretive trend with various pioneers demonstrating their work by conducting 'live' sessions with families. However, although family therapists were once happy to show how they worked by showing film clips of their therapy sessions, rules about confidentiality and respect for the privacy of families have curtailed this activity. Thus, if counsellors, social workers, mental health nurses, clinical psychologists and even beginning family therapists want to learn about 'what family therapy looks in practice', they have to fall back on verbatim transcripts or theory laden papers.

This book is a response to this context. We aim to *show* readers what family therapy looks like so that they can learn how to put it into practice. The written text is only half of the product: Chapters 3 to 10 are presented with a film that demonstrates a skill and method outlined in the text. In our experience, this is what practitioners want. The film and the text are two sides of one coin. Because of this emphasis, the book is a practical resource for all those who work with families.

On a broader level, the book highlights and examines the skills and techniques that family therapy has brought into the world of psychotherapy. What we have chosen to do is to take a defining 'technique' from a number of family therapy schools and demonstrate it both in print (including film transcripts) and in film. We have therefore dissected the range of family thera*pies* and the techniques from those schools into isolated, bite-sized examples. We are well aware that this way of presenting the skills could be seen as reductionist. It seems to presume that 'all' each school provided was the one skill we choose to emphasise in the film. This is obviously not what we want to achieve. We hope the more rounded description in the chapters will go some way towards reducing this risk. We also hope that our zeal for these schools of family therapy transmits itself to the reader, and the music of family therapy guides him or her back to the original ideas and thus see how complex and innovative the approaches are.

Despite these reservations, there are a number of reasons why we feel it is important to return to these skills in the contemporary world. Some of these are to do with the external context within which all the psychotherapies function. Other reasons are connected to internal contexts.

An external reason is that these skills are all around us: adopted by other psychotherapies (and sometimes forgotten by family therapists). But such adoption often misses the context, or the deeper skill implicit in the initial description of the technique. For instance, 'reframing' was originally developed within Strategic Family Therapy (Chapter 6) but has been adapted by many other psychotherapies. In its original version, it included the idea of *gradual* reframing – this has been lost within these other adaptations. We use the film to demonstrate an example of this gradual reframing.

Another external reason for such a pragmatic approach to teaching family therapy skills is that evidence-based practice has introduced an integrative model of family therapy, which we discuss in Chapter 4. This model embeds family therapy techniques in such a way that it can be difficult to extract them, to discern them and to emphasise them. Students learning these models therefore need help in seeing these techniques in action so that they can themselves develop those skills and apply them in practice.

A last reason is that psychological therapies have been undergoing something of a renaissance with various attempts to widen access to them in populations that have traditionally been excluded. Family therapy has been central in this development especially within children's services because of its established evidence base. There is, therefore, a hunger for the transmission of family therapy skills within parenting programmes, cognitive behavioural training and in children and young persons' mental health (e.g. www.minded.org.uk/). These new students want practical skills rather than elite trainings for the select few.

There are a number of internal reasons for a pragmatic approach to teaching and learning family therapy skills. One is to challenge the traditionally complex theories with which family therapists are so enamoured, which may be fascinating but rarely contribute to accessibility for trainees or newcomers. For instance, the more obscure aspects of social constructionism (see Chapters 2 and 7) do not help a family-based support worker faced with an angry parent, where reframing (Chapter 6) or enactment (Chapter 5) might. An equally potent reason for this book's emphasis is the way that family therapists are trained in the contemporary world. Family therapists used to train their students by supervising them in a live context. This involved a number of ways in which the supervisor could guide the therapist *in vivo* during a session. One of the authors (Mark Rivett), for instance, worked with an ear bug in his ear so that he could hear a running commentary on the therapy session from his supervisor who was observing from behind a one-way screen. This traditional way of training has declined because of the influence of collaborative approaches and 'reflective teamwork' (see Chapter 10). Thus, it is rare for family therapists to examine their own skills in this 'dissected' way.

Fact box

In vivo relates to an event, which takes place in real time, in real world conditions. Here it refers to a supervisee being supervised whilst they work with a family.

Despite these valuable reasons for presenting family therapy skills in this way, we also recognise there are some major pitfalls. The first is that often a film comes to represent something that it is not necessarily intended to represent. As therapists, we have had to come to terms with our anxiety about how the films will be received both within the family therapy world and within the broader counselling or psychotherapy world. We need therefore to presage our 'embodied' work with a caveat of humility. These films of family therapy practice are offerings that aim to stimulate discussion, practice and constructive analysis. They are not meant to be perfect examples of 'how to do it' but are rather catalysts for 'how could I have done it better?' The films, in this sense, are a challenge to the reader or watcher. They are not meant to be a finished product despite a process that implies that they are. It is, after all, the great reward of a teacher to have a student who surpasses his or her own competency.

In this context, it is important to explain how the films were made. Over a period of two days, a group of actors met the authors of this volume and created families for us to work with. Each scenario had a basic script to orientate actors and therapists, but very quickly the sessions came to rely on improvised dialogue. Such a way of producing clinical films obviously does not fully re-create clinical practice. For instance, 'in real life' the therapists would not be so persistent, nor would they 'only' work with one technique at a time. Equally, all clinical practice needs to attend robustly to questions about risk, safety and duty of care, which is not demonstrated in these films. However, at times, as the sessions proceeded, a quality of reality did descend in the room, which shows that these are valuable and applicable skills in the everyday reality of clinical work with families.

This book is designed with students and clinicians who have not experienced a 'mentoring' or 'apprenticeship' in family therapy. It is designed for use in social work training, counselling courses and the recent Children and Young People's Increasing Access to Psychological Therapies (CYP-IAPT) courses. However, we are aware that students who have already completed some family therapy training will notice a gap. There is little representation from the social constructionist or dialogical forms of family therapy. Although the influence of these schools of family therapy is strong in Chapter 7 and Chapter 10, we have not given them a stand-alone chapter. There are at least two reasons for this. One is that these schools of family therapy (which are particularly popular in Europe and the UK) have purposefully *not* emphasised 'techniques' because such an approach is contradictory to their philosophy. This makes them very difficult to demonstrate in a short 15 to 20 minute film. The second reason is that the evidence-based integrative models rarely explicitly refer to these more philosophical, amorphous and hard to encapsulate approaches. Because this book has a pragmatic focus – we want to help readers develop their clinical skills – we have chosen not to elaborate these ideas. We do, however, hope that this book will stimulate enthusiasm that will encourage readers to explore the world of family therapy, and lead them to other approaches that are not foregrounded in this book.

Orientation to the book and films

As we have said, the text of the book needs to be read while accessing the accompanying film. Transcripts of the films are included chapter by chapter, but we would recommend watching the session, if possible. Each film can be accessed using the eResources tab on the webpage for the book, which can be found on the Routledge website: www.routledge.com/9781138831438. Like real-life clinical practice, the book takes the reader through a series of encounters with two different families. Details of the families are provided at the end of this chapter. Chapter 2 establishes the underlying metaphor for family therapy. Although this is a short chapter, it is probably the most important one in the book. Chapter 3 gives a thorough description of how assessment works in family therapy. The film that accompanies it provides one example of how the therapist (Mark Rivett) expanded the assessment with the family. Chapter 4 explores integrative family therapy practice with an emphasis on the therapeutic alliance in family therapy and on how to engage family members in a joint endeavour to improve family life. The film that accompanies it shows the therapist (Mark Rivett) 'talking about talking' with the family. This chapter is crucial because, paradoxically, the rest of the book unpicks the contributions of specific models to help the reader learn them. The paradox is that Chapter 4 more closely represents contemporary family therapy practice rather than the more numerous other chapters. Chapters 5, 6, 7 and 8 concentrate on particular schools of family therapy and their films show (usually) one of the techniques that have been bequeathed by that school. Chapter 9 takes the techniques already discussed into work with individuals. The last chapter (Chapter 10) expands on how a systemic understanding can be used in supervision and reflective clinical practice. Each chapter has a quality of being independent from the others; although in a truly systemic way, 'the whole is greater than the sum of its parts'. Readers can choose to develop their skills chapter by chapter. Each chapter begins with a summary of the key points of theory to help the reader locate subject areas of interest. Throughout the chapters you will find 'Fact' boxes and 'Task' boxes. Fact boxes explain the context of key parts of the text – our aim is that they will conveniently inform the reader as they progress through each chapter. Task boxes direct the reader to expand their learning experientially and hopefully provide a personal reference for the written theory. The text also directs the reader to the film accompanying the chapter. If readers chose not to access the films, each chapter has a verbatim script of the film to guide them. You will also notice, as you progress through this book, that we use metaphors to represent an image of the theory being presented. This is done in the spirit of storytelling, with the hope of igniting your imagination. We also use tables to explain ideas in an as accessible way as possible. This does at times break up the text. However, we believe if the reader takes time to analyse the tables, they will be rewarded.

Below, we introduce the two families who form the backbone of this book. As we have said, you will watch actors in the role of family members. We wish to emphasise that although the general features of these families are similar to families which family therapists may work with, they are not based on any particular family. They are 'representative' rather than 'specific'.

Orientation to the families

Family one (Chapters 3–7) (Therapist: Mark Rivett)

Joel: an example of working with adolescent depression within the context of a blended family (Figure 1.1 illustrates Joel's genogram).

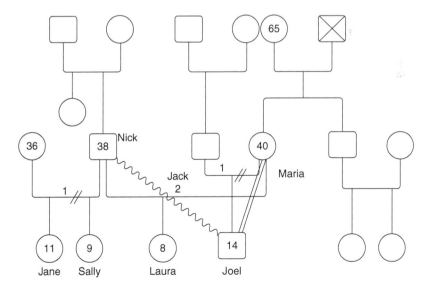

Figure 1.1 Joel's genogram.

Referral information

- Joel is the identified patient. He is a 14-year-old boy who lives with his mum (Maria), stepdad (Nick) and half-sister (Laura), who is five years old.
- He has been referred to the family therapist by his general practitioner (GP) who met Joel when Maria took Joel to the surgery because she was worried about him being 'depressed'.
- The GP noted in the referral letter that Joel's biological father has no contact with him and Maria was from Eastern Europe. The GP also stated that Maria's English was good and there was no need for an interpreter to conduct the session.

Intake information

It is stated that Joel is isolated and unhappy most of the time and at home this can erupt into conflict between him and Nick. Nick is a taxi driver and Maria a teaching assistant in a local primary school. Joel goes to the local comprehensive school and, although he is seen as academic, he doesn't seem to have settled at the school in the last two years.

Fact box

Usually the family therapist will gather further information in a telephone call before meeting the family. This call will ensure that levels of risk are attended to as well as finding out a bit more about the family and context of the referral.

Further family information

Maria came to the UK from Slovakia with her first husband Jack (Joel's father) when she was 22. She is now 40. Jack was a long-distance lorry driver who was rarely emotionally available to either Maria or Joel. Maria and Jack's relationship ended when she discovered he had been having an affair while away working. Jack has had no contact since the end of the marriage ten years ago. Joel was four years old when he last saw Jack. Maria met Nick when he drove her and Joel to nursery in his taxi. Nick and Maria have been married for six years.

Nick has had a previous marriage and has two daughters from that relationship. The daughters occasionally stay with this family. Nick himself had a 'troubled childhood' and was a 'looked after' child, spending time in local authority care.

Maria is the eldest daughter in her family. She has a brother in Slovakia who is a head teacher. Her father, who died when Maria was 18 years old, was also a head teacher. Her mother is still alive and is a retired teacher in Slovakia. Maria returns to Slovakia every year. Joel objects to going and Nick often stays in the UK during these visits too.

Family two (Chapters 8 and 9) (Therapist: Jo Buchmuller)

Jess: an example of working with a young person with a history of an eating disorder within a context of historical parental substance misuse (Figure 1.2 illustrates Jess's genogram).

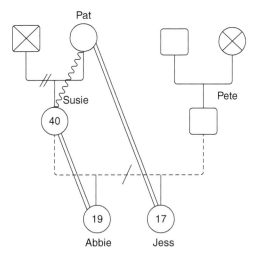

Figure 1.2 Jess's genogram.

Referral information

- Jess is the identified patient. She is 17 years old and lives with her mother Susie (aged 40). She has an older sister Abbie, aged 19. Her maternal grandmother (Pat) lives nearby and is able to join some of the sessions.
- Jess has been re-referred to the family therapist by her GP after her mother took her to the surgery as she was struggling with issues around food and eating. Jess has a history of anorexia but does not meet the criteria for a diagnosis of anorexia at this present time. The GP makes the referral as a preventative step given her previous history.

Intake information

Jess intermittently attends college and is studying for her exams. Susie is struggling in her attempts to support Jess to eat normally, which is putting a strain on their relationship. Susie is very worried about Jess as Jess received inpatient treatment for an episode of anorexia when she was younger. The grandmother, Pat, is supportive of Jess. In the past, Jess attended a drama club but has recently withdrawn from her social activities. Her older sister, Abbie, is away studying at university and will not be able to join the family therapy sessions. Neither Jess nor Abbie has contact with their father, Pete, who left the family after Jess was born.

Further family information

Susie has a history of low mood, depression and reliance upon alcohol.

The relationship between Susie and Pete ended when Jess was a baby and although she has had a few partners since then, she has not had another long-term relationship. Neither Jess nor Abbie have contact with their paternal side of the family. Abbie is close to her mother and is supportive of her. Susie will sometimes use Abbie as a confidante and Jess feels that Abbie and Susie 'gang-up' against her. Pat blames Susie for neglecting her granddaughters' care in the past because of her alcohol dependency. Pat cannot acknowledge that Susie's depression impacted on her ability to parent and that she drank in the past to self-medicate (e.g. cope). Susie has now had a significant period of time not drinking alcohol and is engaged with support services. Pat has a history of depression but struggles to acknowledge a link between her own depression and Susie's experience of being depressed. Susie's father left the family when she was a baby and her parents subsequently divorced. Pat discovered that he had died shortly afterwards.

Chapter 2

Family therapy

Listening to the orchestra

Key points

- Family therapy is a relational therapy that is concerned with the space between people, not what happens inside people.
- The fundamental concept that underpins most family therapies is that of systems theory.
- Family therapy has a rich heritage of ideas, different schools and a wide range of techniques.
- Family therapy has a history that dates back over 50 years.
- The evidence base for the family therapies is growing consistently.

Introduction

When we listen to music, we might adopt one of two approaches. We might focus on the individual instruments: to acutely hear how the violin evokes a feeling, or how the guitar riff ripples through our minds. Or we might focus on the whole sound: putting off appreciation of the individual musicians and immerse ourselves in the experience of how the band or orchestra works together to produce a collective wave of sound that washes over us, leaving us, drenched with a new feeling.

We can see the orchestra, as a metaphor for what family therapy is all about. Over the course of family therapy's history, many metaphors have been used to encapsulate the heart of its message. Metaphors from nature (Rivett and Street, 2009), metaphors from religion (Bateson and Bateson, 1987), metaphors from science (O'Connor and McDermott, 1997) and metaphors from drama (Asen, 1995), all have been drafted in to illuminate its core idea. All have something in common: they are pointing not to individuals but to the *space between* those individuals. These metaphors emphasise that the space between people is not empty. Just like in cosmology the space between stars is not empty but full of hidden, unseen potential (in this case, dark matter). Yet, this potential is hard to grasp. The fact that family therapists have had to use so many metaphors attests to this. At times,

Task 1: Think of yourself as part of an orchestra

Take some time bringing to mind all the relationships you have with the many people in your life. Try to 'categorise them': some close, some distant, some historical or current. Which ones 'define' who you are? Are you a different person in different relationships? Now think about how or if these relationships constrain you. Family therapists sometimes say, "It is the people we love who keep us the same". Does that apply to you?

Figure 2.1 Gregory Bateson.
Credit: Bateson Idea Group.

it feels as if they are pointing at nothing. This might be partly because what is being pointed at is invisible. But as Gregory Bateson (1972: 434), seen by many as the founding theorist of family therapy, said, it might also be because human beings seem "blinded to the systemic nature" of themselves. In other words, the mind has to make an *effort* to notice those spaces.

Family therapy requires a discipline of mind that ensures that a person is seen not as a solid, discrete structure but as a web of connections, a conduit for energy that passes from person to person. A person is a *process of relationships*. From this perspective, all our lives are infused with patterns, with relational memories that influence the present and with cultures that offer us interpersonal stories about those relationships.

This understanding about human life has emerged throughout the millennia of human history. When it emerged within psychotherapy in the 1950s, it presented a radical and challenging view that contradicted the accepted orthodoxy of the time. Rather than looking for 'a damaged childhood' or 'neurotic thoughts' and working only with individuals, family therapy looked for relational patterns that maintained (or caused) psychological difficulties. Family therapists insisted on working with family groups. They eschewed much of the Freudian or Rogerian psychological theory. They adopted behavioural and practical ways of changing the patterns of connection within families, and they insisted that they could heal where other psychotherapies had failed – with entrenched psychosis and eating disorder diagnoses (for a fuller history, see Bitter, 2009; Dallos and Draper, 2010; Doherty and McDaniel, 2010; Goldenberg and Goldenberg, 1996; Lawson and Prevatt, 1999; Nichols and Schwartz, 2012).

Systems theory

We have noted that holding a 'relational mind' is difficult. Most of the time, human beings think in terms of themselves and the world around them rather than their relationships within the world. In terms of an orchestra, mostly we think about how we are performing and rarely think about the collective or about how our performance connects to the people next to us. Family therapists sometimes describe this way of living our lives as being *linear* rather than *circular*. Again, metaphors can help us: we behave as if there is a 'solid' snooker ball (us) that bounces around a table hitting into other balls (others/the world). So, there is a linear relationship between one ball hitting another and the other ball moving. What circular thinking would tell us is that the balls are not solid but fluid and each ball merges into the other balls as they move around the table in a pattern sometimes determined by the way they merge. They therefore have a far less predictable pattern of interaction and this is called a 'circular pattern'.

Fact box

Linear: a sequential progression of acts, which advance step by step.
Circular: moving to join a circle.

This description is essentially what systems theory is all about. Systems theory is a body of ideas about how groups of individual elements interact. Family therapists use systems theory to help them remember to concentrate on patterns and relationships. When they first 'discovered' systems theory, family therapists took it very seriously (see Watzlawick *et al.*, 1967) and at times seem to have overemphasised it as a scientific model for therapy. In this book, we want to see systems theory (and its cousin cybernetic theory) as essentially a metaphor that helps us to stay focused on relationship, interaction and process rather than a 'true scientific description of reality'.

Fact box

Context is the description of the setting in which something happens which helps to explain its meaning.

Systems theory (see Dallos and Draper, 2010, for a fuller description) maintains that both mechanical and living organisms function as an amalgam of relationships. It argues that because of these relationships 'the whole is greater than the sum of its parts'. Becvar and Becvar (1999: 6) comment that:

> The systems perspective would have us see each member of a family in relation to other family members, as each affects and is affected by the other persons.

There are a number of 'ancillary' consequences of thinking from a systemic perspective. One is that all behaviour can only be understood within the context of the human system within which it is embedded. To take an example, traditional psychotherapy might understand anger towards a parent as 'caused' by an unresolved emotional experience from the past. But systemically, we would want to see what interactions were happening before the expression of anger, after the anger and also the interpersonal meaning of expressing anger towards parents within this family (and even the wider culture). This aspect of systemic thinking is why family therapists talk about *context* a lot.

The second consequence of systems theory are a number of ideas about *how systems work*. We outline some of these in Table 2.1.

(For a fuller description of systems theory and its relevance for family therapy, see Smith-Acuña, 2011.)

Task 2

Think of your family, current or past, and map out how the above aspects worked within the family. What was communication like? Who made the decisions? What kinds of rules were there?

Systems theory and cybernetics (systems theory applied to machines) clearly sounds very mechanical. It was, therefore, not long before a number of family therapists questioned how it was being applied to family systems (or human systems in general) (Rivett and Street, 2003). What therefore emerged in the 1970s was something called 'second order cybernetics' (what went before was called 'first order cybernetics'). Here, theorists noted that the observer of any system

Table 2.1 How do systems work?

'Quality' of systems	Explanation of the term	Application to families
Systems have boundaries that control the influence between them and other systems around them.	These boundaries might be firm (rigid) or loose (flexible). There may also be internal boundaries between parts of the system.	Some families are very 'private' and find coming to therapy very difficult. Others seem to be amorphous and hard to pin down in terms of 'who is in the family?'
Communication is significant: within and between systems.	Once we start to see relationships between people, we notice the importance of communication. Communication or 'information exchange' is often what provides the essence of a relationship.	Some families communicate a lot. Others don't. Some talk about some things but not others.
Feedback.	This is a form of communication but specifically is the response within a system or between systems when 'new' information or when communication occurs. Feedback can be positive or negative.	If a family member does something different, others will provide feedback on this but perhaps not consciously. The feedback might stop the new behaviour or promote it.
'Homeostasis' or staying the same.	Systems theory suggests that most systems try to maintain an equilibrium and stability. Few systems are in constant enduring change (although change also occurs and is called 'morphogenesis').	Families will strive to 'keep things going' even if a family member is seriously impaired by other events.
Within a system any behaviour is a form of communication that evokes feedback.	The principle is that it is impossible not to communicate within a system. Moreover, different parts of the system will interpret that communication differently.	Let us say that a father comes home from work in a mood. His partner might interpret this as a sign that home life is not satisfactory. A child might interpret it as rejection.
'Causality' in systems is circular and mutually influential: there are recursive feedback loops.	This refers to linear and circular ideas about interaction.	For example, a child feels depressed and his mother blames herself. The child then feels responsible for mum's upset and gets more depressed. Here it is impossible to differentiate start from finish. We might arbitrarily punctuate a sequence. But this doesn't respect the circular pattern.

Table 2.1 Continued

'Quality' of systems	Explanation of the term	Application to families
Systems have history and shared meanings.	Systems rarely 'just emerge' so their shared experience matters.	A family might define itself in a similar way throughout the generations. The same cultural ideas might affect how family members think.
The whole of life is composed of systems that interlock with each other.	Ecology and understanding about human culture shows us that one system nestles into another. Systems 'go all the way up and down'!	A family is not an isolated system. It connects to the wider society and community. How it functions is influenced by social processes (also systems) like gender, race, politics, etc.
Systems have structures and internal rules of behaviour.	Within all systems there are hierarchies and cross related interactions.	Families are hugely diverse across the human species. Yet all families have patterns that establish a structure. Parents make most decisions for younger children; sibling groups have alliances or conflicts, etc.

was not outside that system but seeing what they were 'pre-determined' to see according to their own experiences or systems. To take an example: a therapist sees a family in which the child openly disagrees with her parents. If the therapist comes from a family, or a culture, that places importance on the authority of parents, she will see this family as 'dysfunctional'. But if the therapist places a value on young people being heard and being raised to have an independent voice, then this arrangement is far from dysfunctional. Again, if we take this family and place them in a different context, such as a war zone, then the ability of the young person to be part of family decision-making, to actively help in survival, would indicate a perfectly functional family. This more nuanced understanding of systems theory led to some new words being introduced to family therapy language. The idea that there are many different perspectives that can be taken on any family came to be called 'multi-perspectives' or the 'multi-verse' of realities. Second order cybernetics also encouraged family therapists to be humble about what they thought they knew. With this humility came an appreciation that many family systems are doing well within the confines of what they think they need to do. It brought a respect for human systems that at times questioned the 'invasive' assumption that therapy can make improvements (Keeney, 1983).

Task 3

Think about your family again. Come up with different ways of thinking about it. How would neighbours have described it? How did different family members describe it?

It is fair to say that family therapists have continued to debate the value of systems theory in their ways of thinking (Rivett and Street, 2003). During the 1980s when Postmodern ideas came into the field, a number of clinicians adopted less mechanical ideas. It was argued that human systems were not 'actual' systems but 'linguistic systems' that comprised a series of meanings that had built up over generations (Anderson and Goolishian, 1988). In this version of family therapy, the therapist used conversation, rather than a theory about how families worked, to help families change. Therapy was about changing 'meanings', not changing systems.

The criticisms of systems theory have sometimes become reasons for some family therapists to abandon systems theory altogether. A number of the people, who we will talk about in this book, have largely 'forgotten' systems theory because of these criticisms. So White and Epston (1990) (see Chapter 8) adopted a narrative rather than systems model for their approach. However, we would want to return, at this point, to the opening metaphor for family therapy. Systems theory is a way of thinking. It is a way of learning how to think in a certain way: it is not necessarily 'true' in the scientific way of truth. Bateson is renowned for saying that "*the map is not the territory*", by which he meant how we describe something is always an approximation and rarely totally sums up the essence of what we are describing. From our perspective, systems theory is a map. It is a way of learning to listen to the orchestra. It isn't the orchestra itself.

An orientation to the world of family therapy

In this section of the chapter, we want to offer a brief orientation to the models and sources of the various schools of family therapy that will be developed in the following chapters. Let's say that if family therapy itself is the orchestra that we are listening to, it is time to hear a little from the instrumental solos! We are not providing a comprehensive explanation of the history of family therapy here and we refer readers to other works for this (Bitter, 2009; Dallos and Draper, 2010; Doherty and McDaniel, 2010; Goldenberg and Goldenberg, 1996; Hoffman, 2002; Lawson and Prevatt, 1999; and Nichols and Schwartz, 2012). Nor can we mention all the significant people who have contributed and continue to contribute to this inventive branch of psychotherapy. We have chosen to present this orientation through a version of a 'family therapy family tree' (see Figure 2.1). We recognise that this is only one version of this type of tree and other commentators have produced their own versions (Bitter, 2009).

A Family Therapy Family Tree

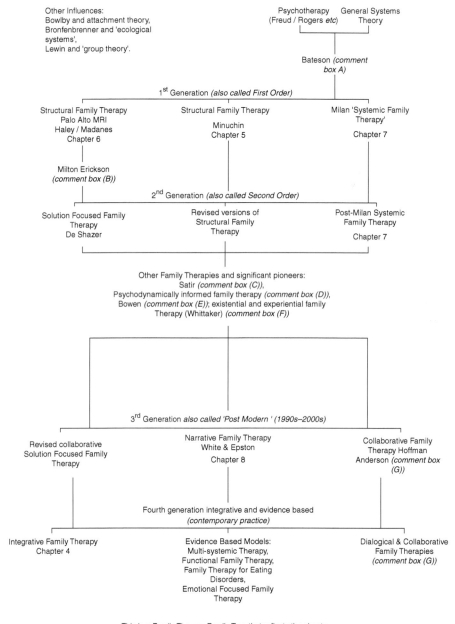

Other Influences:
Bowlby and attachment theory,
Bronfenbrenner and 'ecological
systems',
Lewin and 'group theory'.

Psychotherapy   General Systems
(Freud / Rogers *etc*)   Theory

Bateson *(comment box A)*

1st Generation *(also called First Order)*

Structural Family Therapy
Palo Alto MRI
Haley / Madanes
Chapter 6

Structural Family Therapy

Minuchin
Chapter 5

Milan 'Systemic Family
Therapy'

Chapter 7

Milton Erickson
(comment box (B))

2nd Generation *(also called Second Order)*

Solution Focused Family
Therapy
De Shazer

Revised versions of
Structural Family
Therapy

Post-Milan Systemic
Family Therapy

Chapter 7

Other Family Therapies and significant pioneers:
Satir *(comment box (C))*,
Psychodynamically informed family therapy *(comment box (D))*,
Bowen *(comment box (E))*; existential and experiential family
Therapy (Whittaker) *(comment box (F))*

3rd Generation *also called 'Post Modern '* (1990s–2000s)

Revised collaborative
Solution Focused Family
Therapy

Narrative Family Therapy
White & Epston

Chapter 8

Collaborative Family
Therapy Hoffman
Anderson *(comment box
(G))*

Fourth generation integrative and evidence based
(contemporary practice)

Integrative Family Therapy
Chapter 4

Evidence Based Models:
Multi-systemic Therapy,
Functional Family Therapy,
Family Therapy for Eating
Disorders,
Emotional Focused Family
Therapy

Dialogical & Collaborative
Family Therapies
(comment box (G))

This is a Family Therapy Family Tree that reflects the chapters
and purpose of this book. It is not intended to be comprehensive.
See *Bitter, 2011,* for a more thorough version. We apologise to all
the innovators and clinicians whose contributions we have not
included

Figure 2.2 A family therapy family tree.

Fact boxes: 'A family therapy family tree'

Fact box A

Gregory Bateson (1904–1980) is seen as 'the father' of family therapy. He became an anthropologist and married Margaret Mead, another famous anthropologist. The influence of this branch of the human sciences is evident in the 'observer' role that family therapists take in relation to families. Bateson turned his attention to family life as a result of central government funding and sought to apply his anthropological perspective to mental health. He founded the Bateson Project that later became the Mental Research Institute in Palo Alto, California. Bateson spent his whole life explaining a systemic approach. His profound insights into communication, play, family patterns, social norms and animal behaviour provide endless material for the enquiring mind. He has been the wellspring for much of the ideas of family therapy, particularly the strategic (Chapter 6) and Milan (Chapter 7) schools. His daughter has produced an excellent film about his life which is recommended (Nora Bateson: An ecology of mind, 2011). His book *Steps to an ecology of mind* (1972) is also invaluable.

Fact box B

Milton Erickson (1901–1980) had a huge influence on a number of family therapists as well as many other branches of psychotherapy (including Neuro-Linguistic Programming (NLP)). He was a psychiatrist in Phoenix, Arizona, and developed the use of hypnotic suggestion as a tool for helping 'patients' change. He also used paradoxical tasks that were designed to disrupt the behaviour that created or maintained symptoms. His unusual approach appealed to many therapists (Geary and Zeig, 2001; O'Hanlon, 1987) but probably Haley (1973) did more to promote Erickson's ideas within therapy generally. There are many books about him including *An American healer* (Erickson and Keeney, 2006). There are also a number of film resources. We would recommend *Wizard of the desert* (director – Alexander Vesely, Noetic Films, 2014).

Fact box C

Virginia Satir (1916–1988) also had connections with Bateson and Haley but was more influenced by 'humanistic' models prevalent in USA during the 1960s. She developed an approach to family therapy that emphasised emotional connection (Satir, 1967). Her works became very popular (Satir,

1972) because they accorded with the counter-cultural expressions of the time. Although her approach is still very influential in USA, it did not have as great an effect on UK or European family therapy practice.

Fact box D

In the UK, Robin Skynner (1922–2000) is the most significant psychodynamically orientated family therapist. He brought group therapy, as well as analytical ideas, into his family therapy practice. He is most famous for his collaboration with John Cleese, a famous British comedian in *Families and How to Survive Them* (1983). Skynner set up a training institute in London, which is still training family therapists.

In the USA, Nathan Ackerman (1908–1971) set up an institute in New York, which is still both a training and therapy centre. He was one of the early psychodynamic therapists to experiment in the 1940s with 'seeing the whole family'. He developed analytical ideas to explain family dynamics with particular reference to the process that caused a family member to be 'scapegoated' (1958; 1966).

Fact box E

Murray Bowen (1913–1990) was another hugely influential family therapist in the USA (Bregman and White, 2011). He was one of the first researchers to study family interactions within a residential setting (Weinstein, 2013) seeking to discover 'rules' that explained what happened in families. In Europe, he is remembered for carrying out a 'living experiment' on his own family, which was designed to allow him to 'differentiate from his family of origin'. His training method for family therapists continued this model and is still popular. His therapeutic methods were equally directive and inventive while drawing on a mixture of systemic and psychodynamic ideas. It was through Bowen that family trees or genograms and family life cycle ideas came into family therapy. Betty Carter (Carter and McGoldrick, 2005) promulgated these methods from her original training in Bowen family therapy.

Fact box F

Carl Whitaker (1912–1995) is often called a 'humanistic-existentialist' family therapist. In many ways, he eschewed any set theory and aimed to make the therapy session an interactive event where families tried out new ways of being, with him coaching them into taking risks. He is reputed to have lain down on the floor during one session and when asked why, he replied, "from this perspective I can see all the c*** you are throwing at each other". His sessions were forms of 'play': in many ways, very similar to Erickson! In *The family crucible* (1978), he and his co-author, Napier, presented the whole therapy with a family that is well worth reading.

Fact box G

The range of family therapies influenced by Postmodern and social constructionist ideas is large. This group of family therapies includes therapies that are called 'collaborative' (Anderson and Gehart, 2007; McCarthy and Simon, 2016), 'dialogical' and 'humanistic'. The various models included in this group are coordinated management of meaning (CMM), appreciative enquiry and therapy informed by Positioning Theory. These family therapies sometimes take a stand against evidence-based practice, arguing that lived experience is more important than statistics. They have, therefore, adopted qualitative and collaborative research methods.

The 'what is' set of questions

As yet, of course, we have not answered the obvious questions that are likely to be asked when it comes to family therapy. The first such question being 'what is a family?' (as in the phrase *family* therapy). The answer is, as can be expected, complex. Initially, family therapists were interested in working with the multi-generational group of people who lived together in family groups. One of the early UK writers stated that "family therapy [is] the psychotherapeutic treatment of a natural social system, the family" (Walrond-Skinner, 1976: 1). Of course, since the 1950s, when family therapy first evolved, the range of families has extended, the assumption that the family is 'natural' has come under fire and the 'fit' of a 1950s' family therapy designed for a 'nuclear family' has shrunk. Moreover, family therapy has been used with families that don't live together (e.g. grandparents or separated parents) and with families that have fostered or adopted children where there is no generational connection between family members. Accordingly, family therapy has continued to evolve. Family therapy now encompasses work with whomever people determine is their 'family' and beyond: friendship networks, community members and work teams included. Equally, family therapy has grown to recognise how the 'nuclear family' prevented women from reaching their potential and that the early forms of systems theory sometimes maintained racism, ageism and the cultural hegemony of a white western patriarchy (Carter and McGoldrick, 1999; McGoldrick and Hardy, 2008: McGoldrick *et al.*, 2005;

Rivett and Street, 2003). More recently, family therapy has taken into account work with gay and lesbian families, and the growing range of transgendered families (Bigner and Wetchler, 2012).

The second obvious question is 'what is family therapy?' We have already established that we should really talk about family therapy in the plural (Rivett and Street, 2003). There are indeed many family therap*ies*. In this book, we assume that family therapy is a relational therapy that is undertaken with people who either live together or have some emotional connection (past or present). But there is a further element to family therapy (or most of the family therapies) that is significant. On the whole, family therapists have thought that working with the family group *together* offers the best chance of helping change interactive and relational patterns. This is often called *conjoint* therapy, i.e. 'together'. This assumption comes from systems theory itself. According to this theory, the therapist needs to 'see' the system behave as it does normally and then (with agreement) helps 'nudge' or in Bateson's words "perturb" the system, so that it begins to change. Within this description is another implication: family therapy is designed to change things within the family system, at least as a start, within the therapeutic hour. To return to the metaphor of the orchestra, the family therapy session is expected to help the family find a new way of playing together and practise the new tune(s) during the session.

Another important question is to ask how we know if the music we are hearing is family therapy. There are a bewildering number of phrases being used in psychotherapy that refer to 'family'. Commonly, professionals will hear phrases like 'family work', 'family intervention' and 'family based treatment', among many others. Not all of these models are based on systems theory and not all share the idea that it is the *relational space* that is the focus for change. For instance, 'family counselling' may hold to a Rogerian philosophy that believes that helping families verbalise their problems is both necessary and sufficient for change to occur (O'Leary, 1999). Others may assume that doing therapy with one person *in the presence of the family* is what achieves change. Although these are not family therapies, we want to take a pragmatic and inclusive response to this bewilderment. We would regard techniques that have been developed within family therapy to be useful for any form of intervention that works with families. In other words, skilful use of reframing (Chapter 6), enactment (Chapter 5) or circular questions (Chapter 7) can be used widely without necessarily being used within a family therapy session.

References

Ackerman, N. (1958). *The psychodynamics of family life.* New York: Basic Books.
Ackerman, N. (1966). *Treating the troubled family.* New York: Basic Books.
Anderson, H. and Gehart, D. (2007). *Collaborative therapy.* New York: Routledge.
Anderson, H. and Goolishian, H. (1988). Human systems as linguistic systems. *Family Process*, 27, 371–393.

Asen, E. (1995). *Family therapy for everyone.* London: BBC Books.

Bateson, G. (1972). *Steps to an ecology of mind.* New York: Ballantine.

Bateson, G. and Bateson, M. C. (1987). *Angels fear.* Toronto: Bantam Books.

Becvar, D. and Becvar, R. (1999). *Systems theory and family therapy.* Lanham, MD: University Press of America.

Bigner, J. and Wetchler, J. (2012). *Handbook of LGBT-affirmative couple and family therapy.* New York: Routledge.

Bitter, J. (2009). *Theory and practice of family therapy and counseling.* Belmont, CA: Brooks/Cole.

Bregman, O. C. and White, C. (2011). *Bringing systems thinking to life.* New York: Routledge.

Carter, B. and McGoldrick, M. (1999) (Eds). *The expanded family life cycle.* Boston, MA: Allyn & Bacon.

Carter, B. and McGoldrick, M. (2005). *The expanded family life cycle.* Boston, MA: Allyn & Bacon.

Dallos, R. and Draper, R. (2010). *An introduction to family therapy.* Maidenhead: Open University Press.

Doherty, W. and McDaniel, S. (2010). *Family therapy.* Washington DC: APA.

Erickson, B. A. and Keeney, B. (2006) (Eds). *Milton H. Erickson: An American healer.* Sedona, AZ: Ringing Rocks Press.

Geary, B. and Zeig, J. (2001). *The handbook of Ericksonian psychotherapy.* Phoenix, AZ: The Milton H. Erickson Foundation Press.

Goldenberg, I. and Goldenberg, H. (1996). *Family therapy: An overview.* Pacific Grove, CA: Brooks/Cole.

Haley, J. (1973). *Uncommon therapy.* New York: Norton.

Hoffman, L. (2002). *Family therapy: an intimate history.* New York: Norton & Co.

Keeney, B. (1983). *Aesthetics of change.* New York: Guilford Press.

Lawson, D. and Prevatt, F. (1999). *Casebook in family therapy.* Belmont CA: Brooks/Cole.

McCarthy, I. and Simon, G. (2016). *Systemic therapy as transformative practice.* Farnhill: Everything is connected Press.

McGoldrick, M., Giordano, J. and Garcia-Preto, N. (2005). *Ethnicity and family therapy.* New York: Guilford.

McGoldrick, M. and Hardy, K. (2008). *Re-visioning family therapy.* New York: Guilford.

Napier, A. and Whitaker, C. (1978). *The family crucible.* New York: Harper and Row.

Nichols, R. and Schwartz, R. (2012). *Family therapy: concepts and methods.* Harlow: Pearson Education.

O'Connor, J. and McDermott, I. (1997). *The art of systems thinking.* London: Thorsons.

O'Hanlon, W. (1987). *Taproots.* New York: Norton & Co.

O'Leary, C. (1999). *Counselling couples and families.* London: Sage.

Rivett, M. and Street, E. (2003). *Family therapy in focus.* London: Sage.

Rivett, M. and Street, E. (2009). *Family therapy: 100 key points and techniques.* London: Routledge.

Satir, V. (1967). *Conjoint family therapy.* Palo Alto, CA: Science and Behavior Books.

Satir, V. (1972). *Peoplemaking.* Palo Alto, CA: Science and Behavior Books.

Smith-Acuña, S. (2011). *Systems theory in action.* New Jersey: Wiley & Sons.

Skynner, R. and Cleese, J. (1983). *Families and how to survive them.* London: Methuen.

Walrond-Skinner, S. (1976). *Family therapy: the treatment of natural systems.* London: Routledge & Kegan Paul.

Watzlawick, P., Beavin Bavelas, J. and Jackson, D. (1967). *Pragmatics of human communication.* New York: Norton & Co.

Weinstein, D. (2013). *The pathological family.* Ithaca, NY: Cornell University Press.

White, M. and Epston, D. (1990). *Narrative means to therapeutic ends.* New York: Norton & Co.

Chapter 3

Assessment

Finding out what we need to know

Key points

- An assessment is a description of the current position of a family and should encompass all family members: their strengths and challenges. This description informs the formulation.
- Assessing family relationships is not straightforward and there is no definitive way to describe them: this reflects the fact that there is no definitive way of conducting an assessment.
- During the assessment, it is helpful to keep in mind these three questions:
  1. What do we need to know about the family?
  2. How has the family influenced the problem?
  3. How has the problem influenced the family?
- There are helpful tools for assessing families, e.g. genogram, family life cycle. Additionally, there are a number of research-based assessment models.
- Assessment involves exploration of how family patterns have contributed to what is currently happening in the family (contributing factors) and exploration of what is happening presently that may maintain the difficulties (maintaining factors).

Introduction

In Buddhist philosophy, 'Indra's Net' is the fabric, made up of gossamer thin strands, that binds the universe together. The Net is infinite, imperceptible, full of unexpected undulations and essentially indefinable. This metaphor perfectly fits the very idea of 'assessment' in family therapy. Families are so complex in their permutations and so individual in their understandings that placing a structure on assessing them seems to be both improper and impractical. Moreover, choosing to describe (which is essentially what assessment is) one part of the Net in isolation could mean other sections are overlooked leaving the therapist or assessor blind to the remaining sections and therefore the Net as a whole.

This is a poetic way of explaining that when it comes to assessment, family therapy has a number of challenges. The first challenge is that, as we have explained in Chapter 2, family therapy is interested in relationships. Assessing these is never straightforward because different family members may 'see' their relationships differently. So, the family therapist has to take into account a bewildering variety of descriptions and understandings. The second challenge is that family therapists have traditionally been hesitant in asserting that their descriptions are 'better' than those used by their clients. We will explain this notion further in Chapter 7 (The Milan and Post-Milan Approach), but remember that systemic thinking implies humility about how we interpret what we see in relationships (the Milan team called this *curiosity*). A third challenge, also implied in the Indra's Net metaphor, is that because a family interview might span from past family patterns to future family patterns, from parental, to sibling, to couple interactions, from gendered understandings to age understandings, from behaviours to thoughts and feelings – in fact an infinite variety of topics – it is almost impossible to encapsulate this within a neat assessment framework.

Fact box

Hypotheses are ideas, which can be tested through questioning and experimentation.

It is, therefore, not surprising that many family therapists have chosen not to talk about how they assess and instead talk about a narrow framework within which they analyse their interventions. As an example, in the coming chapters we will explore *structural family therapy* and *strategic approaches to family therapy*. Both set out a narrow area in which they assess: in the case of structural family therapy it is the structure of the family; in the case of Strategic Family Therapy, the way problems are maintained by forms of communication. Because this book presents a largely integrative approach to family therapy, we have chosen to provide an 'Indra's Net' model of assessment, e.g. present a range of aspects of family life all of which may prove helpful to the therapist in working with the family. This integrative model has a number of fundamental elements, which are significant. Let's explain this using the metaphor of the chapter. First, at each intersection of the weave of the Net, the myth suggests that there are jewels. In a family assessment, the therapist may come across the 'legitimate' jewel, which provides an explanation and a way of intervening that is significant. Second, the act of assessment involves the capacity to *punctuate*, i.e. mark out a particular section within the larger, complex warp and weft of the fabric even though this risks missing other sections. Third, the 'outcome' of the assessment is to construct a description that guides both the therapist and the family in a direction that leads to a hopeful future less constrained by problems. The Milan team called these descriptions *hypotheses* and warned that the therapist needed to remember that they were temporary and approximations of the 'truth'. In this chapter, we are going to use the more general word *formulation* for this description. We choose this word largely because it is the word adopted by other psychotherapies (Johnstone and Dallos, 2014). All psychotherapies recognise that however complex human experience is, the therapist needs to have a map to guide the family or client away from the waste ground or desert of difficulties. Of course, family therapists quote Bateson when they think about such maps. He famously asserted, "The map is not the territory". But nevertheless, therapists and families need and like maps, however approximate they may be!

Fact box

Gregory Bateson (1904–1980) was an English anthropologist whose ideas have influenced systemic family therapy theory and practice.

This chapter will be structured around three assessment tasks, which we explain in quite colloquial ways: 'what do we need to know about the family?' 'How has the family influenced the problem?' and 'how has the problem influenced the family?' At the end of the chapter, we will return to the construction of a formulation.

Fact box

A formulation is a way of explaining the information gained during a psychological assessment which is based upon theory.

Finding out about the family

Assessment instruments

During the history of family therapy, there have been a number of empirical methods that help therapists assess family life. Many of these have been 'patented' by their authors and have been used in research studies. Some of them are based on the family filling out a questionnaire. Others might include an *observational tool* in which the therapist observes how the family behave. An example of an observational tool, for instance, would be to ask the family to solve a problem and observe what happens, e.g. 'imagine you won some money: discuss how you would decide to spend it'. Table 3.1 is not exhaustive but provides a reference for readers to follow up (for greater detail, see Lebow and Stroud, 2012).

Table 3.1 A brief summary of assessment instruments

Name of assessment questionnaire	Aspects of family life it assesses	Summary of the ways it has been used
The Family Assessment Device (The McMaster Model)	The assessment covers family problem solving, communication, family roles, emotional responsiveness, emotional connection and behavioural control strategies.	The model enables therapists trained in its use to target interventions at whatever dimension the 'problem' is located. The model has been widely used in research (Ryan et al., 2005).
Family Adaptability and Cohesion Scale (The Circumplex Model)	This assessment covers family cohesion (closeness/distance), flexibility (rigid/chaotic), and communication.	There is a wealth of research based on this model, which grew out of structural family therapy ideas. It has an observational scale used by therapists (Olson, 2000; 2011).
The Beavers Systems Model	This model covers family competence and family style.	This measure was one of the earliest attempts to demonstrate that there was a connection between individual difficulties and family difficulties (Beavers and Hampson, 2000).
SCORE (Systemic Clinical Outcome and Routine Evaluation)	This short self-report questionnaire measures strengths and adaptability; feeling overwhelmed by difficulties and disrupted communication.	This is less a way of assessing families and more of a way of evaluating change in how the family experience family life. It is largely used in the UK. See The Association for Family Therapy's website (www.aft.org.uk) for a full description of research, films about its use and the measure itself (Stratton et al., 2010).

Fact box

Empirical means derived from experiment or observation as opposed to theory.

Conversational ways of finding out about the family

Most family therapists may use one of the methods listed in Table 3.1, but will usually rely upon a conversation because, after all, therapy is about 'meeting' another person! Haley (1976) proposed that the initial assessment session with a family comprised a "social stage" in which the therapist helped the family settle into the session and learned about their lives generally. Some family therapists will simply ask, "What do I need to know about your family before I can help you think about what's going wrong for you?" Even in this 'finding out' phase, the therapist is noticing who speaks most, who talks to or about whom, and the general atmosphere within the family. The therapist will often resist 'problem talk' for a while, perhaps saying: "I don't want to talk about difficulties just yet, but really want to find out about you all first". This initial conversation is more likely to be about strengths, fun and family interests. For instance, one family member might be asked to describe another family member. What is interesting about such an opening discussion is that it immediately introduces relationships into the conversation.

The family tree or genogram

The most common tool that helps the therapist and family orientate to each other in the early assessment session is the genogram or family tree. This is a visual representation of 'who is in the family', with the possibility of drawing up a large number of variations, events, patterns depending on how complex the therapist choses to make it. It can always be returned to in later sessions. Indeed, some therapists will have the family tree on show every time they meet the family. Again, this gives a systemic message: we are here to help the family resolve the problems rather than here to help one individual. Often, young people will have drawn a family tree in school, so the process will be familiar to them. There are a number of conventions and symbols to represent family members and relationships on a family tree (McGoldrick, 2011; McGoldrick et al., 2008). In Figure 3.1 we provide a simplified version of a selection of such symbols.

> In the Assessment film the family tree has already been done and is visible to the family.

There is also software available to help therapists draw up family trees, for example, Smart Draw, I-family tree and Genogram Analytics (see Figure 3.2).

Task 1: Draw up your own family tree/genogram

Spend some time noticing patterns such as names, occupations and gender roles, and even see if you can work out any 'trans-generational scripts' such as approaches to emotional expression, rules about parenting and any cultural assumptions.

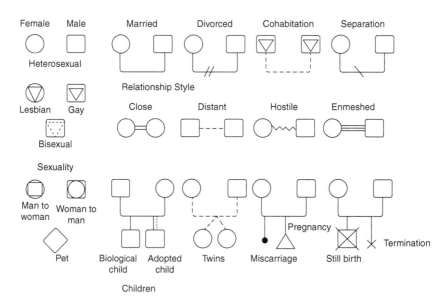

Female Male   Married   Divorced   Cohabitation Separation

Heterosexual

Relationship Style

Lesbian Gay   Close   Distant   Hostile   Enmeshed

Bisexual

Sexuality

Man to Woman to
woman   man   Pregnancy
                                                                    Termination
Pet   Biological Adopted   Twins   Miscarriage   Still birth
         child   child

Children

Figure 3.1 Family tree symbols.

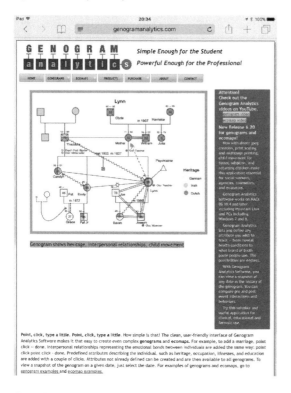

Figure 3.2 Reproduced with kind permission of Genogram Analytics.

The family life cycle

Because family therapists think about families as a unit, they prefer to think about the *family* moving through time rather than individual family members growing older. Therefore, as part of the 'finding out' phase, the therapist will explore how the family fit into what is called the '*family life cycle*' (Carter and McGoldrick, 1999). This model proposes that families tend to share similar developmental phases (just like individuals do). In Table 3.2 we demonstrate one version of the 'typical' life stages of families. It is important to recognise that different families might have different challenges in these stages and indeed not every family experiences all the stages. For instance, adoptive families might 'skip' the 'early childhood' stage. So, the model is not prescriptive nor is it universal. But it provides a guide to the therapist about the types of 'normal' challenges the family might be facing (Day, 2010; Walsh, 2012). The model also suggests that families need to adapt as they move from one stage to another. A typical example would be how parenting needs to change for young children as opposed to teenagers (who need to experience growing independence). The *family life cycle* suggests that transitions between stages might lead to family problems. However, it also suggests that if there are unexpected *vertical* stressors on the family, then the family will need to have greater resources to overcome them. At this point, many families will present to therapists. Examples of a vertical stressor include illness, unemployment or external social pressure such as institutional racism (see Carter and McGoldrick, 1999: 6).

Task 2

Write out where you think your family is on the family life cycle. What kinds of challenges are your family facing? What resources are helping the family manage these challenges?

How has the family influenced the problem?

Throughout the 'finding out' phase, the therapist will be exploring with family members how they connect with the problem. For instance, if a mother says her son was 'great' before he became depressed, the therapist might ask her "how did you first understand his depression?" as a way of helping the mother recognise how she influenced the 'discovery' of the depression. However, there are many more aspects to family life that the therapist may be interested in. These aspects range from parenting approaches, to family 'scripts' (Byng-Hall, 1998), to the way the family interacts. There are also two other dimensions that the therapist is interested in exploring. One is how family patterns *contributed* to what is happening in the family in the present (contributing factors). Some family therapists dislike this emphasis on 'psychological archaeology' and argue that it blames the family for the problem (Eisler, 2005; Roffman, 2005). Although this perspective

---

Fact box

John Byng-Hall was a pioneering English psychiatrist and family therapist. Like others, he suggested that families follow patterns set by earlier
generations.

Table 3.2 Life cycle stages (Carter and McGoldrick, 1999)

Family life cycle stage	Emotional processes of transition; key principles	Changes required for the family to proceed developmentally
Leaving home: single young adults.	Accepting emotional and financial responsibility for self.	Differentiation of self from family of origin. Development of intimate peer relationships. Establishment of work and independence.
Joining of families through cohabiting/ marriage.	Commitment to new relationships.	Forming a new family system. Realignment of relationships with family and friends.
Families with young children.	Adjusting from a dyad to triads and larger system.	Making space for children in the relationship. Creating a team to bring up children. Realignment with family and friends (grandparents).
Families with adolescents.	Increasing flexibility to allow for growing independence and reviewing aging family members.	Shift to allow children to develop outside relationships. Adjust to midlife issues: career, etc. Care for older generations.
Launching children and moving on.	Accept changes in the family system.	Renegotiate the intimate partnership ('empty nest'). Develop adult relationships with children. Deal with issues of older generation.
Families in later life.	Accept changes in generational roles (from caring to being cared for).	Maintain relationships during physical challenges of growing older. Support middle generation. Deal with loss.

has some value, it neglects the argument that systemic thinking avoids blame and
it also ignores the common human wish to 'find a cause'. Many family therapists
find that parents, in particular, blame themselves for their young people's problems irrespective of any 'rational' assessment. Indeed, the initial stages of family
therapy often have to address this blame so that it does not interfere with therapy.
The second dimension that therapists explore concerns what is happening at present that may *maintain* the difficulties (maintaining factors).

We present some areas that the therapist will assess under these categories in Table 3.3. This is not exhaustive, and as mentioned previously, in the course of the assessment, the therapist may discover a different issue of significance.

It should be clear that many of the above processes might *both* contribute to *and* maintain family difficulties. There are however a few extra processes to examine that are particularly significant in maintaining problems (see Table 3.4).

Once more it is important to recognise that many of these factors may contribute to the problems experienced by the family. But like Indra's Net, it is almost impossible to describe every aspect that might be relevant.

Task 3

Choose one of the dimensions discussed in Tables 3.1, 3.2 and 3.3 and apply it to your family. Write out your responses to the dimension. Spend some time thinking about 'how your family works'.

How has the problem influenced the family?

As we mentioned, a number of family therapists are uncomfortable thinking that families *cause* difficulties. They are more likely to concentrate on what is maintaining difficulties. A variation on this is to consider how the problem has influenced the family. This makes sense because systemic thinking encourages therapists to see circular patterns rather than linear patterns. Often families will present to therapists and will genuinely be surprised that any problem has developed. In these situations, the therapist should spend a lot of time thinking about how the family has adjusted to the problem and how it has shaped their current typography of relationships (see Table 3.5).

Task 4

Think about something that has happened in your family such as a family member having an accident, or getting a poor grade in school. How did the event change family life for a while? Did family members 'adjust' to the event? Were the adjustments helpful? Did they contribute to the event lasting longer than it needed to?

Table 3.3 Contributory family processes to explore in family assessment

Family pattern/area of interest	How it might contribute to the current problems	Example
Generational patterns: sometimes called 'family scripts'.	In some families, there are expectations that certain family members will have problems or exceed the achievements of the elder family members.	The individual who feels this pressure may conform to it, or rebel.
Models of parenting.	Parents may have differing styles of parenting which can give confusing messages to the children.	A child 'misbehaves' for one parent because the other parent permits that behaviour.
Parental cohesiveness.	Sometimes parents might inadvertently side with a child against the other parent. Unhappy couples often affect children.	In cases of domestic abuse this pattern is common where the abusive parent encourages one child to disrespect the other parent.
Intergenerational structures.	Sometimes grandparents will care for children and this might encourage children to disregard their parents' styles/rules.	Children may 'yo-yo' between different homes and thus lose stability and a sense of an adult being in overall charge.
Levels of closeness.	Each family member will have their own capacity to manage closeness/distance in relationships. Sometimes a child feels 'smothered' or 'not cared for'.	Adolescent children often want to develop greater distance from their parents but their parents may interpret this as them 'not caring' and the levels of hurt may escalate conflict.
Communication styles.	Many family problems arise because family members don't talk with each other about their worries. Families vary in what they are able to talk about with each other and how they talk about it (e.g. very volatile/ understated).	Not talking about worries can be experienced as 'being alone in the family' by some family members or even 'not really belonging here'.
Family rules.	Sometimes rules haven't adjusted to family life cycle changes. Sometimes they are implicit but not fully understood.	Children may behave in ways that are labelled 'wrong' but may not understand what is expected of them, e.g. 'taking'/ stealing food out of the fridge.
Family beliefs.	These operate at quite a deep level and may be influencing many problems. They may be general beliefs about what kind of a family this is, or specific about how people should think.	Some families have a view that everyone outside the family is 'bad'. Thus, family members won't ask for help from the outside world and will stay confined to a narrow family context.

Table 3.3 Continued

Family pattern/area of interest	How it might contribute to the current problems	Example
Vertical stresses on family life.	Deaths in families can be particularly significant and can lead to problems developing. These may be because communication is affected between family members. Other stresses too may contribute to difficulties, such as parental separations.	Losing a grandparent for instance might compromise the parenting of one of the parents and may distress a child. In this scenario, the distress may not be contained because of the grief of the parent. This, in time may lead the child to feel uncared for/unsupported.
Gender expectations.	All families have implicit and explicit gender expectations. These may influence what is expected in terms of behaviour, expression of feelings and how family members should think about each other.	Sometimes gender expectations cause limitations on what family members believe they can do/be. There may be a clash with role expectations, sexual orientation or transgender experiences. This can cause much distress.
Cultural expectations and wider societal responses to them.	Cultural diversity is part of family life across the globe. With it comes varieties in the way each family incorporates itself into a wider culture. Within the crucible of the family, cultures might clash. But equally wider society may judge such cultures and may react to them in negative ways.	Institutional racism, for instance, constrains and oppresses certain family members. Young black men in Western societies may experience huge pressures to 'conform'. In other families, the younger generations balance cultural differences between their parents and the wider society.
Family flexibility.	Families vary in the degree to which they can be flexible and change in response to life cycle changes or external challenges.	If a parent is made redundant, the family will need to adjust how they manage to contain individual family needs whilst providing security for the children.

Creating a formulation

The purpose of the assessment session, and it may extend over two sessions, is to create a description of what is happening in the family both in terms of contributory and maintaining factors. This description can be called a *formulation*. The formulation is a shortened analysis, which gives direction for intervention. In family therapy terms, it has to be relational (systemic) and it has to be tentative (in Milan words, *curious*; see Chapter 7). Some authors have adopted the phrase 'progressive formulation' (Dallos and Stedman, 2014; Dallos and Draper, 2010) to emphasise that the formulation is often changing as it is co-constructed with the

Table 3.4 Maintaining family processes to explore in family assessment

Family pattern/area of interest	How it might maintain the current problems	Example
Family responses to the problem.	Often, how we try to solve a problem ends up maintaining it. So, the therapist wants to know what the family members have done to resolve the issue. In systemic terms, we often do 'more of the same' when confronted with problems and ignore evidence that what we are doing doesn't work.	For instance, some parents will become more 'punitive' when children 'misbehave'. Usually, this reinforces the behaviour because children, not knowing how they should behave, rarely cause it!
Engrained family patterns such as 'triangulation'.	Triangulation is where a family member seems to help two other family members maintain their relationship.	For instance, sometimes a child has problems because this keeps the parents focused on the child instead of their troubled relationship.
Life cycle issues.	Here the 'problem' seems to help the family stay in a life cycle change that they perhaps should have transitioned through.	A child might help parents avoid facing the 'empty nest syndrome', where they need to reinvest in their relationship rather than be focused on the child.
Adjustment to changes in the family.	It is not unusual for families to struggle to manage change in family composition.	For instance, where a new partner/parent joins an existent family, children may express loyalty to their other parent by misbehaving for the 'new' partner.
Family 'ideology' about the problem.	How families understand the problem they have, might also maintain it.	For instance, some families may 'expect' boys to be difficult: so, it is not surprising if they have difficult boys. Other families may assume their children will have mental health problems like their parents: so, their expectations may maintain the problem.
Wider societal contexts.	Events in the wider society may be maintaining internal family difficulties.	In traumatic contexts, e.g. war, it is appropriate for family members to protect each other even if they are in later stages of the family life cycle.

Table 3.5 Areas to explore when addressing how the problem has affected the family

Area to explore	How this might affect family relationships	Example
The original 'discovery' of the problem.	When the problem is first noticed, it might act as a way of separating family members from each other: secrets might be kept from each other.	For instance, if a child is found to be depressed, often he or she will ask one parent not to tell the other parent or siblings. This introduces secrets into family life.
Trauma of discovery.	The problem might seriously undermine the 'world view' or self-understanding of family members.	For instance, if a child is sexually molested, her parents will often suddenly lose their faith in their ability to protect their child.
Adjustments to the problem.	Sometimes over time, the family will adjust to the problem and stop trying to change it, or accept its presence in family life (it can act as another member of the family).	Where a family member has a chronic illness, family patterns adjust to accommodate the illness. Perhaps family meals change: who spends time with who can change: what family members do for each other changes.

family. These authors also argue that systemic formulations have evolved from seeing the problem as *functional,* to being "centrally concerned with exploring the meanings, understandings and explanations that family members hold about their problems" (Dallos and Stedman, 2014: 94).

Fact box

A 'function' means that the problem achieves an outcome for the family. For instance, a child's illness keeps the parents together as a couple.

The formulation should also make sure that *family strengths* are assessed because these can mitigate the problems and help the family deal with them. Traditionally, a formulation would be quite complex, taking into account the range of factors that have been discussed. But it should also be sensible to the family (to whom it applies): it needs to be constructed in a *collaborative* way. An example from the accompanying film for this chapter would be:

"It seems as if Joel has been unable to access help from his parents because of a number of factors. On the contributory side, his stepfather Nick has not experienced an emotionally rich childhood himself and so he is unable to relate to Joel's experience. This, in turn, reflects very different parenting styles between his Mum and Nick and in some way his depression helps his parents avoid facing their differences. The family is a very 'split' family, in some ways with Maria in a strong alliance with the children, which itself excludes Nick. There is a general level of disappointment in family relationships, which may maintain the inability of Joel's parents to help him. However, both Joel's parents and his half-sister are willing to come to therapy and to work through the issues that they recognise. There are strong indicators that Nick wants to be a better parent than the parent he experienced as a child and Joel's half-sister is able to understand her brother's feelings".

Task 5

There are other formulations that could be constructed about Joel's family and his experiences. See if you can create your own formulation and then consider how you might explain it to the family.

Willingness to change

Assessment is not over when the therapist constructs a formulation. In many ways, the most important next task is to engage the family in change. There has been considerable research (Robbins *et al.*, 2016; Sotero, 2016) that shows that working with the family group increases the motivation of all family members even if they come into the session doubting the value of therapy. The therapist will have worked hard to help the family accept a *relational reframe* of their problems and will seek to show them that any problem is better resolved by collective family action. However, not every family is either willing or capable of working in this way, and in Table 3.6 you will see examples of obstacles to working with change in families.

Task 6

Think about reasons why families might not have the ability or capacity to work together to resolve difficulties or might not want to change.

It is always possible that at the end of the assessment, the family therapist will conclude that the family can't benefit from family therapy. This is rare, but family therapists should remember that humility is an important aspect of the systemic sensibility.

Task 7

If your family was going to go to family therapy, would any of the obstacles mentioned in this chapter exist? What could the therapist do to help your family overcome the obstacle?

Table 3.6 Obstacles to families working together to resolve difficulties

Kind of obstacle	Situations where it may occur	Possible ways of managing the obstacle
The family isn't living together.	Where the local authority looks after children.	Therapists can still (with relevant permission) attempt to help separated families work together in the long-term interests of the children.
Parents are hostile to each other.	Some couple separations can lead to engrained hostilities.	Therapists can meet the parents separately to help them understand how they can help their children.
Factors that prevent family members having the capacity to work on psychological issues.	Where family members have severe mental health difficulties, substance or alcohol misuse problems, these may prevent them being able to work together in therapy.	In these circumstances, the family therapy may have to work in tandem with other interventions such as substance misuse programmes.
Contextual pressures.	Financial pressures, overcrowding, social challenges, major family trauma.	Again, family therapy needs to be seen as part of an intervention in multi-stressed families alongside supportive services.
Family members are very stuck in blaming another family member or possibly an outside system and cannot accept any responsibility for making change happen.	Some parents in particular are unable to see how their behaviour can affect their children. Some authors have argued that these attitudes are part of a 'developmental closure' of the relationship (Street, 1994). This process has also been called 'scapegoating'.	Family therapists may have to recognise the impact these attitudes have on family members and invoke safeguarding procedures.
Some families just don't want to change!	Sometimes 'the devil we know is better than the devil we don't!'	In these situations, the task is to spend some time uncovering why it is so hard to change and the risks of not changing. But in the end, the family have to choose.
The therapist struggles to work with the family.	Sometimes families present difficulties that spark issues for the therapist. They might be going through a similar crisis to the therapist, or the family might evoke very strong emotional reactions that 'get in the way' of the therapist's work.	Therapists should receive supervision (see Chapter 10). But sometimes in the interests of the family, the therapist may need to ask a colleague to take on the case.

Conclusion

This chapter has attempted to give some shape to Indra's Net: the complex number of processes that need to be analysed within a family therapy assessment. Readers will appreciate why many family therapists have concentrated upon one aspect of this assessment: there are a huge number of areas to cover. In Chapter 7 we will explain how a Milan style approach helps temper the 'certainty' of amassing this volume of information and reaching towards a formulation. Inevitably, family therapists will have their 'usual' ways of assessing and may ignore some of the factors we have described. Ultimately, the assessment is only of use if it makes sense to the family and contributes to a solution that the family and therapist can work towards together. In other chapters, we will explore particular kinds of interventions and particular ways of assessing families from certain schools of family therapy. These are demonstrated in the accompanying films.

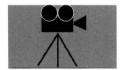

Please access the film using the eResources tab on the webpage for the book, which can be found on the Routledge website: www.routledge.com/9781138831438

Watch film: Assessing Families – understanding family patterns

Introduction to film

In this film Mark, the therapist, has already drawn a family tree and has helped the family think about their family. Now he intends to use the family tree to explore in more detail how the family works. He is keen to find answers to three simple questions: how does this family work; how does the way the family work affect the problem they are experiencing, e.g. making it harder to solve; and how does the problem influence the family? In this clip, Mark is looking for patterns that maintain the problem and what patterns might have caused the problem.

Stepfather Nick has not come to this first session. This means that the therapist has to walk a careful line that does not show any disrespect towards him. It also means that the therapist will need to consider how he can encourage Nick to come to the next session.

01:00 Mark: Does anybody notice anything they hadn't noticed before?
Maria: Well, I knew there were only very few boys in the family, but I had never really thought about it.

Skill note

Therapy relies on helping people notice difference. This idea comes directly from the anthropologist, Gregory Bateson, who believed that we survived by a process of noticing how things differ and then responding to that difference. He argued that therapy needed to help people notice the kind of difference that made a difference.

Mark: Yeah, you're right that Joel is the only youngster and do you think that's affected him? Being the only boy has made a difference to his life?

Maria: I think he may feel lonely. He really only has Nick, as his Dad is no use to him.

Mark: His dad's no use to him? Jack is no use, Jack is not helpful to Joel? So, he only has Nick, so that for Joel do you think, Maria, Nick has turned out to be the kind of father figure that he might have liked?

Maria: No, not really, they fight a lot.

Skill note

Maria has very quickly wondered if Joel is 'lonely' because there are so few men in the family. Notice how Mark makes this an interactive issue by asking if he 'got' the father he wanted. Also notice how Mark avoids 'blaming' Nick by asking if he got the son he expected.

Mark: They fight a lot? So, if we thought about it the other way around, Nick has not turned out to be the kind of father figure that Joel might have thought he'd have had, do you think Joel has turned out to be the sort of son that Nick might have thought he'd have?

Skill note

Mark works hard to establish reciprocity here so neither Nick nor Joel are left 'blamed'.

02:30 Maria: Joel is not the son he chose. He kind of got him.

Mark: But equally he could have been pleased to have a son, he could have done things with him. Do they share interests?

Maria: He tried. He wanted Joel to go out with him to the football. Be interested in cars and stuff. But Joel was too angry then.

Mark: Was too angry, ok right. Is Mum right about that Joel?

03:20 Joel:	Yes … it was a difficult period …
Mark:	Tell me about that. You talked earlier about the time you and Mum were on your own. Are you talking about when Nick joined your family?
Joel:	Yes, there was a large period of adjusting … (*Notice Joel himself reframes the problem.*)
03:49 Mark:	Who found it hardest to adjust? This was before Laura was born, so who found it hardest to adjust?
Joel:	Dare I say it was probably Nick. *I* found it difficult I am sure, so did Mum, but for Nick he was coming in on a family that was already set up. (*Again, notice how Joel is able to see Nick as troubled as well as himself.*)
Mark:	Right, do you think there was a reason why it was hard for Nick to adjust Joel?

Skill note

The reader should now begin to understand what kind of a picture Mark is building up about the family. Take a moment and think about what Mark might be thinking is contributing to Joel's unhappiness and the family conflict.

Possible hypotheses would be that the family never managed to overcome the 're-forming' that happens after separation and divorce. It is possible that the old loyalties between Maria and Joel made it hard for Nick to integrate into the family. Equally, Mark might be wondering if Joel had desperately wanted a father figure only to be disappointed and so he then is angry that he feels 'let down'. Within this complex mix, Maria has loyalties to both Joel and Nick, while also probably being closer to her daughter. This pattern means that there is little demand to solve the undertone of hostility. It is important to remember that these are ideas and Mark will continue to explore throughout the session and will ask the family what they think about his ideas.

04:40 Joel:	I guess he was coming in on a family that was already … I mean … and he suddenly got an extra child to look after.
Mark:	Maria, do you think this is right? Do you think Nick did find it hard to adjust?
Maria:	I think it was kind of equal, but I still think it was harder for Joel. He would have liked to stay with me on his own forever.
Mark:	(*Notice Mark decides this avenue might continue to blame Joel so he moves the conversation elsewhere.*) I'm hearing Joel that you're not the kind of young man that wants to go to football, the kind

Joel: of things Nick likes. What are the kind of things you do that he doesn't get involved in?

Joel: Lots of video games and things. It's easier to play video games and it's more involving that watching football and easier than playing football.

06:35 Mark: So you are playing with friends from school on the games? I heard that you go to your room a lot. I am wondering if you go to your room to run away from other people or because you really enjoy those video games?

! Notice the reframe here of Joel going to his room.

Joel: To a degree, I guess … well I do enjoy them … but maybe it is to run away as well.

Mark: What are you running away from?

Skill note

The reframe allows for an interactive answer: from whom is he running away?

Joel: Probably, the arguments … the general difficult things in life.

Mark: I am going to go back to something your Mum said. I am interested in the 'boy' theory of Mum's: do you think there are burdens or expectations on you as the only boy?

? Why do you think Mark changed direction here?

Joel: Yes, I have to be a man, you have to look after your Mum, that sort of thing. You have to work hard because you have to be like your grandad and your uncle and be a teacher …

08:10 Mark: This is your Mum's Dad and brother?

Joel: I didn't even know my Grandad, and Julian's a teacher.

Mark: Is he a teacher in the UK or in Slovakia?

Joel: I still hardly know him so … I don't pay any attention, I don't feel. I do feel I am the only … other than Nick. It's just.

Mark: A lot of pressure, people expect things of you.

Joel: Yeah.

09:08 Mark: Laura, do you think people expect your brother to be a certain kind of brother?

Laura: Well, it's a bit tricky to explain, but it's because he is older that probably means he is expected to do things …

Mark: Do you sometimes think Mum and your Dad expect a bit too much from him?

Laura: Yes.

Mark: Is that why there are arguments do you think?

Skill note

Mark has begun to layer the patterns in the family: family therapists never see 'one' explanation as enough and seek to help family members see themselves in many different ways. So, Mark is now exploring parental and family expectations on Joel. The implicit message is that this might lead him to be unhappy because it is harder to 'be himself'.

Laura: I don't really know. I haven't thought about that.

Mark: Sometimes in therapy that's what we do. We ask questions of people and they think about things. Sometimes they think on the spot and sometimes they go away and think. Maria do you think there is a certain pressure on Joel? Having just been together for a while, do you think that places a burden on Joel?

Maria: *(Notice that she does not answer the question directly but adds another factor into the discussion: her and Joel's experience of Jack who is Joel's biological dad.)* Maybe … we were very close. I was so unhappy and having Joel made it all worthwhile. Jack was away a lot and when he was back, it was bad and I very much wanted to get out of it. But I couldn't tell my Mum as she always said, "I told you so" when you met him. She didn't even come to the wedding …

Skill note

Again, Maria is adding another layer to the family history. She is explaining why she is so close to Joel and this may explain why Nick finds it hard to get close to him, or why Joel finds it hard to let Nick get close to him.

Mark: So you didn't have any support. Explain something to me. You and Joel were very close and maybe that was how you survived. Now with the four of you, who is closest to whom?

Skill note

Mark is now trying to encourage the family to see how these patterns prevent other patterns from emerging.

Maria: I am equally close to my children. I wanted to be there for my children more than my Mum was. Well, she had to work hard after my Dad died. I know she always wanted me to be a teacher. I might be one day. But my brother gets the prize: she treated us differently.

Skill note

Interestingly Maria interprets the question as implying that she is less close to one of her children, so she defends herself and contrasts the way she is with the way her mother was. What this does, of course, is start to explain why Maria is more comfortable with the pattern that she has: perhaps closer to the children (in contrast to her mother) than to her partner.

Maria: I don't want to make the same mistake as my mother. But sometimes I don't have enough patience as I should have. They fight and I shout at Joel because he is older and he should know better.

Mark: In your calmer moments do you wonder if Laura might instigate problems?

Maria: What do you mean? (*She doesn't understand the question.*)

Mark: Do you think Laura can be mischievous? (*Note a less pejorative word.*)

Maria: I think sometimes she might but ... when I come back from work I am tired, I need to cook dinner, I don't want to deal with them so I never notice that.

13:30 Mark: So there is something in your mind that assumes that the eldest should know better? Is that right Joel? Do you think that is what your Mum thinks?

Mark: I am hearing that there have been issues with the family coming together; I am hearing that there are experiences from the past that are affecting the family now. I am also hearing people have been quite unhappy at times. Have the different generations had to deal with being unhappy? Maria, it sounds as if you have been unhappy with Jack, Joel is having to cope with being unhappy. I wonder if Nick has ever been unhappy. Joel?

Skill note

Mark is seeking to explore the way unhappiness has existed within the family.

Joel: Well, he was in care. He didn't really know his parents. So, I guess to a degree. That's probably got a lot to do with it.

Mark: That seems important. He might not know how to bring you up? He might not know how he was brought up. So, Maria, Nick was in care? Do you think that influences how he thinks about Joel?

! The therapist must always avoid taking sides when a family member is absent: their positive intentions must be noted rather than negative traits.

15:10 Maria: I think it has. Nick didn't have any role models or he hasn't experienced how families should function. He tried his best. But um … As I said in our first session, he doesn't know how to talk about it either.

Mark: Is there a connection then with his finding it hard to talk and his experience in the past? Are they connected in any way?

Maria: Yes. He hasn't learnt how to communicate in a family.

Mark: People sometimes are frightened to communicate in case they make things worse … I sometimes wonder if Joel is frightened to say too much in case it makes things worse … is that right, Joel?

Joel: Well yes … there is a lot of tension in the family unit … it feels like anything could sort of topple it (*Notice this extreme language*).

Mark: So everyone is kind of walking on egg shells. Do you think sometimes that the family is going to break up?

Skill note

Mark is taking a risk naming something that might be a fear for some family members. He needs to show the family that these fears can be talked about in therapy: carefully.

Joel: Well, I don't think it is that … far … I don't think … (*Notice how close Joel comes to using the phrase 'that far gone'.*)

Mark: Maria, do you worry about that?

Maria: Yes, I sometimes am piggy in the middle and that the children would be happier if I left Nick …

Skill note

This conversation has proceeded gently until Mark asks the paradoxical question about whether the conflict distracts everyone from the fear that the family might separate. Maria agrees that worrying about Joel means she worries less about Nick and the family. Here Mark is exploring an interactive cycle that may be kept going because it has a 'function'. So, the more Maria worries about Joel being depressed, the less she worries about the family breaking up. Mark then asks if Maria and Joel had the same pattern when Jack was in the family. She agrees. So, we can see that the close relationship between Joel and Maria has been a protective factor for them.

17:30 Mark: 'The children' – both Laura and Nick?
Maria: Yes.

! This is a crucial moment. But this is an assessment session and Nick is not here. Also talking about this *may* be very difficult for the children especially Laura. Mark chooses to note it and move on.

Mark: How does the fact that Joel and Nick have conflict, and Laura and Joel have conflict … how does that influence your worry or your thinking that the children would be happier if you left Nick?

! Mark chooses not to directly address the issue but 'paint in' the shades of the relationships around the issue.

Maria: I think there would be less tension. So, Nick and Joel wouldn't have a view, that is the main issue, there would be less tension … at the same time I would worry because Laura would miss her father …
18:40 Mark: I am also wondering if being worried about Joel distracts from the other worry. Does the fact that you worry about Joel being stuck in his room, being unhappy, does that mean you worry more about him than you worry about Nick?
Maria: Yes. (*Notice how Maria answers this question: she has thought about it.*)
Mark: Tell me something, Maria, was that the same thing that happened when you were with Jack? Was it like you and Joel were very close and that meant you didn't get so worried about Jack?
Maria: It was very much the same.

19:40 Mark: OK, I am going to summarise where we have got to. I am trying to see how Joel's difficulties fit into the family pattern. It sounds like being the only boy, having lots of expectations, being close to his Mum, having a stepdad, neither of whom have adjusted to getting together, I think I've heard that there was a pattern between Joel and Maria and this pattern influences Nick, and I'm hearing that people have had hard times, that patterns from the past affect the way people behave in this family. Is that summarising quite well? Have I forgotten anything?

Maria: That is pretty much it.

Mark: Laura, have you heard anything about your family that you weren't expecting to hear?

Laura: Not really.

Mark: Did you know about Dad's background?

Laura: Not about that. I have heard him talk to Mum about his parents but not the rest.

Mark: So that is kind of new. Did you know about Mum and Joel being really close before Dad came into the family?

Laura: Yes.

Mark: Do you sometimes think they are so close that it stops you being as close as you want to be?

Laura: A couple of times. Not much.

Mark: Joel, have you heard anything new?

Joel: I guess it has put everything into perspective. The majority is stuff I knew but putting it altogether …

Mark: Does it help explain why you have so many worries?

Joel: Yeah.

Mark: Maria, have you heard anything today that's made you understand things differently?

Maria: Yes. I think I feel better already. I think we can work it out and Joel can get out of his depression.

Mark: So you think things can change in the family that will help Joel use the family to get out of his depression. Great. I am looking forward to seeing you next time.

Summary

The end of the session statement is essentially a formulation about what interactive processes are going on in the family that influence Joel's experiences. Mark might follow this up in a letter so that his ideas can be shared and discussed with all family members (including Nick). Mark has spent very little time talking about Joel's depression in the session clip. In a real situation, time would be spent finding out about the risks posed by his depression (e.g. suicidality) but that would be inappropriate in front of Laura. Also, more time would have been spent on tracking the family members experience of the depression. This would have established the resources, if any, this offered to Joel. Mark finishes the session by asking family members to remember what was new in what was said. He is interested in establishing what Bateson called "news of difference".

Task 8

There are always different ways an interview can go. Mark has pursued some themes in his assessment but not others. What other ideas from this chapter could he have used in assessing this family?

References

Beavers, R. and Hampson, R. (2000). The Beavers Systems Model of family functioning. *Journal of Family Therapy*, 22: 128–143.

Byng-Hall, J. (1998). *Rewriting family scripts*. New York: Guilford Press.

Carter, B. and McGoldrick, M. (1999). *The expanded family life cycle*. Boston: Allyn and Bacon.

Dallos, R. and Draper, R. (2010). *Introduction to family therapy*. Maidenhead: Open University Press.

Dallos, R. and Stedman, J. (2014). Systemic formulation. In Johnstone, L. and Dallos, R. (2014) (Eds) *Formulation in psychology and psychotherapy*. London: Routledge, pp. 67–95.

Day, R. (2010). *Introduction to family processes*. New York: Routledge.

Eisler, I. (2005). The empirical and theoretical base of family therapy and multiple family day therapy for adolescent anorexia nervosa. *Journal of Family Therapy*, 27: 104–131.

Haley, J. (1976). *Problem solving therapy*. San Francisco: Jossey Bass.

Johnstone, L. and Dallos, R. (2014). *Formulation in psychology and psychotherapy*. London: Routledge.

Lebow, J. and Stroud, C. (2012). Assessment of effective couple and family functioning. In Walsh, F. (Ed) *Normal family processes*. New York: Guilford, pp. 501–528.

McGoldrick, M. (2011). *The genogram journey*. New York: Norton.

McGoldrick, M., Gerson, R. and Petry, S. (2008). *Genograms: assessment and intervention*. New York: Norton.

Olson, D. (2000). Circumplex model of marital and family systems. *Journal of Family Therapy*, 22: 144–167.

Olson, D. (2011). FACES IV & the circumplex model: a validation study. *Journal of Marital and Family Therapy*, 37: 64–80.

Robbins, M., Alexander, J., Turner, C. and Hollimon, A. (2016). Evolution of Functional Family Therapy as an evidence-based practice for adolescents with disruptive behaviour problems. *Family Process*, 55: 543–557.

Roffman, A. (2005). Function at the junction: revisiting the idea of functionality in family therapy. *Journal of Marital and Family Therapy*, 31: 259–268.

Ryan, C., Epstein, N., Keitner, G., Miller, I. and Bishop, D. (2005). *Evaluation and treating families*. New York: Routledge.

Sotero, L., Major, S., Escudero, V. and Relvas, A. (2016). The therapeutic alliance with involuntary clients: how does it work? *Journal of Family Therapy*, 38: 36–58.

Stratton, P., Bland, J., Janes, E. and Lask, J. (2010). Developing an indicator of family function and a practicable outcome measure for systemic family and couple therapy: the SCORE. *Journal of Family Therapy*, 32: 232–258.

Street, E. (1994). A family systems approach to child parent separation: developmental closure. *Journal of Family Therapy*. 16, 347–366.

Walsh, F. (2012) (Ed). *Normal family processes*. New York: Guilford.

Chapter 4

Integrative family therapy

A contemporary practice

Key points

- Integrative family therapy draws together many of the techniques from other schools of family therapy.
- Integrative family therapy incorporates ideas and methods from the wider psychotherapy world.
- Many contemporary evidence-based models of family intervention are examples of integrative family therapy.
- Integrative family therapy is particularly focused on the therapeutic alliance between family and therapist.
- Collaboration between therapist and family is the basic foundation of this approach.

Introduction

The basic assumption of this book is that contemporary family therapy practice is 'integrative' and so, although each subsequent chapter will describe and give examples of techniques from specific schools of family therapy, this chapter provides an overview of how these techniques are blended into a coherent clinical practice. Having said this, it is probably harder to define 'integrative family therapy' than any other model. This is largely because it has functioned as a chameleon throughout the history of family therapy. What we mean by this is that it has adapted as family therapy has evolved, i.e. changing colour and shape. For instance, in the 1980s, integrative family therapy could mean either an integration of family therapy with psychodynamic approaches (Will and Wrate, 1985) or an integration between structural and strategic approaches (Treacher, 1988). Most recently, Lebow (2005: XV) has argued, "today's approaches [include] a generic core of strategies and interventions derived from the first generation of models". He further suggests that contemporary integrative family therapy has a "biobehavioral-psychosocial foundation". In other words, it incorporates research findings and practice from a range of therapies and interventions. An example of this is that most of the evidence-based models of family therapy have incorporated ideas and techniques from the 50 years of family therapy practice and literature. Here, the way integrative family therapy works is to integrate *inside* the field of family therapy.

Integrative family therapy is also chameleon-like because it has not been averse to swallowing up ideas and techniques from other psychotherapies as it has gone along. Just like the chameleon that gobbles up the insect! When this happens, for instance in the use of attachment theory, integrative family therapy adapts the ideas to suit a systemic framework. Here the way integrative family therapy works is to integrate ideas from *outside* the field of family therapy.

Unfortunately, when the chameleon is sitting on a branch, it can be nigh on impossible to see it. Similarly, integrative family therapy is often hard to define and observing it in the practice of clinicians is something of a challenge. Having said that, all integrative clinicians would assert the paramount importance of what is called the 'therapeutic alliance' in their work. This will, therefore, be the primary focus of this chapter, although we will first describe Lebow's outline of integrative family therapy and take attachment theory as an example of an approach that has been integrated into family therapy. We will also consider one example of the new evidence-based approaches to demonstrate how integrative these models are.

Figure 4.1 Jay Lebow.

Lebow's integrative family therapy

Jay Lebow (see Figure 4.1) undertook his family therapy and clinical psychology training in Northwestern University, Chicago, and at the Family Institute, Chicago. Both of these institutions have a strong profile of empirical research and its application to clinical practice. This explains why Lebow has continued to promote evidence-based practice (Lebow, 2006). Lebow is now a Professor at Northwestern and editor of the most significant family therapy journal, *Family Process.* One of the major influences on his development was William Pinsof, who developed the first coherent integrative model of family therapy called 'problem centred integrative therapy' (1995). Together, and with the Faculty at Northwestern, Pinsof and Lebow have created a range of methods for evaluating family therapy, including both the Systemic Inventory of Change and a measure that helps therapists track the therapeutic alliance.

Lebow (2003) highlights the complex definitions involved in integrative practice. He notes that *integration* can so easily mean *eclecticism*, in which the clinician has no overall way of formulating the problems presented in therapy and simply uses a 'tool box' of techniques with no coherent approach. He also recognises that "there (are) not one, but many integrative family therapies" (Lebow, 2003: 206). He argues that they all share a number of core understandings:

- They all have a coherent theory of change.
- They all function under the umbrella of a systemic understanding, including attending to multiple levels of experience.
- They all give attention to the 'common factors' found across psychotherapies.
- They utilise behavioural, cognitive and emotional methods for change.
- They rely on research and are part of building evidence-based interventions.
- They use relational language and 'relational diagnoses'.
- They use various methods to track the effectiveness of therapy and thereby are pragmatic in seeking to change focus to achieve a required outcome.
- They all accept the need to individualise treatment to different families while taking into account diverse family structures, cultures and orientations.

Lebow (2014) explains that integration can have theoretical or technical aspects to it. A theoretical integration would involve an overarching theory within which the therapy is undertaken. For instance, the 'Integrative Systemic Therapy (IST)' model (Pinsof, 2011) provides an updated version of Pinsof's 'problem centred therapy', in which a series of hypotheses are constructed about the 'constraints' that prevent the solution to the presented problem. Intervention is a 'stepped' model targeting various parts of the client system. Technical integration, on the other hand, is where the therapist uses whatever technique is required without necessarily adopting the theory attached to this technique. Indeed, technical integration can slip over into assimilation where the technique is soon seen as part of the original model. Lebow comments on how mindfulness has become part of a cognitive behavioural therapy (CBT) model (Germer *et al.*, 2005; Tirch *et al.*, 2016) as an example of this process (see Table 4.1).

Table 4.1 Underlying conceptual ideas within Lebow's integrative family therapy

Concept	Lebow's description of the concept	How it impacts family therapy practice
Bio-behavioural-psychosocial foundation.	We now recognise that the family environment is not the only influence on difficulties. There are also genetic, cultural, psychological and social influences.	This is clearest in severe mental illness where ideas about family *causation* have been disproved. In such situations, the family therapy is aimed at increasing resilience and changing any behaviours that maintain difficulties not at causative factors.
Systems theory, cybernetics and ecological systems theory.	Lebow (2014: 41) repeats the axioms of systems theory: "to understand behaviour, one needs to understand context". However, he also argues for a "nuanced view".	Family therapists still use the idea that the symptom 'fits' into the family system and the idea that circular causation is useful.
Family structure, communication style and family life cycle.	Lebow sees these as integral to the way family therapists understand families.	Understanding the research about expressed emotion (Kuipers *et al.*, 2002) and communication in couple relationships (Gottman, 1999) informs how family therapists help families communicate for instance.
Ethnicity, culture and the wider system.	"Almost all couple and family therapy today integrates understandings of culture into therapy" (Lebow, 2014: 47).	We can only understand a family if we see them within their culture. This includes social justice perspectives about how the dominant culture might oppress minority families.
Social contexts such as social roles, gender, ideas about social learning and social 'exchange' (e.g. conscious choice in behaviour).	Gender, in particular, is a dominant influence on behaviour in society and in families.	Family therapists must take into account how these factors influence individual family member's behaviours. Is the family patriarchal and does it limit the life choices of its members?
Individual personality.	Previous family therapy models rarely thought about the 'individual' (Rivett and Street, 2003) and how personality influences behaviour. Strong psychological research confirms the significance of these factors (Kagan, 2010).	Family therapists must include ideas about how family members can manage their personalities rather than 'change' them.

Table 4.1 Continued

Concept	Lebow's description of the concept	How it impacts family therapy practice
Postmodern theories.	Lebow asserts that despite these influencing family therapy in differential ways, they help bring into the field ideas about uncertainty and social justice.	Family therapists need to regard their 'truths' with suspicion and always be open to challenge on what they think is 'right'.

Fact box

The 'stepped' model of intervention is clinically attractive for therapists. The idea is that the initial intervention is the 'simplest', for instance, teaching parents to impose consistent sanctions where their child is misbehaving. If the behaviour continues, then the therapist might decide to help the parents add 'rewarding good behaviour' as well. These are behavioural interventions. If the behaviour continues, then the therapist may move into 'meanings' and look at what is preventing the parents from applying these techniques. In this stage, family scripts, gender scripts, and many family therapy ideas would be used. If the behaviour still continues, the therapist will explore if the couple relationship is impacting on the parenting system. Here emotional issues may emerge which reinforce the inability of the family system to change the behaviour.

Of course, in a full integrative model the biological and social would also be taken into account: are there reasons why the child/parents can't help or are there cultural/social influences which interfere?

Fact box

Bowlby was a psychiatrist and psychoanalyst who worked at the Tavistock in London. Best known for his work on attachment theory, which was said to be fuelled by his own experience of being parented by a nanny.

Attachment based family therapy: an example of a theoretical integrative family therapy

Attachment based family therapy (ABFT) (Diamond *et al.*, 2014) is an example of a theoretical integration as defined by Lebow. It is not the only such model (see also Crittenden *et al.*, 2014; Dallos, 2006; Dallos and Vetere, 2009; Hughes, 2007 and 2011; Vetere and Dallos, 2008). Attachment theory was 'created' by the British psychoanalyst Bowlby (1988; Bretherton, 1992). As such, the adoption of attachment ideas within family therapy represents a 'softening' towards psychoanalytic ideas that has had other repercussions on family therapy practice (Flaskas and

Pocock, 2009; Pocock, 2006). He argued that the quality of attachment between child and parent affected not only how they developed but also had long-term consequences on their future psychological functioning in life. Since his original proposal (based on a clinical sample), researchers have produced various 'types' of attachment that children have with their caregivers. Initial categorisations included secure, anxious, avoidant and disorganised attachments, but these have been further extended within Crittenden's Dynamic-Maturational Model (DMM) (Crittenden *et al.*, 2014).

Task I

There are scientific ways of assessing attachment style. But just ask yourself who in your family appears to hold which style: secure, anxious, avoidant or disorganised? What do these words mean to you (have a look at the literature recommended for more information)?

There have been a number of reasons why family therapy has been historically reticent to adopt attachment theory. First, certainly as originally described by Bowlby, the focus was very much on the dyad of mother and child. Thus, it was not systemic in recognising either the role of other significant adults in children's lives (especially fathers) or the role of the wider culture. In fact, it could be argued that by focusing on mother and child, the theory was determined by a patriarchal model that blamed mothers for children's problems. Second, attachment theory could easily be interpreted as deterministic and labelling. Bowlby had originally studied 'delinquent boys' who he thought had been damaged by early attachment injuries (notice the words used). Family therapy has always sought to avoid such negative language and has wanted a theory that was hopeful rather than predictive of problems. Third, the more Postmodern family therapies have opposed 'grand narratives', arguing that any theory is a social construction. Attachment theory fits a narrative of the scientific revelation of truth that bolsters a social system that constrains much human potential. It purports to be global, applying to all human beings regardless of age, culture or gender. Interestingly, even attachment researchers suggest that a third of people have an insecure attachment, which makes it hard to think of such an attachment as a problem. Fourth, and connected to the previous point, attachment theory functions as a 'tautological' system in that it is not possible to disprove it scientifically. What we mean here is that researchers 'assume' that attachment theory is 'true' and therefore their observations confirm that it is 'true'. As such it does not conform to Popper's argument that empirical theories should be *disprovable*. Other childhood researchers (Kagan, 2010) have argued that there are alternative ways of understanding childhood behaviour and parental responses. Finally, it may be worth commenting that in this book we will be exploring a range of family therapy schools that have designed interventions to help children and families: none of them 'needed' attachment theory to underpin their work.

This being said, ABFT is undoubtedly the most coherent and well-researched family therapy model (Diamond *et al.*, 2016) that uses attachment ideas to help adolescents who are self-harming and depressed. The fundamental premise of ABFT is that one way of helping depressed and self-harming adolescents is to attend to *attachment ruptures* between themselves and their caregivers. Diamond *et al.* (2014: 3) comment:

> 'A secure base provides the essential context for growth and development throughout childhood'.

However:

> 'For adolescents who become depressed, life is dark and lonely. The world becomes unsafe, and they begin to view themselves as unworthy. To protect them, they often retreat from parents, friends and activities ... Lacking the expectation that parents will understand their pain and provide a safe haven, depressed adolescents use emotional overregulation to protect themselves from more hurt. Some are ambivalent about their parents, wanting love but fearing rejection'.
>
> (Diamond *et al.*,2014: 5)

ABFT therefore seeks to help adolescents turn to their parents for support and to heal whatever attachment rupture may have been present before the depression or as a result of the depression. ABFT aims to provide a 'corrective attachment experience'. The model has five phases of treatment or tasks (see Figure 4.2).

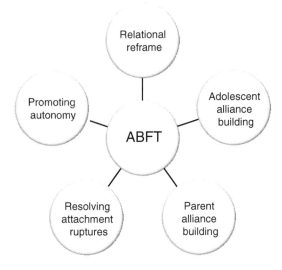

Figure 4.2 Stages of treatment in ABFT.

The first establishes the relational purpose of the work. The second and third involve separate sessions for adolescent and parents with the aim of coaching them towards a 'corrective attachment' conversation. The fourth phase includes family sessions in which the adolescent verbalises their needs and their disappointments and the parents respond. Finally, the therapy begins to address the developmental phase of autonomy building.

From Table 4.2, it is clear that ABFT is an integrative family therapy model, which incorporates many systemic concepts within the 'wrapper' of attachment theory. It has most recently been developed for use with lesbian and gay adolescents (Diamond and Shpigel, 2014; Levy *et al.*, 2016) and eating disorders

Table 4.2 How does ABFT integrate family therapy techniques and ideas?

Technique/idea from family therapy	How does ABFT use this technique/idea	Example
Reframing (Strategic school).	The initial session is about a 'relational reframe'.	'How come you find it so hard to ask your parents for help?'"Why do you think your child can't turn to you for help?'
Families are systems where patterns build up over time (general systems theory).	ABFT avoids blaming parents for the attachment rupture but does not avoid conversations about 'what has gone wrong?'	'When did you first notice that your child stopped confiding in you? What was happening in the family then?'
Change occurs through interactive processes (general systems theory).	ABFT sees Phase Four as the crucial change event: where patterns can be talked about and altered.	'What would you have to hear from your parents to feel you could turn to them again?'
Enactment (Structural school).	Phase Four is an extended enactment: ABFT 'facilitates dialogue' to ensure a 'corrective attachment experience' occurs.	'I'd like you to start by telling your parents about some of the things that we have been discussing that get in the way of you going to them' (Diamond et al., 2014: 168).
Setting tasks (Strategic school).	ABFT wants change to happen outside the therapy room as well as within it.	'What would you have to do to keep this new relationship working?'
Family structure (Structural school).	ABFT assumes that parents are responsible for helping their children grow up safely.	'I know it will be hard hearing what your young person wants to say. What do we have to do to help you with this?'
Family narratives (Narrative school; see also Dallos, 2006).	ABFT explores meanings including how family members understand how they have reached the place they have.	'How do you understand that your child can't turn to you? Does this seem to remind you of your experience growing up?'

(Wagner *at al.*, 2016). One of the primary assumptions of ABFT is that the 'therapeutic alliance' is a crucial element in creating the 'corrective attachment experience'. Indeed, close attention (if not obsession) to the therapeutic alliance is central to all integrative family therapy approaches.

The therapeutic alliance

If integrative family therapies are chameleon like, then the therapeutic alliance is the skeleton of the lizard: the skin colour may change but the essential elements of the creature remain the same. Throughout the history of psychotherapy (Safran and Muran, 2000), the therapeutic alliance has been conceptualised in different ways. Essentially, it is the way that therapist and client (in family therapy terms, the family) work together to achieve a mutually agreed goal. Rogers (1957) also famously argued that a good therapeutic alliance was the "necessary and sufficient" condition of therapeutic change. Bordin (1979) systematised the previous thinking by talking about three elements to the alliance: tasks, goals and bonds. While other forms of psychotherapy were attending to the alliance, family therapy lagged behind. Although some might argue that the alliance was an assumed basis for Minuchin's work (Simon, 1995), it was never described as such, although 'engagement' was. However, by the 1990s, a number of family therapists began to formulate a specific *systemic* understanding of the alliance. Some of these approached the alliance from a psychodynamic as well as a systemic perspective (Flaskas and Perlesz, 1996). While others, including Lebow and colleagues at Northwestern, brought a strong empirical quality to their thinking (Knobloch-Fedders *et al.*, 2004; Pinsof *et al.*, 2008). Indeed, since the 2000s the 'common factors' debate within family therapy has taken a number of complex turns with some researchers questioning how important the role of the therapist is in creating a 'good' alliance (Sexton, 2007; Simon, 2012), while others maintain that the therapist's model is less important than 'matching to clients' (Blow *et al.*, 2012). More recently, a 'moderate' approach has been proposed (Sprenkle *et al.*, 2009), which recognises the central role of the therapeutic alliance while agreeing that the therapist has a significant part to play as do the range of specific models for specific difficulties, e.g. the approach has to fit the problem rather than a generic 'alliance focused' intervention being enough.

Research confirms that the quality of the therapeutic alliance in family therapy is a significant indicator of both lower 'drop out' and better outcomes (Friedlander *et al.*, 2011). Thus, it is important for clinicians to cultivate the skills that are required to foster a good alliance. The best model for teaching these skills is that developed by the System for Observing Family Therapy Alliances (SOFTA) (Friedlander *et al.*, 2006). This method of understanding, recording and learning how to build alliances in family therapy has a range of studies confirming its value (Carpenter *et al.*, 2008). What is unique about SOFTA is that it provides a set of behavioural indicators that therapists can use to evaluate the alliance they have with each family member and the family as a whole. Building on these indicators,

Table 4.3 The dimensions of the therapeutic alliance as defined by SOFTA and what the therapist can do to improve them in therapy

Dimension	Description	What the therapist can do to improve the dimension
Emotional connection to the therapist.	This refers to Bordin's emotional bond dimension. It means that each family member must trust the therapist and on some level 'like' them.	Although this is perhaps culture specific, the therapist must come over as a human being who cares for the family members. The therapist may disclose something about her life or may ask about family members without reference to 'problems'.
Engagement with the therapeutic process.	This refers to the willingness of family members to commit to using therapy to help them change and improve life.	The therapist needs to help the family have clear commitments to the therapy. The therapist may have to negotiate multiple and varied thoughts on what the therapy is 'for'.
Safety within the therapeutic space.	This refers to the family members being willing to talk about difficult things, to feel safe enough to disagree with each other and verbalise differences.	The therapist needs to make clear what the 'safety rules' are for the conversation and also find ways of ensuring that conflict doesn't spread from the therapy room to the home.
Shared sense of purpose.	This is the only dimension that requires a family 'global' score. The family as a whole has to see the point of them all working together and helping each other or even one family member.	The therapist needs to foster collective responsibility. S/he needs to encourage the family to look at joint agendas not just one relating to an individual/family member.

it provides guidance on what the therapist can do if one aspect of the alliance is less secure (see Table 4.3).

Clearly, the therapeutic alliance between one therapist and one client is a wholly different phenomenon than that between one therapist and a family. The quality of the alliance will inevitably vary between family members, and indeed it is often

---

Task 2

Imagine your family (current or your family of origin) was going to family therapy. Who might be most anxious? Who might want to say the least? What would you all want from the therapist? Are there qualities you would look for? How would you want the therapist to manage any differences between you?

Task 3

Imagine your family was in therapy and one family member did not want to be there. What could the therapist do to change this?

---

the case that one family member 'wants' to bring the family to therapy more than other family members. Thus, in family therapy, the therapist has to work at the inherent dimensions with every family member! The research on the alliance has pinpointed another important process: *split alliance scores*, e.g. where one family member's score is very different from another's, as these are also indicative of dropout and poor outcome (Robbins *et al.*, 2003). This means that the therapist needs to be alert to the way she or he relates to family members throughout the sessions and make adjustments to keep individuals on board during the therapy.

The therapist in an explicit or an implicit way might undertake these techniques, which are designed to ensure that the alliance is strong. SOFTA, for instance, largely trains the therapist to behave in ways which can maximise the alliance without necessarily talking about it. In fact, SOFTA has a software programme that helps the therapist map what is happening in a session on each of the dimensions, so that she or he can consciously decide, for instance, to improve her or his 'emotional connection' scores with the family. However, alliance building behaviour can also be explicit and live and this is the kind of behaviour demonstrated in the film that accompanies this chapter (see film: Integrative model – talking about talking and building the therapeutic alliance). Here the therapist is asking the family how they can 'collaborate' together in the therapy and is seeking advice from the family about how he should work with them.

Fact box

CYP-IAPT is an NHS England training programme that aims to improve the community Child and Adolescent Mental Health Service (CAMHS), which are National Health Service-funded services that address children and young people's mental health, by improving access to evidence-based psychological therapies and improving service user participation.

Clearly, 'collaboration' can mean many things: from just asking for permission to do something, to fully creating something *with* someone. Family therapy has been very alive to these varying descriptions of what it means to collaborate (Anderson and Gehart, 2007; Sutherland and Strong, 2011; Zimmerman, 2011). Moreover, the spirit of participation and customer input into services has strongly influenced current family therapy practice (Howe, 1989; Reimers and Treacher, 1995). An example can be seen in the focus of participation as a core principle in the Children and Young Person's Increasing Access to Psychological Therapies (CYP-IAPT) Systemic Family Practice curriculum (www.hee.nhs.uk/our-work/hospitals-primary-community-care/mental-health-learning-disability/mental-health/children-young-people%E2%80%99s-improving-access-psychological). Family therapy retains its view that there are multiple perspectives, and the therapist's perspective is one of these. For instance, family therapists may be working with people who have mental health conditions that threaten their lives (e.g. anorexia). Here the voice of the 'ill' person needs to be tempered with other voices, although they clearly have a role in how therapy proceeds (Fernández *et al.*, 2007).

One of the ways that family therapists can explicitly address the therapeutic alliance is to actually ask about how they should work with the family. Such an approach seems quite obvious but may also seem a little unusual to the family. However, contemporary social constructionist theory would promote such a transparent practice (Anderson and Gehart, 2007).

Task 4

Imagine you went to family therapy with your family, would you want the therapist to ask for your ideas about how you could work together? Might it seem a bit strange to start with that question?

This kind of way of discussing the alliance with families has come to be called 'talking about talking' within the family therapy world. Burnham (2005) translated this phrase into 'relational reflexivity', which describes what the therapist has to do to make the conversation with the family therapeutic. He recommends that family therapists ask about the minutiae of what they do with the family. For instance, he asks if the questions he is using are hard/easy, helpful/unhelpful! Talking about talking is also a very subtle and complex intervention. On one level, it is exactly what it is describing: enquiring about how the family and therapist are going to cooperate with each other. But on another level, it is itself an intervention. For instance, the therapist may ask, "How should we manage if someone in the family gets upset?" Or "What topics do you really not want to talk about?" In both of these, the therapist is inviting a collaborative 'solution' to emerge but is also commenting on what might happen! Strategic therapists who have been influenced by Ericksonian ideas (see Chapter 5) might comment that by mentioning these possibilities, the therapist is making them less likely. Elsa Jones (personal communication with Mark Rivett) used to talk about using these conversations to 'fill in gaps' which cannot be directly addressed. In the following example, the therapist almost inoculates the family about talking about a particular subject, so that when it is talked about, it is okay.

Therapist: I am wondering if there are any topics you just don't want me to raise in these sessions?

Mother: Yes. I don't want to talk about the past and about the kids' father.

Therapist:	OK, I respect that. But you know what us therapists are like! I might unintentionally 'wander' into that zone. How can we manage when I do that?
Mother:	I could tell you to butt out!
Therapist:	Yes, that might work but it might be tough for you to do that. I am sure you would not want to be rude! (To stepfather) Do you have any ways of helping your partner when the conversation goes into those issues?
Stepfather:	Yes, I just change the subject.
Therapist:	OK, so if we are talking and one of you suddenly starts talking about the weather, I will know I have strayed somewhere where we have to get out of?

In this segment, although the therapist and family have named how they will collaborate when a difficult topic is discussed, they have also talked about that subject! Jones calls this "colouring in the outline" of a difficulty without actually talking about what is in the middle. Much like a child completing a dot-to-dot picture: without directly drawing in the conventional sense, step-by-step an image finally appears.

So far in this chapter we have discussed various aspects of the integrative family therapies. We have highlighted the general features of such approaches and we have emphasised the role of the therapeutic alliance in them. Our metaphor of integrative approaches is that they are chameleon-like. We therefore will close this chapter by considering the most recent transformation of the chameleon, which is that of evidence-based practice models. We cannot describe all these models but will take one as an example of the others.

Evidence-based practice models as integrative family therapies: family therapy for adolescent eating disorders

> ### Fact box
>
> Ivan Eisler is a clinical psychologist and researcher whose work in the treatment of eating disorders at The Maudsley Hospital, London, is widely published.

There are two evidenced-based family therapy models for adolescent eating disorders (Eisler et al., 2016; Lock and Le Grange, 2013). Each of them have a wealth of research behind them and indeed there are even studies exploring which type of family therapy is the most effective (Eisler, 2005; Eisler et al., 2015; Agras et al., 2014). Lock and Le Grange (2013:21), for instance, argue that:

> The theoretical understanding or overall philosophy of FBT [family based treatment] is that the adolescent is embedded in the family and that the parents' involvement in therapy is vitally important for ultimate success in treatment.

Eisler *at al.* (2016: 27) state:

> The systemic model for treatment of anorexia nervosa should not be thought of as a distinct model of family therapy … but rather as an application of a general integrative systemic family therapy approach to the treatment of a specific condition.

Both these approaches are integrative in the sense that we have already described. Each insists on the centrality of the therapeutic alliance, each retains an overall systemic perspective in the treatment and each brings into the treatment techniques from a range of family therapy schools. In Table 4.4, we provide a fuller analysis of the manualised Maudsley model as an integrative family therapy.

In our earlier description of integrative family therapies, we noted Lebow's argument that some models integrated theoretically by bringing systemic ideas underneath an alternative 'umbrella'. Others integrated by bringing many systemic and family therapy ideas within one model: technical integration. Both family-based treatments for adolescent eating disorders function as technical integrations under a fully systemic umbrella. They are, however, not alone. Most, if not all, the evidenced-based models that exist within the field of family therapy are technical or theoretical integrations (see Table 4.5).

The examples in Table 4.5 are guides. There are many other integrative evidence-based family therapies. We would recommend readers review a number of texts, which carry fuller descriptions of these models (Bray and Stanton, 2009; Lebow, 2005; Sexton *et al.*, 2003).

Table 4.4 Table outlining how the Maudsley approach functions as an integrative family therapy

Idea/technique integrated from other schools of family therapy	How this is described in the Maudsley manual	Clinical example
Family systems theory.	Eisler *et al.* (2016) argue that rather than the eating disorder being a "function" of family dysfunction, it *causes* changes in the family.	Families where a young person has an eating disorder often 'reorganise' around the illness. Meals become the focus of functioning, the family life cycle is frozen and patterns emerge that *maintain* the problem.
A systemic understanding of change.	The approach assumes that change occurs through changes in *individual* and *relational* patterns/ understandings.	Families are helped to think about how the eating disorder limits their development. They are asked to change how they behave towards each other.
An emphasis on meanings within the family (Milan school).	Beliefs about the eating disorder are an "important focus" so that change can occur.	Ideas about 'why?' the young person has an eating disorder will be discussed and analysed with the family. How these beliefs block change will be explored.

Table 4.4 Continued

Idea/technique integrated from other schools of family therapy	How this is described in the Maudsley manual	Clinical example
Systemic formulations (development of Milan school).	The formulation will evolve over the course of the treatment but it provides a framework for change.	For instance, part of the formulation may be that the young person's parents are separating and thus cannot come together to help the young person and the young person feels 'in the middle' of them.
Parents need to be helped to 'take the lead' in working to restore health to their child (Structural school).	Intervention 'requires rapid learning on the part of the parent'.	Parents are encouraged to take responsibility for managing their child's eating.
Externalisation (Narrative school).	The eating disorder is externalised to 'separate problems from the individual'. This helps galvanise the family against the eating disorder not against the young person. The approach recognises that there are also pitfalls to externalisation.	The therapist will explore questions like: "When did this eating disorder first get in the way of family relationships?"
Experiential intervention is a way of in-session learning (Structural school).	The approach favours a 'family meal' in which the therapist and family work together to learn what works and what doesn't work in helping the young person eat.	The therapist might ask: "How much distraction works during meal times?" Or "I notice you are what I might call 'encouraging' a lot. Your daughter might call it 'nagging'. Can you tell me when it works and when it doesn't?"
Recognising that as treatment progresses, the therapist becomes less expert and aims to help the family manage 'safe uncertainty' (Mason, 1993) (Social constructionist schools).	The approach is divided into four 'phases'. The early phases concentrate on 'food as the medicine' but in later phases, the therapy changes to exploring 'normal development' and managing anxiety.	The therapist might start to ask about how the family know that some behaviour is from the eating disorder rather than from 'just being an adolescent'.

Table 4.5 Examples of other evidence-based integrative family therapies

Name of model	What kind of integration is it?	What main family therapy schools does it draw on?
Multi-Systemic Therapy (MST) (Henggeller *et al.*, 2009). Treatment of anti-social behaviour.	Theoretical in that MST has a fundamentally systemic approach to anti-social behaviour in young people. It has also been adapted for work with sexually harmful behaviour and mental health difficulties.	Structural and Strategic. MST also favours a view that the therapist needs to work to find 'fit' with the family and its goals.
Functional family therapy (FFT) (Sexton, 2011). Treatment of anti-social behaviour.	Theoretical although FFT has more of a family intervention focus than MST.	Structural and Strategic. FFT have a range of elegant ways of reframing.
Multidimensional family therapy (MDFT) (*Liddle et al.*, 2005). Treatment of adolescent drug misuse.	Theoretical balancing intra-familial and extra-familial interventions.	Structural in particular but also a strong use of alliance concepts.
Brief Strategic Family Therapy (BSFT) (Horigian *et al.*, 2005). Initially treatment of substance misuse in young people but now applied more generally. The first evidence-based model to be designed for an ethnic minority ('Hispanic youth').	More of a technical integration bringing many family therapy techniques into a coherent whole.	The title gives away the primary influence: strategic school ideas.
Emotionally focused couple therapy (EFT) (Greenberg and Johnson, 1988; Woolley and Johnson, 2005). An evidence-based model for couples' therapy.	Theoretical integration, which like ABFT, uses attachment theory as an overarching guide to practice.	Attachment systemic schools.

The legacy of integrative family therapy

Now we are at the end of this chapter, you will hopefully grasp why we chose the metaphor of a chameleon to epitomise integrative family therapies. The variety and difference between all these family therapies is astonishing. Yet, they all share some central components and attitudes to family intervention. A key element to them all is a focus on the therapeutic alliance and an emphasis on systemic, relational processes. In each of our subsequent chapters, we attempt to summarise what has been gained from the different schools of family therapy (as well as visually demonstrating this in the films) and consider where those skills will lead to in future family therapy practice. In some ways, we believe that the 'legacy' of integrative family therapies is all around us in contemporary practice. Its legacy is current and growing. Earlier on we talked about the chameleon eating 'insects' and assimilating them. This is perfectly apt in the current climate of evidence-based practice built on consumer collaboration. We can predict that these models are likely to expand; family therapists will need to learn them and even perhaps become accredited practitioners in them. However, as these integrative models expand, there is an increasing gap between these and the more 'socially constructionist' models of family therapy. This gap will only be filled if socially constructed family therapy expands its own research base and creates its own forms of integration-or if the as yet unformed integrative family therapies choose to eat these up too!

Please access the film using the eResources tab on the webpage for the book, which can be found on the Routledge website: www.routledge.com/9781138831438

Watch film: Integrative model – talking about talking and building the therapeutic alliance

Introduction to film

This is the second section of a family therapy session devoted to assessment. After the therapist (Mark) has gathered enough information to begin to construct a hypothesis about the relational factors that are influencing the behaviour of the family members, he begins a conversation that elicits how the family and he are going to work together. The clip shows a few minutes of 'talking about talking'.

1.26 Mark: It is important for me to know what I need to know about you and how I need to behave so that you can get the most out of these sessions. Does anyone have any ideas about what I should think about when I am working with you?

Skill note

Here Mark uses very general language, which allows for any issue to be raised and also any person to speak. In some ways, his question may be too complex for Laura to grasp (readers might ask themselves how it could be said in a way which she might understand). But the assumption is that she will 'catch' up as the conversation unfolds.

Maria: Neither Nick nor Joel are very good at talking about their worries and problems.

Skill note

Maria comments that the men in the family are less likely to talk in sessions. This represents a stereotypical gender role situation (see Featherstone *et al.*, 2007). Therapists need to recognise that men and women will have different ways of managing these issues.

Mark: So neither Nick nor Joel are good at talking? Is that right, Joel?

Skill note

It is important that Joel has a voice in this conversation. Mark has already picked up that he is reticent and also quite a careful thinker before he speaks. This may or may not be related to symptoms of depression but makes it doubly important that he is allowed to have space to talk and think through what he wants to say.

Joel: Yes, I guess.

Skill note

Mark connects the process of 'talking about talking' to why the family are struggling at home. Here he is painting the background to the problem as referred to above. Doing this means any conversation about how to handle the sessions is an indirect conversation about how to change things at home.

Mark: I might guess that this is one of the reasons you are here, that talking is difficult.
It's hard to talk about what is worrying people. If that is an issue for Joel and Nick, and Nick's not here so someone might have to help me think what I might have to do for him. So, what do I have to do to make them feel more comfortable talking here?

Skill note

Mark is asking for the family to help him manage this issue. It is not his 'problem' alone but shared: this is collaboration in action.

Maria: Go slowly; give them time to come around.

Mark: (Sees Laura nodding) Do you agree Laura? Are you better at talking than Joel or your dad?

Laura: Not really ... I get a bit nervous when I am around people I don't really know.

Mark: Does that make it difficult sometimes for you? So, this means it might be hard for you to talk here too? OK, so everyone's a bit nervous about talking; they maybe haven't learnt how to talk in these settings (*note reframe here*). Maria, you say I need to go slowly, is there anything else I can do? For instance, Joel is sitting here, is there anything else I can do to help him feel more comfortable apart from going slowly?

Maria: I think he may be worried to get blamed.

Mark: So, Joel, your mum is saying two things: Nick is not very good at talking and he might need me to go slowly, and she is also saying you might feel blamed. Could you help me understand what that's about?

4.43 Joel: It's like I sort of feel if I'm talking about something, people might assume it's my fault ... I guess. I don't know.

Mark: Do you think I might blame you?

Joel: No. It's mostly Nick.
I feel he blames me for a lot of things.

Mark: So what do you think I can do to help you speak more, feel less blamed and do something about that experience you have that feels as if Nick is blaming you?

Skill note

Here Mark again asks for the family to help, but notice he does not give the experience a 'truth' value. He asks what can be done about the experience not the 'fact'.

Joel: I guess tell Nick to be quiet ...

Mark: So when Nick is here, I have to be very sensitive to when he says something that you might interpret as blaming you and try to calm it down. Now Nick is not here, he can't answer for himself. Do you two think Nick will be 'up' for me doing that?

Joel: I don't know. Probably not. He feels like the sort of person who doesn't listen to anyone ...

Mark: So he doesn't find it easy to talk and he struggles to listen (*note reframe*).

> **Skill note**
>
> It is important for the therapist not to 'take sides', nor to allow how other people in the family view each other to affect the therapist making their own relationship with that person. Often, perceptions are contextual: determined by repetitious patterns and do not actually summarise the person at all.

Mark: Are the two connected do you think (listening and talking)? Maybe he's not used to listening very well so he is not used to talking very well.

> **Skill note**
>
> Here one family member names that they feel blamed by an absent family member. Mark must behave ethically now. He must not agree to this idea because doing so may make it harder to work with Nick when he comes but also such behaviour lacks respect for someone who is not here and able to speak for himself.
>
> Note: Laura looks uncomfortable about her dad being talked about like this.

Mark: We are talking about your husband, Maria, and about what I have to do to help Joel feel more involved here. Is what Joel is saying about Nick fair or is it something else I need to think about?

Maria: It sort of is. He is not used to doing this sort of thing … talking and when he has something in his mind, I really have to drag it out of him. It's very difficult.

Mark: So I have to drag things out of Nick and help keep Joel feel less blamed. That's a tall order. What about yourself? Joel, you tell me about your mum. What do I need to do to help your mum feel she can contribute here, that she can say things?

(Joel doesn't really know how to answer this question. So Mark offers an idea that as a system, if one member doesn't talk, another will likely talk too much.)

Mark: Do you think I might end up relying on your mum too much because she might have to talk for you and Nick?

Joel: Well, I like kind of think, yes, she does try to fill in for other people. If that makes sense?

Mark: Do you think this is going to work if the only person who talks is your mum?

Joel: No!

> **Skill note**
>
> This is a semi-humorous question designed to encourage Joel to say No! Again, the process is encouraging responsibility taking amongst all family members. Once this is established, Mark makes sure that the youngest family member has a place to contribute. Notice that all family members must be included.

Mark:	So somehow, we have to help her be a bit quieter, and help you and Nick say some things. What about Laura? What do I have to do to help Laura feel she can contribute to these sessions and get something from them?
Maria:	As she says, she is a bit shy around people she doesn't know and she can't concentrate for too long. But she likes drawing.
Mark:	Would you like to do some drawing now, Laura? What would you like to draw?
Laura:	Why don't I draw pictures of like what you are talking about and how much you are talking (see Combrinck-Graham, 2006; Wilson, 1998, for working with children in family therapy).
10.00 Mark:	That sounds good. See what you can do. And we will talk about that later, yes? So, for us to work together and for people to feel safe here, I have to help Nick listen and talk more. I have to help Joel feel less blamed. I have to help mum speak but not for other people. I have to make sure that Laura has got a chance to contribute in her own way. How about … I am hearing there is tension in the family. Joel is saying there is a bit of tension between Joel and Nick. What do you think I need to do, we all need to do, to manage that tension between family members in the family? If there was a big row, would that be helpful or not, and what would you want us to do about that?
10.40 Maria:	Maybe we should ah … try to listen to each other and understand each other properly and react differently.
Mark:	OK, so we are building up a few rules, ideas … that we try to listen, we try to react differently, that we make sure that things stay calm. If things did get very difficult, what do you think I should do? Let's say, Joel, you two started to exchange words and say rude things to each other; what should I do?
Joel:	Tell us all to shut up!
Mark:	So you give me permission to do that, Joel? And Maria? And when Nick comes, will he give me permission to do that, do you think?
Maria:	I think so. Laura, will you give me permission? Did you hear what we are saying? Yes, OK.

Skill note

Mark establishes that each family member gives him permission to do this. He will have to check this out with Nick also.

Mark: (To Laura) Do people start to shout at each other at home sometimes?
Laura: Ummm, quite often.
Mark: Does that get frightening?
Laura: Sometimes.
Mark: Does it upset you?
Laura: Sometimes, not that often though.

Skill note

Mark is assessing here as well as working out how to manage conflict in the session.

Mark: Sometimes but not that often. OK. If it happens here, I have permission to ask people to stop. What about people crying? Who is most likely to cry in these sessions?
Joel: It's mum.
Mark: Ok, does mum get upset a lot at home? Does she cry at home when things are difficult?
Joel: Yes.
Mark: Do you mind when she cries?
Joel: It feels sort of bad.
Mark: Is it bad because she is crying because something has gone wrong, or does it just upset you when she cries?
Joel: Yes, it probably…
Mark: Upsets you? Laura, do you get upset when mum cries?
Laura: I don't really like it when mum cries because it makes me sad all the time.
Maria: It sounds like I am a fountain.

Skill note

It is important that family responses are validated and not given a negative description. Mark points out how the young people experience the crying but does not judge, nor does he imply Maria shouldn't cry in sessions.

Mark:	I don't think we are saying that but … what is your advice to me? Therapy can be difficult; people can say things that are hurtful because we find out about things that they are unhappy about. (*Mark normalises crying in therapy.*) What shall we do with this … is it OK to cry a bit, can we manage a little bit of upset, do I need to give you tissues or what?
Maria:	Well, I will try to control myself but maybe to give me a time when I cry it really releases stress. I am luckily not upset for long; when I cry I can come back to normal, you know. Just give me some time and tissues!
14.10 Mark:	The other thing in my head that we need to talk about. You are Slovakian so is there anything I need to understand about how you think about family life and bringing up the children that I might not be used to, might not know about?
Maria:	Maybe just, I may not understand everything you say, some phrases I haven't heard of before and idioms.

Skill note

Many family therapists have written about culture in therapy (Krause, 2012; McGoldrick and Hardy, 2008). It is important for the therapist to take responsibility to raise the issues of how different cultural experiences and expectation might influence therapy.

Mark:	Do you feel confident you could say to me, Mark, I don't understand?
Maria:	Yes.
Mark:	(To children) Is that something that happens in the family? Joel, do you use a phrase that your mother doesn't understand? Or is it quite rare?
Joel:	It is rare, but it does happen every now and then.
Mark:	When you think about your mum with a Slovakian heritage, do you think she has particular attitudes about family and about how children should grow up that you notice?
Joel:	I don't really notice anything; it's been my whole life.
Mark:	So when you talk to your friends at school, they don't say we do it this way and your mum says you should do it another way?
Joel:	It isn't something we talk about.
Mark:	Maria, is there anything I need to know about, any words about family I should learn?
16.00 Maria:	No.
Mark:	So it is just a matter of language.

Skill note

Although family therapy is 'just talk', it is meant to make a difference to family members' lives. So, building the therapeutic alliance also needs to address goals. The family have to find a use for coming to *therapy*.

	So, our final discussion about how we are going to work together is to work out what our goals are. What do you want to achieve, what do you want to see in your family that we can work on in these sessions? Who would like to start? (*Asks Laura*) What would you like to change in the family?
Laura:	To start with everyone to stop arguing.
Mark:	I might write these up on the board. Laura's goal is to have less arguing or stop arguing. Laura? *(Note: Mark seeks to establish a realistic goal: arguing is usually part of family life!)*
Laura:	Less. And also, if Joel could play with me sometimes or help me with my iPad.
17.00 Mark:	You'd like a bit more help from your brother. Joel, what would you like to achieve in these sessions? How would you like your family to change? Things to get better?
Joel:	I think I would like people probably to sort of calm down, I guess. Though that comes with the less arguing.
Mark:	It is very similar to your sister's. Anything else?
Joel:	Can't think of anything that would go against what you have on the board.
Mark:	Have I heard that your relationship with Nick isn't as good as it could be? Would you like to improve that?

Skill note

Goals are co-constructed: the therapist can also suggest some as Mark does here.

Joel:	Yeah …
Mark:	And Maria? How would you like things to change? What would your goals be?
Maria:	I would like Joel to feel better and get out of his depression, come out of his room more so we can have a family dinner. More family time.
Mark:	If Nick were here, does anybody have an idea about what he might want to get out of these sessions? *(Absent family members should not be left out).*

Maria: I think he'd want pretty much the same, and that Joel would have a different attitude towards him as well. Yes, both ways. (*Mark emphasises reciprocity*).
Mark: So what has Laura drawn to show us? Would you like to share?
Laura: I've done bigger blocks for people who have said more and smaller boxes, and I've put a dash in it every time someone has spoken.
Mark: Who have you missed out?
Laura: You!
Mark: Yes! Where would I be? Would I be saying more than mum or less than mum?
Laura: Probably a bit more.

Summary

This short film demonstrates a number of key factors in building the therapeutic alliance and how 'talking about talking' contributes to this process. Pace has been addressed. Issues about strong emotional expression have been covered. Cultural issues have been mentioned, although it is true that the family did not have a lot to say about these. Lastly, children's contribution to building the alliance has been encouraged by the simple use of pen and paper!

References

Agras, W. S., Lock, J., Brandt, H., Bryson, S., Dodge, E., Halmi, K., Booil Jo, Johnson, C., Kaye, W., Wilfley, D. and Woodside, B. (2014). Comparison of 2 family therapies for adolescent anorexia nervosa. *JAMA Psychiatry*: 1279–1286.
Anderson, H. and Gehart, D. (2007) *Collaborative therapy*. New York: Routledge.
Blow, A., Bavis, S. and Sprenkle, D. (2012). Therapist-worldview matching: not as important as matching to clients. *Journal of Marital and Family Therapy*, 38: 13–17.
Bordin, E. (1979) The generalizability of the psychoanalytic concept of the working alliance. *Psychotherapy: Theory, Research and Practice*, 16: 252–260
Bowlby, J. (1988). *A secure base*. London: Routledge.
Bray, J. and Stanton, M. (2009). *The Wiley-Blackwell handbook of family psychology*. Chichester: Blackwell.
Bretherton, I. (1992). The origins of attachment theory: John Bowlby and Mary Ainsworth. *Developmental Psychology*, 28: 759–775.
Breunlin, D., Pinsof, W., Russell, W. and Lebow, J. (2011). Integrative problem-centered metaframeworks therapy I: core concepts and hypothesizing. *Family Process*, 50: 293–313.
Burnham, J. (2005). Relational reflexivity: a tool for socially constructing therapeutic relationships. In Flaskas, C., Mason, B. and Perlesz, A. (Eds) *The space between*. London: Karnac: 1–18.
Carpenter, J. Escudero, V. and Rivett, M. (2008). Training family therapy students in conceptual and observation skills relating to the therapeutic alliance. *Journal of Family Therapy*, 30: 411–421.
Combrinck-Graham, L. (2006) (Ed). *Children in family contexts*. New York: Guilford.

Crittenden, P., Dallos, R., Landini, A. and Kozlowska, K. (2014) *Attachment and family therapy.* Maidenhead: McGraw-Hill.

Dallos, R. (2006) *Attachment narrative therapy.* Maidenhead: McGraw-Hill.

Dallos, R. and Vetere, A. (2009) (Eds). *Systemic therapy and attachment narratives.* London: Routledge.

Diamond, G., Diamond, G. and Levy, S. (2014). *Attachment based family therapy for depressed adolescents.* Washington DC: APA.

Diamond, G, Russon, J. and Levy, S. (2016). Attachment-based family therapy: a review of the empirical support. *Family Process,* 55: 595–610.

Diamond, G. and Shpigel, M. (2014). Attachment based family therapy for lesbian and gay adolescents and their persistently nonaccepting parents. *Professional Psychology,* 45: 258–268.

Eisler, I. (2005). The empirical and theoretical base of family therapy and multiple family day therapy for adolescent anorexia nervosa. *Journal of Family Therapy,* 27: 104–131.

Eisler, I., Simic, M., Blessitt, E. and Dodge, L. (2016). Maudsley service manual for child and adolescent eating disorders. www.national.slam.nhs.uk/wp-content/uploads/2011/11/Maudsley-Service-Manual-for-Child-and-Adolescent-Eating-Disorders-July-2016.pdf.

Eisler, I., Wallis, A. and Dodge, E. (2015) What's new is old and what's old is new: the origins and evolution of eating disorders family therapy. In Loeb, C., Le Grange, D. and Lock, J. (Eds) *Family therapy for adolescent eating and weight disorders.* New York: Routledge: 6-42.

Featherstone, B., Rivett, M. and Scourfield, J. (2007). *Working with men in health and social care.* London: Sage.

Fernández, E., Cortés, A. and Tarragona, M. (2007). You make the path as you walk: working collaboratively with people with eating disorders. In Anderson, H., and Gehart, D. (Eds) *Collaborative therapy.* New York: Routledge: 129–148.

Flaskas, C. and Perlesz, A. (1996) (Eds). *The therapeutic relationship in systemic,* pp. 425–442.

Flaskas, C. and Pocock, D. (2009). *Systems and psychoanalysis.* London: Karnac.

Friedlander, M., Escudero, V. and Heatherington, L. (2006). *Therapeutic alliances in couple and family therapy.* Washington: APA.

Friedlander, M., Escudero, V., Heatherington, L. and Diamond, G. (2011). Alliance in couple and family therapy. *Psychotherapy,* 48: 25–33.

Germer, C., Siegal, R. and Fulton, P. (2005). *Mindfulness and psychotherapy.* New York: Guilford.

Gottman, J. (1999). *The marriage clinic.* New York: Norton.

Greenberg, L. and Johnson, S. (1988). *Emotionally focused therapy for couples.* New York: Guilford.

Henggeller, S., Schoenwald, S., Borduin, C., Rowland, M. and Cunningham, P. (2009). *Multisystemic therapy for antisocial behaviour in children and adolescents.* New York: Guilford.

Horigian, V., Suarez-Morales, L., Robbins, M., Zarate, M., Mayorga, C., Mitrani, V. and Szapocznik, J. (2005). Brief strategic family therapy for adolescents with behaviour problems. In Lebow, J. (Ed) *Handbook of clinical family therapy.* New Jersey: Wiley & Sons, pp. 73–102.

Howe, D. (1989). *The consumer's view of family therapy.* Aldershot: Gower Publishing Co.

Hughes, D. (2007). *Attachment focused family therapy.* New York: Norton.

Hughes, D. (2011). *Attachment focused family therapy: workbook.* New York: Norton.

Kagan, J. (2010). *The temperamental mind.* New York: The Dana Foundation.

Knobloch-Fedders, L., Pinsof, W. and Mann, B. (2004) The formation of the therapeutic alliance in couple therapy. *Family Process*, 43: 425–442.

Krause, I.-B. (2012) (Ed). *Mutual perspectives: culture and reflexivity in systemic psychotherapy.* London: Karnac.

Kuipers, E., Leff, J. and Lam, D. (2002). *Family work for schizophrenia.* London: Gaskell.

Lebow, J. (2003). Integrative approaches to couple and family therapy. In Sexton, T., Weeks, G. and Robbins, M. (Eds) *Handbook of family therapy.* New York: Routledge, pp. 201–225.

Lebow, J. (2005). Preface. In Lebow (Ed) *Handbook of clinical family therapy.* New Jersey: Wiley & Sons: xv–xvii.

Lebow, J. (2006). *Research for the psychotherapist: from science to practice.* New York: Routledge.

Lebow, J. (2014). *Couple and family therapy: an integrative map of the territory.* Washington DC: APA Books.

Levy, S., Russon, J. and Diamond, G. (2016). Attachment based family therapy for suicidal lesbian, gay and bisexual adolescents. *Australian and New Zealand Journal of Family Therapy,* 37: 190–206.

Liddle, H., Rodriguez, R., Dakof, G., Kanzki, E. and Marvel, F. (2005). Multidimensional family therapy: a science based treatment for adolescent drug abuse. In Lebow (Ed) *Handbook of clinical family therapy.* New Jersey: Wiley & Sons, pp.128–163.

Lock, J. and Le Grange, D. (2013). *Treatment manual for anorexia nervosa.* New York: Guilford.

McGoldrick, M. and Hardy, K. (2008). *Re-visioning family therapy: race, culture and gender in clinical practice.* New York: Guilford.

Mason, B. (1993). Towards positions of safe uncertainty. *Human Systems,* 4: 198–200.

Pinsof, W. (1995). *Integrative problem centered therapy: a synthesis of family, individual and biological therapies.* New York: Basic Books.

Pinsof, W., Breunlin, D., Russell, W. and Lebow, J. (2011). Integrative problem-centered metaframeworks therapy II: planning, conversing and reading feedback. *Family Process,* 50: 314–336.

Pinsof, W., Zinberg, R. and Knoblock-Fedders, L. (2008). Factorial and construct validity of the Revised Short Form Integrative Psychotherapy Alliance Scales for family, couple and individual therapy. *Family Process,* 47: 281–301.

Pocock, D. (2006). Six things worth understanding about psychoanalytic psychotherapy. *Journal of Family Therapy,* 28: 349–366.

Reimers, S. and Treacher, A. (1995). *Introducing user-friendly family therapy.* London: Routledge.

Rivett, M. and Street, E. (2003). *Family therapy in focus.* London: Sage.

Robbins, M., Turner, C., Alexander, J. and Perez, G. (2003). Alliance and dropout in family therapy for adolescents with behaviour problems. *Journal of Family Psychology,* 17: 534–544.

Rogers, C. (1957). The necessary and sufficient conditions of personality change. *Journal of Consulting Psychology,* 21: 95–103.

Safran, J. and Muran, J. C. (2000). *Negotiating the therapeutic alliance.* New York: Guilford.

Sexton, T. (2007). The therapist as moderator and mediator in successful therapeutic change. *Journal of Family Therapy,* 29: 104–108.

Sexton, T. (2011). *Functional family therapy in clinical practice.* New York: Routledge.

Sexton, T., Weeks, G. and Robbins, M. (2003). *Handbook of family therapy.* New York: Bruner-Routledge.

Simon, G. (1995). A revisionist rendering of structural family therapy. *Journal of Marital and Family Therapy,* 21: 17–26.

Simon, G. (2012). The role of the therapist: what effective therapists do. *Journal of Marital and Family Therapy,* 38: 8–12.

Sprenkle, D., Davis, S. and Lebow, J. (2009). *Common factors in couple and family therapy.* New York: Guilford.

Sutherland, O. and Strong, T. (2011). Therapeutic collaboration: conversation analysis of couple therapy. *Journal of Family Therapy,* 32: 1–23.

Tirch, D., Silberstein, L., and Kolts, R. (2016). *Buddhist psychology and cognitive-Behavioral Therapy.* New York: Guilford.

Treacher, A. (1988). Family therapy: an integrated approach. In Street, E. and Dryden, W. (Eds) *Family therapy in Britain.* Milton Keynes: Open University Press: 171–194.

Vetere, A. and Dallos, R. (2008). Systemic therapy and attachment narratives. *Journal of Family Therapy,* 30: 374–385.

Wagner, I., Diamond, G., Levy, S. Russon, J. and Lister, R. (2016). Attachment based family therapy as an adjunct to family based treatment for adolescent anorexia nervosa. *Australian and New Zealand Journal of Family Therapy,* 37: 207–227.

Will, D. and Wrate, R. (1985). *Integrated family therapy.* London: Tavistock.

Wilson, J. (1998). *Child focused practice.* London: Karnac.

Woolley, S. and Johnson, S. (2005). Creating secure connections: emotionally focused couples therapy. In Lebow (Ed) *Handbook of clinical family therapy.* New Jersey: Wiley & Sons, pp. 384–405.

Zimmerman, K. (2011). Commentary: is collaboration a viable target for family therapists? *Journal of Family Therapy,* 33: 215–223.

Chapter 5

Structural family therapy
Creating a new dance with families

Key points

- Structural family therapy was founded by Salvador Minuchin.
- Minuchin proposed that families were complex systems with their own unique culture and individual structures.
- Minuchin recognised boundaries between systems and subsystems as being important in the role of family life. He felt that problems arose if they were too flexible or too rigid.
- Structural family therapy has been enduringly influential and continues to be practiced, although it has been adapted and indeed integrated within many of the evidence-based approaches.
- Structural family therapy has been criticised both for being too 'expert-led' and for ignoring issues of power, race, gender and culture.

Introduction

The word 'structural' in the title of this version of family therapy implies something that is solid and probably steely in nature. Indeed, ever since this description of the model was invented, its founder has proceeded to insist that its practice is far from solid and steely! (Minchin and Nichols, 1993; Minuchin *et al.*, 2006.) In deference to this founder, Salvador Minuchin, we are going to suggest that, like Minuchin himself who was born in the heartland of the Argentinean tango, a metaphor from dance is more apt for his model rather than one implying concrete and walls. What is useful about the title is that this form of family therapy is indeed all about family structure. But the elegance of its theory (like a series of footwork moves) and the fluidity of its practice, belie the solidity of its name. Structural family therapy is an experiential process: something *happens* in the therapy session that offers families alternative ways of behaving towards each other. Minchin talks about therapy being a place for spontaneity (Minchin and Fishman, 1981). The therapist takes on a succession of roles in this process: conducting family dramas, personally dancing with family members and sometimes simply observing, like an anthropologist, and reflecting back what is seen. Unlike the psychoanalyst, the training for which Minuchin undertook early in his career, the therapist is personally fully present in the therapy session (Minuchin *et al.*, 2006). With this presence comes the freedom to improvise with the steps, to create whatever needs to happen to help the family to take risks within the safety of the therapy space. In the light of this description, perhaps it is best to imagine that the theory of structural family therapy (the 'solid' bit of its nature) is the hidden music that the family are dancing for which the therapist has to use intuition, connectedness and a sixth sense to hear. This then guides the moves, the dance and the steps.

Foundations

Although a number of other clinicians have contributed to the development of structural family therapy (including Fishman, 1993, Aponte,1994 and Montalvo [Minuchin *et al.*, 1967]), it is Salvador Minuchin (see Figure 5.1) unquestionably who stands out as the main founder, the main theorist and the main promulgator (See Minuchin, 1993, for his own description of his development). Indeed at 96 years old, he is still presenting at conferences and teaching within his own institute.

Minuchin was born in Argentina in 1921. One of three children of Russian–Jewish immigrants, he was raised in a small rural Jewish community. Initially, his family were prosperous but when the Great Depression hit Argentina, the family were forced into poverty. As a result, Minuchin experienced first-hand the impact of social hardship and inequality on family and community life. He began his career by studying medicine in Argentina. In 1944 during his medical training he became involved in revolutionary activities, which resulted in a short prison

Image 5.1 Dr Sal Minuchin.
Courtesy of Minuchin Center for the Family

sentence. When he qualified in 1946, he worked initially in paediatrics although he already had an interest in psychiatry.

Following the establishment of the state of Israel in 1948 and the subsequent Arab–Israeli war, Minuchin travelled to Israel and joined the army to work as a doctor caring for wounded Jewish soldiers. At the end of the conflict, he relocated to the United States to continue his studies under Nathan Ackerman (1958), who was a psychiatrist and a psychoanalyst but had also begun to work with families (see Chapter 2). After a further stay in Israel, Minuchin's interest in psychoanalysis resulted in him returning again to New York, and between 1954 and 1958, he trained in that discipline. Shortly afterwards, he took the post of medical director at the Wiltwyck School for Boys, which was to prove a transformational experience for him. He soon realised that helping these 'juvenile delinquents', who were mostly black Americans from poor families, as individuals was ineffective: psychoanalysis did not have the techniques to give them a better chance in life. So Minuchin began to experiment with working with the families of the boys. The roots of this bold move (the usual view was that these young people were better off 'without' their families) may have come from Ackerman or the branch of psychoanalysis that he had preferred (the 'interpersonal psychiatry' of Harry Stack Sullivan). It was this work, with disadvantaged and multiply stressed families, that led Minuchin to attend to family structure. He noticed, repeatedly, that these families seemed to lack parental authority and there were permeable (loose) boundaries between the generations (Minuchin et al., 1967). During this stage in his career, Minuchin also visited Palo Alto and made a strong friendship with Haley (Chapter 6).

In 1965, Minuchin joined the Philadelphia Child Guidance Center where he took the post of director. Under his direction, the centre became a worldwide respected child guidance clinic and family therapy training centre. Other prominent family therapists such as Jay Haley came to work with him (see Chapter 6; Minuchin and Nichols, 1993). Finally, in 1981, he established his own family therapy centre in New York that was renamed the Minuchin Center after his retirement in 1996. It continues today.

We mentioned that the structural family therapist is attentive in the therapy session. This extends to understanding what attitudes the therapist brings to the therapy. Not surprisingly, Minuchin has traced some of his ideas about family life to his own experience. The Argentinian–Jewish family that he grew up in was very hierarchical. The generations respected the eldest family members and looked to them for guidance. He admits that it was patriarchal. Each family member knew what other family members expected of them. This experience clearly influenced Minuchin's ideas about 'family functioning'.

Even during the early years of developing structural family therapy, it was criticized for promoting an idea about what a 'healthy' family 'should' look like. This is not surprising, given Minuchin's own experiences. However, even the limited history already outlined should alert readers to Minuchin's own personal understanding of the variety of families, the hardships experienced by many families and the hugely significant role of culture in family life (see Minuchin, 1984). It would, therefore, be a simplification to see structural family therapy as an apologist for the nuclear 'functional' family.

Key ideas in structural family therapy

Minuchin, influenced by his experiences of working with families from different cultures and continents, recognised families as complex systems with their own structures. He suggested that family members relate according to certain arrangements, which are rarely explicit. He believed each family had 'rules' that determined how family members related to each other and to the outside world. In fact, these patterns evolve over time: they govern how individual family members interact and they regulate the family's daily functioning. These transactional patterns, which often arise from hierarchical arrangements, serve to regulate the behaviour of family members. He recognized that families are not static – new family members are born whilst others may die. Ideally, the family adapts to accommodate these changes, but if the family structure is inflexible and cannot accommodate to change, problems can arise. Minuchin saw the role of the structural therapist as helping the family to find a more 'functional' way of managing relationships.

Task I

Using your own family, think about family rules. How might these help/ hinder the family?

Family structure

Minuchin (1974: 51) argued that all families have a structure:

> Family structure is the invisible set of functional demands that organises the ways in which the family members interact. A family is a system that operates through transactional patterns. Repeated transactions establish patterns of how, when and to whom to relate, and these patterns underpin the system.

He also says, "in truth, there is no such thing as a family structure", which is qualified by "I have found structural constructions useful" (Minuchin *et al.*, 2006: 35). Over the course of his career, Minuchin categorized the structure of families by thinking about them along two separate dimensions (Minuchin *et al.*, 1978; Minuchin *et al.*, 2007). The first is to do with their *emotional closeness*. This dimension has too 'opposite' poles: the '*disengaged*' family and the '*enmeshed*' family. In disengaged families, emotional connection is loose. Therapists might hear these families describe relationships like 'ships that pass in the night' or 'home is really a hotel'. The implication is that there is very little 'heart' to family

Table 5.1 Boundaries in structural family therapy

Rigid Boundary	Clear Boundary	Diffuse Boundary
Disengagement	'Normal' Range	Enmeshment
———————	– – – – – – – – – –	. . . .

life. Minuchin thought these kinds of families were more likely to have problems containing young people who might engage in risky antisocial behaviour. At the other extreme are 'enmeshed' families. These families describe themselves as 'living in each other's pockets'. Family members struggle to develop a life outside the family and sometimes appear to be telepathic about each other's needs. Minuchin thought these kinds of families were more likely to have young people who had psychosomatic problems (Minuchin *et al.*, 1978).

These terms applied to both the internal family structure but also to how the family related to the outside world. Minuchin noted that such descriptions were only useful inasfar as they helped orientate the therapist *and* they made sense to families. He would often ask: "Do you think you are too close/too distant?" as a way of helping the families see themselves from this perspective.

This model of family structure also contained an idea about *boundaries.* Again, Minuchin applied this concept to boundaries around a family, e.g. in relation to the outside world, and within a family e.g. between family members. Structural family therapists often map the family relationships in order to consider what the family needs to do to function more effectively. To do this, they use a kind of descriptive shorthand (see Table 5.1).

Another aspect of family structure that Minuchin emphasised was that of the systems within the family – or subsystems. He argued that the different subsystems within families might have different rules or cultures and may also have differing relationships to each other. He enumerated a number of family subsystems:

1   **The partner subsystem:** This subsystem includes the partners who bring their own internalized values and scripts (learnt in their families) into a new relationship. The partners need to reconcile their differences for the relationship to continue harmoniously. This subsystem will also form a role model for the children of the family when they become parents themselves (Minuchin, 1974).

2   **The parental subsystem:** This is different from the partner subsystem because the members may be parents but not necessarily partners (e.g. through separation/divorce or surrogacy). Parents draw on their own experiences of being parented and, if this is very disparate, will require negotiation and compromise. If the parental subsystem is divided, a number of processes may occur. First, each parent may form a bond with the children *against* the other parent (e.g. 'life would be great if your father/mother would just butt

out'). Second, they may distract from parental conflict by allying *against* one of the children (e.g. 'our relationship has been ruined by this child's behaviour'). Third, the parents may look for support from their own families (e.g. 'You would be a great dad if it wasn't that you married that woman!').

3   **The sibling subsystem:** If the family is large, this may consist of several subsystems according to developmental stages. This provides an opportunity for children to experiment with relationships and practice the effectiveness of social interactions.

Task 2

Consider your own family and describe the various subsystems within it. Try to work out how these subsystems 'relate' to each other.

Figure 5.2 illustrates how there may be a number of subsystems in one family, with the same family members belonging to different subsystems, each one of which will have its own set of rules and values. This complexity can often cause conflict and confusion. The family illustrated consists of two sets of grandparents where the youngest daughter of one set has married the eldest son of the other. This couple have given birth to a daughter and three sons.

1.   Shows the youngest sibling subsystem
2.   Shows the parental subsystem
3.   Shows the male subsystem
4.   Shows the maternal subsystem

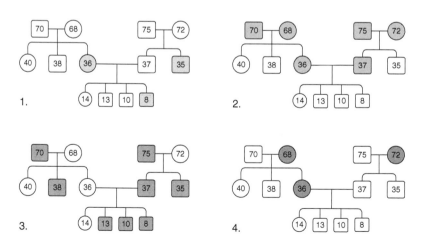

Figure 5.2   Variations in family structure.

Minuchin argued, like systems theory would suggest, that the way the subsystems inter-related was designed to maintain equilibrium: to keep the family stable even if the form 'stability' took was not helpful to individual development. This gave rise to a number of transactional patterns that were often repeated across many family systems. Again, structural family therapists adopt a novel way of showing these patterns (see Figure 5.3).

Task 3

Can you suggest other possible subsystems within this family? Think about values, beliefs, culture, sexuality, education, etc.

Mother (M) and father (F) have clear boundaries between them and their son (S) and daughter (D). This is a pattern seen in many 'functional' families.	M F ⌐ − − − − − − − D S
Mother, father and the children have no clear boundaries. The adults are not in control and there is a degree of enmeshment or co-dependency between them.	M F · · · · · · · · · · · D S
Mother is very close to children to the exclusion of father.	M ╲ F · · · · · · · · · ╱ D S ╲
Mother and daughter have an enmeshed relationship where mother does not parent the daughter and the daughter is like a mini-adult. The father and son have a 'normal' relationship, but they are disengaged from mother and daughter.	M F · · · · · · ╱ − − − D ╲ S
Mother and stepfather (SF) have a normal boundary between them and the children of her first marriage. They also treat the birth father (F) appropriately. But he has an over-familiar relationship with his children and there are no clear boundaries, so they behave like 'three children' when they are together.	M SF − − − − − − − − − D S ┊ F ·

Figure 5.3   Transactional patterns from a structural perspective.

Task 4

Bring to mind your own family and see how these transactional patterns may have been replicated.

The second major dimension of structure that Minuchin saw as essential was that of *adaptability*. Again, this dimension has two poles. On the one end are families that are 'rigid' and apply the same rules consistently even though the reason for them might have gone. An example might be a bed time for a child that is no longer developmentally necessary, or a curfew time that separates the young person from their peers. On the other end of the spectrum are families where there are no rules: almost anything goes. These families are sometimes described as 'Mardi Gras' families because it seems as if there is a carnival all the time. These families never eat meals together, don't have 'set' bed times and are very inconsistent when they impose rules. In his early work, Minuchin was not interested in the cause of these family systems: he was focused on change (largely behavioural). However, his later work took much more interest in why families had chosen to adopt these positions (Minuchin *et al.*, 2006, 2007, 2014). See Table 5.2 for a summary of family structure aspects in structural family therapy.

Table 5.2 Summary of family structure aspects in structural family therapy

Aspect of family structure	Meaning of the description	How might the therapist explore the aspect?
Emotional cohesion: Closeness.	This encompasses aspects of connection.	Who in the family would know if Joel was depressed? Might that make them depressed too?
Emotional cohesion: Distance.	This includes how disconnected family members are from each other.	Do you ever think about your mum, what she is feeling?
Adaptability: Rigidity.	This involves finding out about who makes decisions, if there are set ways of doing things.	So, who in the family makes up the rules? Are these negotiable?
Adaptability: Chaotic.	This involves finding out what families might do if things happen.	Who would know if your son was taking drugs? Do you think most families would be unaware of what is going on in their children's lives?
Subsystems.	The therapist will want to understand how each subsystem works and how each relates to other subsystems.	So, when the children fight, how important is it for you as parents to intervene?

Techniques designed to change family structure

We have established that structural family therapy is an active and quite directive form of family therapy. Minuchin lays down a number of preferred behaviours from the therapist in the full range of his works. In these he draws on other family therapy schools such as promoting 'joining' with family members and reframing (Minuchin and Fishman, 1981). However, each is re-described with a structural perspective. For instance, he maintains that joining includes avoiding exclusive alliances because the therapist has to be manoeuvrable, e.g. join with other family members and sometimes do the unexpected! There are, however, a number of key techniques solely developed by the structural school (see Table 5.3 for Minuchin's own words on the preferred behaviours).

Enactment

Enactment has often been seen as the cornerstone of this model of family therapy (Davis, 2004; Nichols, 2000). It literally means 'enacting' a piece of interaction and making it alive and available in the therapy session. It entails a number of 'phases' as described by Minuchin himself and subsequent structural therapists (Minuchin and Fishman, 1981; Minuchin et al., 2014). First, the therapist encourages the family to replay the same behaviours and patterns that they engage in at home. During this phase, the therapist observes what happens to work out what is maintaining a problematic pattern and what kind of intervention would help the family change the pattern. Second, the therapist intervenes to help the family resolve the pattern in a more fruitful way. Third, the therapist debriefs the family and works out how they can keep the 'new' pattern going at home rather than resort to the old habitual pattern.

Example:

- A mother and father say they never have time to discuss how to manage the children. The therapist says, 'Now is your chance: off you go' and gets them to talk. The therapist suspects that they 'never talk', not because of time but because they have disagreements that they don't want to air. By helping them talk, the disagreements can be faced.
- A family say they want things to be different but don't know what to do, so the therapist asks them to 'sculpt' (a physical image placing family members where they think they 'are') where they are now and where they would like to be in the future. This gets some energy moving, helps family members see what needs to change in relationships and provides a strong emotional impact.

There is some evidence that these active interventions have been influenced by drama therapy and Minuchin's exposure to Satir's methods (see Chapter 1).

Unbalancing

The structural therapist attempts to perturb the homeostasis of the family by trying to change the hierarchical and relationship patterns between family members. For example, this might be done to change a subsystem between a child and parent in order to re-establish the parent in a role of executive control.

Examples:

- The eldest daughter of a single parent mother has aligned herself with her mother as co-parent. This has interrupted the development of the sibling relationship with the younger daughter, leading the youngster to rebel and the older sister enforcing strict rules around her sister's risky behaviour. The therapist selectively supports the mother to take back control from the eldest daughter and re-establish the separate parent/child subsystem.
- Father interrupts when others are talking. The therapist might impose a new rule of 'no interruptions' in the sessions.

Intensification

Intensification is probably the hardest technique to learn that has been developed by the structural school. This is partly because it requires the therapist not to shy away from conflict and to use his or her personality to stimulate intense emotional experiences. In many ways, this is 'counter' to therapeutic training, which encourages the containment of conflict and the careful uncovering of emotion. In intensification, the therapist notices what the family choose not to talk about, and then guides them into talking about it. It requires persistence, confidence (that the therapist can help the family handle the consequences) and skill in finding the 'right' topic. The therapist might amplify an observed interaction which is 'ignored' by the family. The therapist might encourage conflictual family members to sit together (and even hold hands). The therapist might choose to sit in between family members or may decide to 'talk' for a silent family member. Sometimes this process unbalances and enacts all at the same time!

Example:

- If the therapist notices a parent overlooking a child's challenging behaviour she may say, "I see that your son is happy to ignore you, what do you think of that?"

The legacy of structural family therapy

Of all the first-generation schools of family therapy, structural family therapy was probably the most criticised for being 'first order' and prescriptive within the family therapy world (Hare-Mustin, 1987; Klassop, 1987). Yet, like the other two main first-generation schools, it has had a profound influence not only on subsequent practice within family therapy but also outside of family therapy. This influence can be broken down into a number of elements. The first is the impact of the idea about 'structure'. Almost any psychotherapist will now consider 'how the

Table 5.3 Minuchin in his own words

Theme	Quotation
Enactment	"Enactment is a process during which the therapist acts like a traffic agent, directing members of the family to enter dialogues in his or her presence … when two family members talk to each other in this context, the conversation is no longer spontaneous. It slows down and becomes an encounter". (Minuchin *et al.*, 2014: 5)
Certainty	"The family's certainty is an enemy of change … An important function of the therapist is to challenge the family's certainty." (Minuchin *et al.*, 2014: 4)
Unbalancing	"Unbalancing … facilitates change by creating stress for some units …while supporting others, then shifting over time." (Minuchin *et al.*, 2014: 7)
Intensification	"The therapist may have gained their [the family's] attention … but they do not hear." So, the therapist must "increase the affective component of the transaction." (Minuchin and Fishman 1981: 118)
Role of the therapist	The therapist "joins families, as healer, teacher, and resonator for an experiential journey." (Minuchin *et al.*, 2006: 15)

family works' and terms like 'enmeshment' are common. This is largely because such language is easily translated into a number of therapy approaches even though it began within family therapy. The second impact is the one we referred to earlier in this chapter: structural family therapy is an active form of family therapy. It provides licence for the therapist to stand up, move around, ask the family to try out something new. Although its name implies a static quality, its actual practice is innovative and creative (like dance itself). Third, there is an enduring value to recognising that therapy should not be totally comfortable. In structural family therapy, this becomes explicit and expected. Last, as we have highlighted in Chapter 3, many of the contemporary evidence-based models of family therapy have been hugely influenced by structural family therapy. For instance, although Attachment based family therapy (ABFT) has added to enactment, its way of repairing attachment ruptures still relies on this fundamental technique. We hope something of these qualities emerge in the film demonstrating enactment.

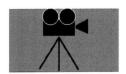

Please access the film using the eResources tab on the webpage for the book, which can be found on the Routledge website: www.routledge.com/9781138831438

Watch film: Structural school – Enactment

Introduction to film

This is the second time that Nick has come to the family therapy sessions. If the therapist is working with a structural framework, he has a responsibility to help Nick (and all family members) learn something new from the sessions. He has already made a formulation, which includes the idea that the way the family works and communicates doesn't help Joel escape his depression or feel he has his family's support in managing it. Conflict between Joel and Nick furthers their views that the other is at fault, and also perpetuates the isolation that prevents the resolution of the depression. The therapist therefore decides to address family communication and verbalisation of emotional experiences. Structural methods are very helpful in such situations because they help families try new behaviours and challenge them to go beyond their normal styles.

00.00 Mark: Welcome back. It is really nice to have you, Nick, here today. Thanks for coming along. I am wondering if anyone noticed that things had been different after our last session?

Skill note

The *therapist* begins by tracking change from the last session.

Joel: I think Nick was a bit nicer to me and my Mum didn't go on at me all the time.

Mark: So some kind of changes … do you think they have done anything different? Do you think they know they have done anything different?

Skill note

The therapist wants the change to be conscious change: then the family can keep making the changes happen.

Joel: I don't know, ask them.

Mark: (To Maria and Nick) OK, so Joel is saying you have been on at him less, and what was it you said Mum was doing?

Joel: I said Nick was nicer.

Mark: Did you notice that?

Nick: They were certainly better than they were before, yeah.

Mark: Any ideas about how that happened?

Nick: Perhaps I was more tolerant because of what we have been doing here.

! Notice the words of *change*: tolerance which will re-occur later in the session.

Mark: OK. I am wondering who in the family is able to recognise that they are most able to change and who finds it very hard to accept that they have changed?

> **Skill note**
>
> The therapist tries to work out why the question is so hard to answer.

Maria: Nick.

Mark: So, you think Nick finds it hardest to accept that he has changed? Do you know why that might be?

Maria: I think he wants to think it is all Joel's or my fault that we have problems in the family. And he is quite stubborn when he thinks he knows something.

Mark: (Some stumbling around what to ask) Do you think there is a reason why he finds it hard to think he can change, do something?

Maria: 'Cos I think as a man, as a father, as a man, he doesn't want to think he hasn't done a good job.

> **Skill note**
>
> This is an important moment: vulnerability is put into words. The therapist intensifies this.

Mark: So are you saying that even coming here it feels like he has failed in some way? He has failed Joel. OK. Does that connect at all with this thing about finding it hard to talk?

Maria: Yes (sighs as if that is important).

Mark: Is it hard for you to talk as well? About what has gone wrong and what you need to do to improve things?

Maria: Yes, it just came into the family, and we just don't talk and we are used to it now.

> **Skill note**
>
> The therapist hears that communication is a problem in the family.

Mark: I will tell you what I would like to do (to Joel) because I am hearing these two aren't very good at talking. And we have a golden opportunity here today for you two to talk to your heart's content about things that matter, not just about Joel or about what people are going to have for dinner. It's an ideal opportunity just to do it now in front of me and Joel. So, Maria, would you mind coming over here for a moment please? (Re-seats Maria opposite Nick)

Skill note

The therapist sets up an enactment. Enactment is unusual. It needs preparation and collaboration. Families need to understand why they are being asked to do it.

04.00 Mark: I would like you two, in front of us, to have a conversation about why it is so hard to talk, what you think you could do to make it easier to talk, are there some things that are harder to talk about, can you talk about other things ... that kind of thing. Try to have that conversation so we can listen and you get practice at talking to each other.

Maria: (To Nick) So why is it so hard for you to talk openly about your problems and worries?

Nick: I think it is just easier to get on with life. Than to talk about these things. It is a bit weird sat around like that.

Maria: Why is that weird?

Nick: I don't know. We just never did it. I just have no experience of spending time talking.

Skill note

The enactment is successful if things are said that aren't said at any other time. Here a lot is being revealed.

Maria: But I tried a couple of times when I saw you were upset or unhappy. I tried to drag it out of you, but you just wouldn't talk.

Nick: Yes, I guess you are probably right there. There is one person I can really rely on and that is myself. And that is why perhaps I find it harder to talk. I get on with things.

Maria: That makes me feel a little bit uncomfortable. If you think the only person you can rely on is you. Why can't you feel you can rely on me?

Skill note

One of the skills in enactment is not to 'rescue' the family members too soon. The therapist has to let hurtful things be said and see if the family can move to a resolution.

Nick: I can see how you must feel. Yeah. And I am sorry for that.

Maria: I think after the few sessions we have had, we wouldn't even need to be here if we talked at the first place.

Nick: Perhaps that is right and I didn't think we needed to be here anyway in the first place.

Maria: Why?

Nick: Because it was something I think we could have solved.

Skill note

Again, the therapist could respond to this 'resistance' to therapy. But it is best left.

Maria: But how, you weren't able to talk and you just really wanted to blame Joel or me for …

Nick: I don't think I really wanted to blame Joel all the time; if he behaved better I wouldn't have to say anything.

Mark: (To Maria) Why don't you ask him if he blames himself?

Skill note

Conversations where blame is attributed are unlikely to be fruitful. The therapist intervenes to divert attention from blame.

Maria: Do you blame yourself?

07.00 Nick: Well, perhaps lots of things are my fault. I find it difficult. Family life is difficult. That's the way it is. So perhaps there is something there. (Silence) I don't mean to (to Joel) blame Joel all the time, I really don't.

Maria: Well, it seems like you do. I think you are worried that the fact that you are not his real dad, it affects your relationship in the first place …

(Talking over each other)

Nick: Of course it does. He is not my son obviously.

Maria: I think you can try to understand him more. I knew you had a bad time as well as a child; it must have been really tough not to have a proper family; That's why I think you should, you know, create your own family to have something that you haven't had.

Nick: I am here, aren't I? I am trying this.

Skill note

The conversation is about to become an argument. Now is the time to intervene and help the parents learn a new interaction.

08.25 Mark: I am going to stop you for a moment. I can see that it is quite uncomfortable. So, I am going to promise that I will let you do this for a couple more minutes. I hope you have noticed that the way we talk here, I try not to blame anybody, I try to use language that understands where they are coming from, and I also try to make sure it is reciprocal. So, when I am talking about one person's behaviour, I am also talking about how the other person behaves. There is a kind of circular pattern going on between them. I would like to see if for only two minutes you could have a conversation based on those principles. So, understand each other, try not to blame each other and try to understand what you do that contributes to the 'not talking'. Do you think you could do that for only two minutes? (Both agree.) Over to you.

Nick: You must see that I have looked like the outsider, that's quite difficult for me.

Skill note

The intervention has produced a heartfelt confession. The therapist has stayed with the discomfort: intensification!

Maria: Yes, I think the main source of that problem is, I mean the source is that you have been in care but, for example, I've also thought about how I have similar feelings. Like about how I let my parents down, like sometimes I wonder why my dad had his heart attack and I know my mum blames me for it. Well, she never says, but she does.

Nick: I know that. It's tough. I understand that. I really do.

Maria: I am really … for example, you come home from work and I see you are tired and unhappy and I try to talk to you but you seem unreachable to me and then I see you and Joel who is mini-you … kind of …

! The couple soon change the subject of conversation. It is painful talking about their feelings of failure.

Mark: He is a mini-Nick? OK, I didn't quite get that.

Skill note

This is important use of words: it connects rather than divides Nick and Joel.

Maria:	He might have picked up …
Nick:	My anger, my intolerance.
11.00 Maria:	Not just the anger, but the thing that he wouldn't talk about things. He may have picked it up from you. Maybe from me as well. I don't know.
Nick:	Yeah, we are both not good at communicating and talking and perhaps understanding each other's feelings.
Maria:	Maybe we should try to see things from each other's perspective as well.
Nick:	Yes. (Nods)
11.45 Mark:	That is really helpful. Do you think the two of you have understood a bit more about each other and about the situation in the family as a result of that conversation?
Nick:	I think I have.
Maria:	Me as well. I think also instead of blaming each other, we should try to understand each other.

! Maria makes use of the words of the therapist.

12.12 Mark:	I want to check with Joel. When you heard that, were there any thoughts that went through your mind, were you surprised by anything Nick or your Mum said?
Joel:	Not particularly. I mean it was kind of weird to sort of see them having a private conversation.
Mark:	Which wasn't private! Are you willing to try something else now? Are you willing to have a conversation with Nick and have me and your mum watch, about how you can improve your relationship? (Joel is a bit reticent.) I promise I won't let you have an argument with each other.

Skill note

The therapist sets up another enactment. Joel is cooperating but clearly finds it hard putting his feelings into words.

Joel:	OK.
13.00 Mark:	So change places with Mum. I'd like the two of you to talk about what you can do to improve your relationship. Mum and I are just going to listen.

Nick: It would be really good if you did what you were told sometimes. That would really help me.

! Nick starts with a veiled demand.

Joel: Uhmm…
Nick: I know that might not be easy for you.
Joel: I think at the same time there are a lot of situations where you don't listen to me.

! Joel responds in an assertive but negotiating way.

Nick: You are probably right there, and when I am tired I don't feel I have the same patience. And I am really sorry that I hurt you so much in that way. You've got to believe that.

! Inside this is an apology: a recognition of responsibility.

Joel: Maybe all it takes is if we did a bit more.
Nick: A few things together or something.
Joel: Yeah.
Nick: So perhaps you would come to the football or give it a try anyway.
Joel: Yes, but there are still going to be occasions where there are problems, it is just something.

! Joel knows that what is needed is more than just going to football together.

Nick: Do you think we could talk about it, you won't slam your bedroom door or shut me out?

Skill note

Nick is almost returning to a 'blame' conversation. Joel responds but in a way which opens up options.

Joel: Well, I can't always help it if sometimes I think you are a bit of a nob.

Maria: (Shocked by the language) Joel don't be insulting.

Mark: Maria, let them sort this out. See what happens. But we don't want to be insulting to people, Joel.

Skill note

The therapist sees a 'triangular' pattern where Maria sides sometimes with one and sometimes with the other. This probably doesn't help and also probably means that the disagreements never get fully resolved.

15.20 Joel: What I mean is, there are situations where you say things. For example, when you are telling me what to do. It feels like you're...

Nick: I'm not trying to control you really. I'm just trying to show you my ways. What I think is the right way. I can see that.

! Nick knows what he does.

Maria: He does that because he wants you to do well.

Mark: (To Joel) Does it feel like they are ganging up on you?

Joel: A bit.

Mark: Do you think it is really hard for your mum to let you and Nick sort this out?

Joel: It feels like it, yeah.

Mark: Do you think you and Nick can sort this out without your mum's help?

Joel: I think so, yes.

Mark: So when you call Nick a 'nob', do you think you can explain to Nick that at times he knows, he behaves kind of nobbish?

Skill note

The therapist almost makes a joke out of the language. This makes it less hurtful. He also validates the feelings behind the language.

Joel: Yeah.

Mark: How can you get that through to him, that you are not insulting him but sometimes 'you are over the line, sometimes you don't need to do that', how can you teach him?

Joel: Well, I mean ...

Mark: Talk to him.

Joel: Well, I mean, like I said there are situations where, there are times when I feel like … I don't know.

Nick: You could talk to me. You honestly can talk to me. And if you perhaps weren't angry with me, I might not get as angry back.

! Nick still tends to go back to blame.

Joel: So maybe all it takes is a bit more …

Nick: Tolerance. Maybe you tolerate me when I'm being a nob and I tolerate you when you are not doing what I want you to do.

! Nick now comes back to 'tolerance' and he also incorporates Joel's language so making it 'OK'. Nick also recognises the reciprocal process between them.

17.40 Mark: You did very well, guys. Do you think you can do the same at home? Can you do this and not get angry with each other?

Joel: I think so.

Nick: I think this helps.

Mark: So we might need to keep practising. (To Maria) How difficult is it to let them get on with it?

Maria: Well, when they argue, I tend to protect Joel. But I think it actually gets in the way.

Mark: You are very frightened that they are going to start arguing and, therefore, you want to get in before it happens. But it doesn't always happen. And they can find a way, can't they? I think we have made a good start today, so let's see if you can remember what we have done? What was the first thing that we did?

Skill note

The therapist checks that the family understand the purpose of the enactment.

Maria: We tried to find out why it is so difficult for us to communicate.

Mark: That's right. So that's something you can keep doing. And we can do some more next time. Then what did we do? Joel, what did we try to do?

Joel: Tried to get us talking about issues.

19.00 Mark: That's right and there are lots of issues, aren't there? But you can talk about them without getting into a fight or an argument. So, we can come back to these next time. I hope it wasn't too painful.

Summary

In a short space of time, the therapist has encouraged the family to create two enactments: one between the couple and one between Joel and Nick. The purpose is to help the family challenge habitual patterns of interaction and learn new ways of relating. In this context, enactment enabled 'avoided' interactions to be faced and the 'unsaid' to be said.

References

Ackerman, N. (1958). *The psychodynamics of family life*. New York: Basic Books.
Aponte, H. J. (1994). How personal can training get? *Journal of Marital and Family Therapy*, 20, 3–15.
Davis, S. (2004). Enacting relationships in marriage and family therapy. *Journal of Marital and Family Therapy*, 30: 319–333.
Fishman, H. C. (1993). *Intensive structural therapy: treating families in their social context*. New York: Basic.
Hare Mustin, R. T. (1987). The problem of gender in family therapy theory. *Family Process*, 26(1): 15–33.
Kassop, M. (1987). Salvador Minuchin: a sociological analysis of his family therapy theory. *Clinical Sociology Review*, 5(1), Article 15. Available at http://digitalcommons.wayne.edu/csr/vol5/iss1/15
Minuchin, S. (1974). *Families and family therapy*. London: Tavistock Publications Ltd.
Minuchin, S. (1984). *Family kaleidoscope*. Cambridge, MA: Harvard University Press.
Minuchin, S. and Fishman, H. C. (1981). *Family therapy techniques*. Cambridge, MA; Harvard University Press.
Minuchin, S., Lee, W.-Y. and Simon, G. (2006). *Mastering family therapy*. New Jersey: John Wiley & Sons.
Minuchin, S., Montalvo, B., Guerney, B., Rosman, B. and Schumer, F. (1967). *Families of the slums*. New York, NY: Basic Books.
Minuchin, S. and Nichols, M. P. (1993). *Family healing: tales of hope and renewal from family therapy*. New York: Free Press.
Minuchin, S., Nichols, M. and Lee, W.-Y. (2007). *Assessing families and couples: from symptom to system*. Boston: Pearson Education.
Minuchin, S., Reiter, M. and Borda, C. (2014). *The craft of family therapy*. New York: Routledge.
Minuchin, S., Rosman, B. and Baker, L. (1978). *Psychosomatic families*. Cambridge, MA: Harvard University Press.
Nichols, M. (2000). The effective use of enactments. *Journal of Marital and Family Therapy*, 26: 143–152.

Chapter 6

Strategic family therapy

Making language therapeutic

Key points

- Strategic Family Therapy follows a problem-centred approach.
- Strategic Family Therapy attends to communication patterns in families.
- Strategic Family Therapy designs strategies to change these patterns and the implicit meanings within these patterns.
- Strategic family therapists argue that attempted solutions often make problems worse.
- Reframing and the use of paradox are two of the gifts that Strategic Family Therapy has given to family therapy in general.
- There are various approaches within the broad 'strategic family therapy' wrapper.

Introduction

Many story-telling traditions around the world have a character that can be described as a 'holy fool' or a 'trickster'. This character often ridicules the pompous behaviour of others and sometimes acts as a critic of those in power. In other stories, she or he helps people change by persuading them to do something positive because they think they will benefit: she or he 'manipulates' their intentions. African and Caribbean traditions have Anansi, the 'man spider' (Marshall, 2012); the Sufi tradition has Mulla Nasrudin (Shah, 1968); the Native American tradition has Coyote (Erdoes and Ortiz, 1999); while perhaps in the UK this character is often an animal such as a fox (Aesop, 1994; Dahl, 2016). In the story of family therapy, strategic approaches could often be described as the 'wily fox'. Of all the approaches, these are the ones that use humour, 'cunning' intelligence and creativity to help families change their patterns of behaviour. But, because they have these qualities, they are the least likely to be taught in contemporary trainings and are most often criticised for failing to be client centred and respectful. In this chapter, we will describe the approaches most often associated with a 'strategic' approach and outline some of the context in which they emerged. We hope to provide evidence that the legacy of these models remains in a number of useful techniques, which are demonstrated on the film clip that accompanies this chapter. We will also suggest that a number of features of Strategic Family Therapy have continued, albeit with changes, within other family therapy traditions.

The evolution of the wily fox

There are two points to make before we examine how strategic approaches arrived on the family therapy scene. First, we need to establish that there are at least three separate (though interconnected) groups who could be classed as 'strategic'. The first is a group of researchers, mental health professionals and therapists who are collectively known as the Mental Research Institute (MRI); one of these was Jay Haley who went on to establish his own school of strategic therapy; the third was Haley's second wife, Cloé Madanes, who also established her own strategic school. So, when we talk about the 'strategic school of family therapy', we are talking about a large den of 'wily foxes'. Second, we need to outline why the school is defined by the word 'strategic'. The best way to answer this question is to quote Haley (1973: 17):

> Therapy can be called strategic if the clinician initiates what happens during the therapy and designs a particular approach for each problem. When a therapist and a person with a particular problem encounter each other, the action that takes place is determined by both of them, but in strategic therapy the initiative is largely taken by the therapist.

Haley (Figure 6.1) also states that this approach means that it is the therapist's *responsibility* to make sure that the conversation is helpful to the family. He argues that the previous *non-directive* methods of therapy such as the client-centred and psychodynamic ones failed to accept this responsibility. Clearly, Strategic Family Therapy is within the 'first order' group of family therapies (see Chapter 2), which is why they may now be out of synch with how services are designed in the contemporary world.

Task I

Where do you think responsibility lies in terms of therapy being useful to families? How much is it the family's and how much is it the therapist's responsibility for the conversation to be helpful?

All the strategic approaches originated in a research programme set up by Bateson in Palo Alto, California, between 1952 and 1962.

Bateson had been given funding by the American government to research 'family communication' with particular relevance to soldiers returning from war zones

Figure 6.1 Jay Hayley.
Courtesy of Mr M. D. Yapko PhD

Figure 6.2 Dr Milton Erickson.
Courtesy of The Milton H. Erickson Foundation

(e.g. Vietnam). He gathered a number of experts in behaviour, mental health and communication around him and spent the next ten years studying family communication. The group included Don Jackson, John Weakland, Jay Haley and Paul Watzlawick. They began by video recording many hours of family interactions and built up a model of how communication worked in families (similar to Bowen: Weinstein, 2013) before some of them set up their own institute, the MRI in 1959.

The focus of the MRI was clinical and not research: the group saw this as an opportunity to practice what they had learnt during the research trials. The MRI is still helping families with mental health problems and largely still utilises the techniques learnt over 50 years ago (Fisch, 2004; Hale and Frusha, 2016). Haley, however, spent the 1950s and 1960s expanding his experience and understanding. While immersed in the MRI (he was director of research). he also became interested in the work of Milton Erickson (Figure 6.2), a psychiatrist from Phoenix, Arizona. Erickson is regarded as the 'father' of contemporary hypnosis practice and also famous for using very unconventional ways to help people escape psychological problems (Haley, 1973; 1984; 1993). For 17 years, Haley (and later many other therapists, O'Hanlon, 1987) studied and wrote with Erickson, bringing from this fruitful interchange a detailed understanding about therapeutic communication.

Haley did not, however, stand still. In contrast to his colleagues at MRI, he began to think about hierarchy within families and how symptoms sometimes reflected problems in how that hierarchy functioned. This led him to begin collaboration with Minuchin (Minuchin, 2001; Chapter 5) in Philadelphia where he once again became the director of research at the Child Guidance Center in the late 1960s. Haley was a prolific writer but perhaps his most famous work *Problem solving therapy* (1976), was written during his years in Philadelphia and it has become the basic guide to strategic therapy. In 1976, Haley and his second wife, Cloé Madanes, set up their own training institute in Washington DC, where he stayed until the 1990s. His later emphasis was on training therapists in his approach, even though he was well aware that it had gone out of fashion (Grove and Haley, 1993).

In this chapter, as in the others, we will briefly describe the essential ideas and techniques that these strategic approaches have bequeathed to family therapy. For ease of discussion, we will describe the MRI and then Haley's approaches separately.

MRI: attending to words and world views

As we have explained, because Bateson wanted to apply his systemic, anthropological ideas to families in crisis, the MRI team spent many hours studying how families communicated. As a result, they began to describe a number of features of communication that they asserted had psychological consequences. The most famous of these was the *double bind*. This way of communicating is characterised by a contradiction between what is said and how it is said (see Example 1).

Example 1

A young man has two ties to wear to go out on a date: a red one and a yellow one. He puts his red one on and asks his father if it looks good. His father says, "What's wrong with the yellow one?" So, he goes upstairs and changes into the yellow one. When he comes down his father asks, "So what's wrong with the red one then?"

This is a classic double bind! He can't win! Or rather he feels criticised whatever he does.

The MRI team suggested that these forms of communication were common in families where a member had schizophrenia (Bateson, 1972) or other mental illnesses, and therefore had a role in causing these problems (for a fuller description see Berger, 1978). In one sense, this argument was echoed in the UK by Laing's ideas (Laing, 1976) and has subsequently been discredited both as a causative theory and because it seems to 'blame' families for the serious mental illness of a family member. However, it has stimulated research, which confirms that certain forms of communication may contribute to relapses in mental disorders (Kuipers *et al.*, 2002). It is also worth noting that such contradictory forms of communication are quite common in everyday relationships. Even though this idea has not blossomed into the significance the original team had expected, the careful attention to how family member's talk and what they *mean* when they talk, remains a strong focus for family therapists.

Task 2

Try to think about times when you have experienced a 'double bind' communication. Examples might be from childhood or from close relationships. They often leave us thinking one thing but feeling unsure what to do for the best: to agree or not to agree with the other person for instance.

This attention to detail and the use of meaning lead to the more significant technique of *reframing*, which is probably the most utilised legacy of the strategic school of family therapy in contemporary practice. The word 'reframing' has of course spread throughout psychotherapeutic schools (see Chapter 2). But, it was first explained by the MRI team (Watzlawick *et al.*, 1974: 95) in their book *Change*:

> To reframe then, means to change the conceptual and/or emotional setting or viewpoint in relation to which a situation is experienced and to place it in another frame which fits the 'facts' of the same concrete situation equally well or even better, and thereby changes its entire meaning.

There are various ways of thinking about reframing. One is to imagine it as a frame around a picture. The frame, however, can be moved to a new picture: literally reframing! Other visual examples are those optical illusions that can be seen in two different ways (see Figure 6.3).

Figure 6.3 An optical illusion representing a reframe.

© *Emily Kear*

The MRI school, however, was more interested in reframing within communication. For instance, they frequently changed the meanings of symptoms such as 'bad behaviour' to 'experimentation'. Sometimes, as in the film, they would introduce intermediate reframes before finding the 'final' one. So, if they wanted to reframe 'bad behaviour' but knew that 'experimentation' was perhaps too fast a change, they might talk about 'strong willed nature' and then 'knowing what you want' and then perhaps 'liking to try new things out' before they reached 'experimentation'. The task box has some examples of reframes.

Task 3

Common language is full of reframes: can you think of a few?

Examples: every cloud has a silver lining.

What doesn't kill you makes you strong.

At least the garden needs rain.

A change is as good as a rest.

Common therapeutic reframes

Sad becomes mad.

Mad becomes sad.

Anger is sadness that can't be expressed in any other way.

Bad behaviour is a sign of strength and individuality.

Arguments are a sign of strong feeling between people.

Unhappiness is a stage in growing up.

A breakdown becomes a break through.

Reframing is one of the basic techniques of family therapy. From the opening words of the session, the therapist will be talking about *family life,* about *family resources* and about *the family working together to manage the problem.* These are themselves a reframe because most families come into therapy with the 'frame' that the problem resides in one individual and that person has to change. Family therapy is, in contrast, about family members *changing together.* In Table 6.1 we outline a summary of the key MRI concepts/techniques.

Task 4

Think of some experiences you may have had in reframing in your life. Perhaps someone has called you stubborn and you have changed that to 'determined'. How often do adults help young children reframe an event: falling over being an excuse for a 'kiss it better', or perhaps unhappiness being tiredness!

Clearly this is a short summary of the MRI approach to family therapy. It is certainly not exhaustive. We would recommend readers go back to the three classic MRI texts to gain a fuller picture of their methods (Fisch *et al.*, 1982; Watzlawick *et al.*, 1967 and 1974).

Haley and Madanes: flirting with change

Although Haley's debt to Erickson was profound and fully acknowledged, it would be wrong to assume that Haley's version of strategic therapy was simply 'Erickson plus systems theory'. Haley retained both the MRI emphasis on communication (agreeing with Bateson that human beings cannot not communicate) plus the willingness to be paradoxical with interventions. In addition, Hayley's explanation of his therapy adopted an understanding of hierarchy in families and a closer awareness of cycles of interaction rather than cycles of communication. He wrote:

> A goal of therapy is to change the sequences that occur between people in an organised group. When that sequence changes, the individuals in the group change.
>
> (1976:105)

Haley did not believe that family members needed to understand the sequences that maintained the problem. In fact, he believed that if they were told about these, then they would actually resist change because "something in the family situation is making the problem necessary" (1976: 44). This is where the analogy of the

Table 6.1 Key ideas and techniques from the MRI strategic school

Key concept or technique	Background explanation of concept or technique	Example
The therapist's task is to help the family solve the presenting problem.	The causes of the problem were not important. What mattered was what was maintaining the problem.	The therapist, therefore, had to design a way of helping the family stop maintaining the problem. However, odd that may be.
Often attempted solutions to problems become the problem.	Families engage in 'redundant' patterns that are a response to a past issue which then create new issues.	When a child is ill, the parents protect her or him more. This protection then becomes an issue that prevents the child developing.
The therapist's task is to help the family recognise they have control over processes that they have come to think are outside their control.	The assumption is that the family experience hopelessness, which in turn maintains the problem.	The therapist 'tricks' the family into realising that they can control things by designing tasks. In the accompanying film clip, the idea that anger outbursts are a sign of being out of control is challenged by 'prescribing' anger at certain times of the day!
Behavioural change is what is crucial. Understanding is less important.	Families are often stuck in doing 'more of the same' because they think this is the solution. The therapist needs to help them get out of that 'groove' and do something different which will catapult them into a new 'virtuous cycle'.	A family use punishments to stop a child behaving badly. The therapist sees this as a 'vicious cycle' and so convinces them to reward the child for good behaviour. The cycle changes!
There are two kinds of systemic change in family life.	One is called 'first-order change' in which behaviour changes but the underlying basic rules that govern the behaviour don't. 'Second-order change' is where the rules also change.	MRI group talked about nightmares when talking about this. In a nightmare, being aware of the nightmare and trying to change it from the inside is first-order change. But waking up is second order. In this example, only if the parents see their child as a 'resilient' child rather than a 'naughty child who is sometimes good' have they reached second order change.

Table 6.1 Continued

Key concept or technique	Background explanation of concept or technique	Example
Utilise the resistance of the 'system' within the therapy.	The therapist assumes that the family has benevolent intentions but is conflicted about grasping for change (which might be scary). So, any ambivalence is framed as part of change.	For example, as young people begin to overcome an eating disorder, their levels of anxiety will rise. This can be described as evidence that they are improving and not a cause to relapse.
The therapist needs to maintain a stance of manoeuvrability.	In the MRI school, the therapist has to alter her behaviour and stance to meet the needs of the family. She should never be 'pigeon holed' into one stance by the family.	A classic position for the therapist should be 'one down'. The MRI mean that the therapist should behave such that responsibility is placed with the family not the 'super competent' therapist. The therapist might say, "I have no idea how you will solve this. After all, what do I know?"
Language is a crucial factor in how symptoms are described and how the therapist responds.	The emphasis on communication means that the minutiae of conversation are to be noted by the therapist.	For example, the way the symptom is described can become a metaphor for the family's approach to the problem. So, a family that talks about someone being angry might be saying that they are 'an angry family'.

wily fox becomes useful: the therapist had to 'trick' the family into changing their sequences so that there is no longer a need for the problem.

> Change occurs by the therapist joining the on-going system and changing it by the ways he participates within it. When dealing with a governed, homeostatic system that is maintained by repeating sequences of behaviour, the therapist changes those sequences by shifting the ways people respond to each other because of the ways they must respond to the therapist.
>
> (1976:119)

In Haley's description, the therapist is pivotal to the endeavour of therapy. Thus, the therapist has to create unique ways of helping each family and find inventive ways of helping the family to *try out a new sequence.*

Example 2

A couple asked Haley to help them because the husband was a chronic hypochondriac and kept taking his temperature with an oral thermometer. The wife got annoyed that this behaviour occurred so frequently. Haley agreed with both of them but pointed out that oral thermometers were not very accurate. He told them to destroy the thermometer and buy a rectal one. The behaviour stopped (Haley, 1984).

As a consequence of this approach, Haley worked very hard to design tasks and strategies that would interrupt those sequences of behaviour and also methods that motivated families to try out something new. His assumption was that these methods were most effective if they were indirect rather than direct. Here, he undoubtedly used many of Erickson's techniques. Erickson was famous for inventing odd and sometimes shocking tasks for his patients. For instance, he coached a young woman who still wet the bed at age 25, to pee on the bed before she lay in it (Haley, 1973). Obviously, his skill at convincing her that this would 'cure' her problem must have been outstanding and he may have used some hypnotic communication methods as well to 'help' her try the solution out. Haley adapted a number of these methods over time. In his book *Ordeal Therapy* (1984) he outlined "unusual ways to change behaviour". Many of these ways were paradoxical. Haley explains the need to use paradoxical tasks by saying that the 'problem' stabilises a family, hence, any attempt to change the problem will be met with resistance. Accordingly, the therapist 'prescribes' the problem that the family are struggling with.

Example 3

A family asked Haley for help getting their child to school. He was unsure that school was really the right place for clever, creative individuals and that he thought school was only likely to deaden the young child's potential. Moreover, he commented that the parents would get very upset to have such a normal child who went to school and so the child should stay home.

The parents went home in horror at the advice given and resolved to get the child to school come what may. They succeeded and showed how useless therapy was to them! (Haley, 1984)

Another paradoxical intervention is to encourage a problematic symptom that the family have presented with. Here the paradox works by actually bringing what is seen as an out of control symptom, to within the families' control. Thus, the therapist might ask the family to practise the problem with wholehearted attention but only for a few minutes a day. Haley is a delight to read as his sense of humour pervades both his therapy and his writing (see Table 6.2).

Table 6.2 Haley in his own words

Haley in his own words	Source
"A therapist should make it more difficult for a client to keep a symptom than to lose it."	Mazza, J. (2001). Haleyisms. In Zeig, J. *Changing directives*. Phoenix: Milton Erickson Foundation, p. 252.
"You cannot defeat a helpless opponent: you only suffer feelings of guilt and exasperation as well as doubt about who is the victor."	Haley, J. (1986). *The power tactics of Jesus Christ and other essays*. Rockville: Triangle Press, p. 40.
"People who have attempted schizophrenia without the correct family background have universally failed."	Haley, J. (1986). *The art of being schizophrenic*. In Haley, J. *The power tactics of Jesus Christ and other essays*. Rockville: Triangle Press, p. 58.
"As a further step to restrain patients who might spontaneously improve, the therapist should focus upon the patient's past."	Haley, J. (1986). *The art of being a failure as a therapist*. In Haley, J. *The power tactics of Jesus Christ and other essays*. Rockville: Triangle Press, p. 87.
"The most common wrong reason to marry is to escape from one's family."	Haley, J. (1986). *How to have an awful marriage*. In Haley, J. *The power tactics of Jesus Christ and other essays*. Rockville: Triangle Press, p. 121.
"Sometimes, you have to make things worse before you can make them better."	Mazza, J. (2001). Haleyisms. In Zeig, J. *Changing directives*. Phoenix: Milton Erickson Foundation.
"If you want someone to stop doing something, give him or her something else to do rather than just asking them to stop."	Mazza, J. (2001). Haleyisms. In Zeig, J. *Changing directives*. Phoenix: Milton Erickson Foundation, p. 253.
"Therapy is not a social situation, so conventional social rules do not apply."	Mazza, J. (2001). Haleyisms. In Zeig, J. *Changing directives*. Phoenix: Milton Erickson Foundation, p. 254.
"A therapist is in the business of making and breaking hypotheses."	Mazza, J. (2001). Haleyisms. In Zeig, J. *Changing directives*. Phoenix: Milton Erickson Foundation, p. 255.

Example 4

In the accompanying film clip, the therapist asks the family to practise being angry at each other. This task is highly ritualised: a few minutes each a day. This achieves a number of things: it encourages communication, which the therapist has established is a problem for the family, it makes the expression of anger a conscious decision rather than an 'outburst' and it hopefully introduces humour into family interactions and thus breaks the sequence of disappointment and seriousness.

Madanes (1981; 1984; 1995) introduced a number of changes to strategic therapy particularly later in her career. She firstly made ordeals and paradoxical interventions more fun for children by asking them to 'pretend' to behave in certain ways. One paradoxical directive was for the child to 'pretend' that he had the same problem that the family had presented with. The result was that the family started to behave differently. Another important contribution from Madanes was to argue for a strong ethical commitment for strategic therapy. This entailed both an emphasis on 'strategic humanism' (Madanes, 1990; Crenshaw and Barnum, 2001) with a view that therapy should increase care and love in families, as well as a belief that therapy should influence social attitudes. For example, in her later work, *The Violence of Men* (1995), she applied strategic approaches to abuse, sexual violence and domestic violence.

Example 5

In a typical 'strategic' intervention, Madanes asked a man who had hit his wife to write a cheque for $20,000 to his mother-in-law. The 'deal' was that the cheque would be cashed if he ever hit his wife again (Madanes, 1995).

We wish to note that this brief summary of Haley's and Madanes' techniques in no way provides a thorough description of their work, nor indeed does it give it full justice. Readers are directed to the attached reference list for further reading.

The legacy of strategic family therapy

Of all the schools and approaches that we outline in this book, Strategic Family Therapy is the one most likely to be underplayed, especially in European family therapy circles. We have already commented that the 'clever' almost 'tricksy' approach does not fit well with some aspects of contemporary practice. The writings of the MRI group and Haley often sound as if 'the therapist knows best', and their view that explaining what they were doing was likely to prevent it actually working means that the principal of collaboration was never interpreted in the way that it is today, e.g. with a transparency. Although these criticisms have a strong flavour of truth to them, we should not forget that similar views were expressed when they were emerging. As we noted earlier, Haley and others (Crenshaw and Barnum, 2001) always argued that these criticisms ignored the real power imbalance in the therapeutic context and that therapy was always about *influence*. They also asserted that it was the therapist's responsibility to ensure that the therapeutic conversation was helpful to the family. We should also note that strategic approaches have strongly influenced the research field and can be said to have a central role in a number of evidence-based models (Horigian *et al.*, 2005; Sexton, 2011).

In the light of these thoughts, what is interesting is how strategic ideas have continued to influence family therapy practice albeit in subtle and often unrecognised ways. In Chapter 2, we proposed a genealogy from Strategic Family Therapy to Milan family therapy, solution focused family therapy and even narrative family therapy. As the generational process progressed, strategic techniques were altered and made more collaborative. Even Madanes' 'as if' techniques used humour to soften the 'tricksy' strategic ideas (Madanes, 1984). The apparently sharp 'prediction of failure' (e.g. a paradox that challenged the family to change) became the more tongue in cheek 'what pitfalls are going to get in your way and can you overcome them?' (which itself seems to have influenced *Motivational interviewing,* Miller and Rollnick, 2002). It is therefore perfectly possible for strategic interventions to be interpreted in a more collaborative and respectful way. The film that accompanies this chapter demonstrates how the paradoxical 'arguing task' can be suggested and taken on by the family in an open, almost playful exchange between therapist and family. Indeed, the playfulness and humour of strategic techniques can bring a different quality to family therapy, which is both dynamic and helpful for families.

Fact box

Motivational interviewing is a way of engaging individuals and families in change. It aims to increase their motivation for change by using a range of methods. Many of these sound very like the methods used by strategic family therapists, e.g. 'rolling with resistance'. The model is based on a 'stages of change' concept: that people often need help moving from thinking about change to actually doing anything. Motivational interviewing grew out of work with individuals with substance misuse issues.

The other significant legacy of Strategic Family Therapy is its emphasis on how people use words. The MRI, Haley and Erickson all studied minutely the language families adopted to describe their situation. Out of a fascination with this, they concentrated on *helping people think differently by changing the words they used.* Thus, reframing is a core skill for all therapists who work with families. Again, this technique has been changed as family therapy has developed. Narrative therapy may talk about 'exceptions to the problem' or 'unique outcomes', but even in these cases, it is the words families use that is the focus of attention. The wiliness of the approach also helps therapists 'play' in other ways with the language families bring to therapy. We call one of these the 'principle of Occam's razor'. This leads the therapist to divide the description offered so that it is no longer a description that seems monolithic and impenetrable. This method provides opportunities to find change where the initial language implies 'stuckness'. For instance, in the film, the therapist discovers 'two kinds of anger', which allows for a far richer conversation than the description that a family member is 'angry'. An equally useful technique is what we call 'seeking the opposite'. Here the therapist holds

Table 6.3 Nuances in using language in therapy

Name of technique	How it works	Example
Occam's razor.	By dividing up what sounds like a definite description of a behaviour, alternative meanings emerge.	A family explains that one family member is *always* depressed. The therapist enquires if the depression is the same kind of depression all the time. Out of this question will often come a relational description of different kinds of depression.
Looking for the opposite.	This introduces uncertainty but also new possible meanings to behaviour.	The therapist might ask, "Is the depression sometimes suppressed anger do you think?" What might emerge again are relational reasons for depression.
'Walking into words' (an idea used in *appreciative enquiry*).	Here the therapist remains very curious and explores the landscape of a word to help families fully appreciate how the word might limit their world view.	The therapist might ask about the word 'depression', what it means to the family, how the family's understanding of it relates to wider social uses of the word, what alternative words there might be for their experience.

in mind that human beings think in polarities (opposites), but often life is simply not like that. So, behind one emotion, is often its opposite. Again, in the film clip, one of the two kinds of anger described is actually a feeling of 'loss of love'. In Table 6.3 we show strategic ways of helping families think differently through the introduction of nuances to the way they talk.

Fact box

Appreciative enquiry is a more contemporary practice that has grown out of Postmodern therapeutic practice. See Cooperrider and Whitney, 2005.

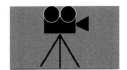

Please access the film using the eResources tab on the webpage for the book, which can be found on the Routledge website: www.routledge.com/9781138831438

Watch film: Strategic school – Reframing

Introduction to film

In this film, Mark has decided to work with family meanings. Specifically, he has decided to work on how Joel's anger is perceived. Although Mark guides the conversation, significant elements of meaning emerge from family members. These allow Mark to uncover a reframe of anger which begins to help the family see both solutions and connections between family members. As the reframe develops, new aspects to anger emerge which give the family more effective ways of thinking about anger rather than 'depositing' it in Joel.

1:07 Mark: Thanks for coming back today. I would like to spend some time understanding those times when Joel seems to be 'down' to family members and also those times when he seems to be an 'angry teenager'. Is that OK?

Maria: Why is this important?

Mark: I think if we can work out what is going on for Joel and you can understand this, then maybe you can manage things differently. Does that make sense? OK? Well, let me ask Laura. If you think about the times you know Joel is unhappy and those times he is just angry, like teenagers can be, how much of the time is he one and how much the other?

Skill note

Mark has already begun to use Occam's razor, a technique that divides descriptions and invites comparisons between the descriptions. This has the effect of limiting 'totalising' descriptions such as 'he is always angry'. It often also functions as a bridge to noticing what other family members do to elicit certain responses from each other.

Laura: He is always angry!

Mark: Is he always angry? OK, is he always angry with you, with Mum or with everybody?

Skill note

Notice Mark does not 'give up' on Occam's razor! He finds another way to vary the description that Joel is always angry. Instead of the initial division, he is looking at the anger being different with different people.

Laura: He is always angry with me. He yells at me to get out of his room. When I want him to help me with my iPad, he says no.

Mark (to Joel):   Is that right?

Joel: I guess … I don't think about it much.

Mark: So, help me think about it now, Joel. Do you think you show your anger to different people in the family and do you think you show your unhappiness to different people in the family?

Skill note

This is a crucial reframe: it seeds the idea that emotions are not 'solid' and constant but that people choose to 'show' different emotions to different family members. If family members can hear this reframe, then the 'problem' starts to change: people's responses as well as choices matter.

Joel: Well yeah, when you put it like that … different people, well … they are different people.

03:20 Mark: Who do you show your unhappiness to the most?

! Joel replies in the negative: not to this person, not to that person. These styles of communication are important for Mark to notice: perhaps he needs to use negatives in his language. This implies a tentativeness, which may suit family communication styles.

Joel: I try not to ... but I guess … probably … I don't think Nick or Laura see my … I think probably Mum.

Mark: So, you show different 'bits' of yourself to different people. So, it isn't a surprise that Laura doesn't see that, and if Nick were here he might say the same, that he doesn't see your unhappiness. Because you don't show them your unhappiness. Let's think about the unhappiness in a little while and stay with the anger.

Task 5

Why do you think Mark decided to work with the 'anger' first?

Mark: We have heard that you show anger to Laura and to Nick, and I suppose Mum sees some of that too. I am wondering if there are different kinds of anger that you show different people?

Skill note

Occam's razor part two! Because it worked the last time, it probably will work again!

05:20 Joel: I guess … at times the anger is more like … I need you. Then at other times it is like, get out of my life … It is different versions of anger.

Skill note

This is gold dust for the therapist! It opens up a large number of options for reframing.

Mark: Can I write this up on the board? There are two kinds of anger. What were the words that you used? 'Get out of my life' and 'I need you'. Maria, is that your experience?

Skill note

Writing words down makes them 'solid': makes it harder to lose them and forget them. The exact words used are important to hold onto.

Maria: I think … now ... when I come back from work, I need to cook and stuff; he is angry and it sounds like 'get out of my life' anger but it can be 'I need you' anger. I don't recognise it. Can't see the difference. I only see the other sort: 'get out of my life' sort.

Skill note

Maria has made the connection before Mark needs to help her to make it! She is introducing a further interactional aspect to these sorts of anger: the different family members may interpret angry differently.

Mark: So it isn't just the anger, it is what people recognise. And sometimes they recognise something that it isn't. (Turns to Laura) … Did you follow this Laura because this is really interesting? What your brother is saying is that sometimes people think he's angry and it's one sort but it's another sort. Is that like you? Sometimes people think you're being angry when you're saying, "I want your help"?
Laura: Mmmm, not really.
Mark: Not really. So if you think about …
Maria: I think it is actually. Sometimes I think she's just annoyed 'cos she didn't get what she wanted but it could be, actually, calling for help or attention.

Mark: (To Laura) Do you hear that? Your mum's saying that she thinks you're angry 'cos you don't get your own way, but she's saying that maybe, when you're angry like that, you're actually asking for help.

Laura: Umm....

Mark: Did you understand that? That's quite complicated, isn't it?

Skill note

It is important to remember that we often don't know what we think until we have talked about it.

Laura: Yes ... I guess.

Mark: Are there times when you want someone to listen to you?

Laura: Well, it's a bit like this. I come home from school and I want to talk about when Cindy, my best friend, stopped talking to me ... all mum does is get on with tea and so I slam the door and she yells at me.

08:25 Mark: So it's very much like what your brother is saying then. Sometimes you're wanting people to listen to you and they don't listen to you and that's what makes you angry. Is that right?

Laura: Yes.

Mark: (Turns to Joel) How about that one Joel ... so what your sister is saying is that it's not just that you give different anger messages to people but also sometimes the anger is a way of trying to communicate with each other ... Yeah? Does that make sense?

Joel: Yeah ... yeah.

Mark: So there's three members of your family – Nick's going to come next time – who's most likely to pick up the message that you give that "I need you"?

Joel: Err, um, well I would feel that it would probably be Mum because we spent so much time together.

Skill note

In systemic therapy, emotions are interactional communications, so Mark is going to make the anger a relational process.

Mark: Right – and does Nick misunderstand the anger and see it as "get out of my life" when it's something different?

Skill note

Mark here assumes that Maria and Nick have different perspectives. If he had been more Milan (curious), he would have checked this out first.

Joel: Yeah … that's most likely.
Mark: Is that the same for you, Laura? Do you feel that sometimes mum does understand that you want to give her a message that you want her to listen and dad doesn't, or do neither of them pick up what you're trying to ask for?
Laura: Well, sometimes it's neither of them but sometimes it's both of them. It's a bit complicated really.
Mark: I bet it is. I bet it's complicated for them too to know what the young people are trying to say.

Skill note

Mark wants to make sure that this process is reciprocal: all family members are 'stuck' in the same pattern and none of them take ownership of that pattern.

Maria: Yes, it is because … especially … and I work with children so it's really tiring, so I can come back home knackered and feeling really, really tired and exhausted and still my … you know … have loads of things to do and so … yes, I should probably listen more to their anger …
Mark: Right, OK … anger is some kind of message. Tell me something – I've got the impression that both of you two sometimes communicate with anger. I wonder if Mum ever communicates with anger and I'm wondering if Nick – Dad – ever communicates with anger?

? Mark could have directed the conversation in other directions at this point: can you think of alternative directions? Why might you have taken these?

Joel: Yeah – at times. It's sort of a … isn't it something that everyone does at times … at times you just feel angry and … I mean … I can't think of any specific examples right now but I know there have been times quite often where, um … I mean there's just … I don't know what I'm trying to say…
Mark: Are you trying to tell me that you're quite an angry family?

> ? Why did Mark go there?

Joel: Yes.

Mark: Do you think that anger is because people haven't got a better way of communicating?

Joel: Quite possibly.

Mark: OK ... so the anger is some kind of way of communicating to people because they've not found another way or they've not been heard ... so the anger is some way of communicating and people get angry because they don't think they're being listened to.

Task 5

Take a few moments to write down how Mark has made the conversation about anger into an interactive, family conversation. Notice where the crucial 'reframing' phrases came in. Spend some time thinking about alternative reframes Mark could have used.

Joel: Yeah.

12:30 Mark: OK, OK ... So, we are talking about anger and everyone in the family seems to have anger. It sounds like anger is a kind of a substitute for another way of talking – Yes? It's a bit like, you know, people say someone is nagging them all the time and in many ways nagging is what you do when the other person is not listening ... OK? So it's like anger is a way of doing something to get people to listen. So it's a kind of a two way thing ... It's not just somebody has got anger, it's like everybody has got a communication problem ... Does that kind of make sense?

(Everybody nods.)

Mark: So we are talking about everybody in your family has a communication problem. It isn't really that anyone in particular has an anger problem. It's that everybody collectively – all together – has a communication problem. OK ... so what can we do to make a change to that? How can we get people to listen to each other, do you think? Have you got any ideas?

Skill note

Mark has now changed the type of conversation. Now he is helping the family think about how to communicate better. This is a whole lot different from blaming someone for having an anger problem! It is also more easily solved because everyone takes responsibility for communicating better!

13:45 Maria: To understand each other properly. To listen and try to recognise the anger and maybe not to get offended by the anger but to try to figure out what could be behind the anger.

Mark: OK ... to see what it's trying to say – what that person is trying to communicate.

Maria: Yes.

14:15 Mark: OK. Alright ... Now there are lots of way of trying to deal with this kind of problem 'cos I've come across it many times and, I guess, one of the ideas I've got is a little bit crazy really. It's about giving you permission to be angry with each other but only within a time frame so that the other person listens. Are you willing to give that one a go? Do you feel that you might enjoy being allowed to be angry for ten minutes each day?

Skill note

Mark is now moving onto a paradoxical task. These tasks have their roots in Ericksonian therapy and are designed to bring out the playfulness in interactions so their serious intentions are changed.

Joel: It's a bit weird but I guess ...

Mark: It is a bit weird, yes ... If we did that, how much time of the day would you need to be angry for people to stop and think about what you are communicating? How long would you need in each day?

Skill note

For a task to work, it has to be spelled out. Frequency, timing, place all need to enter the equation. The therapist can then come back to what has happened and why it may not have happened in the next session.

Joel: Well, I mean ... If it's just sort of ... if everyone is listening ... I mean I feel like 10 minutes is enough.

Mark: Do you want to have a set time of day when you get your ten minutes to be angry and everybody else has ten minutes to listen?

Joel: Erm ... I don't know ... like probably just after school.

Mark: OK, so it's a long time since I was at school, Joel. What time would that be?

Joel: Well actually, I feel probably, I mean that school ends at quarter past three but to actually get home, that's probably about quarter to four ... but ... I don't ... not everyone's ...

Mark:	'Cos everyone has to be there. Nick has to be there, Laura has to be there, Mum has to be there. Mum of course is out at school too, so what time are you all going to be in the house when Joel can have his angry ten minutes?
16:00 Maria:	I would say around five o'clock.
Mark:	Right five? So five o'clock is Joel's angry ten minutes and everybody has to listen to him, just for 10 minutes. OK? So (turns to Laura) Laura, I'm sure you need a few minutes. Do you need a whole ten minutes to be angry?
Laura:	Probably six or seven minutes.
Mark:	OK. Now, do you think you should have your angry six or seven minutes straight away after Joel has had his angry ten minutes, or do you want an angerless break?

Skill note

This conversation probably sounds absurd to you and it is meant to be absurd! 'Angerless breaks?' Notice that the family seem to take it seriously. Mark is guessing they won't when they get home and try it out. They might even laugh and listen to each other!

Laura:	Probably a bit of a break ...
Mark:	OK.
Laura:	Because after Joel, it probably needs a bit of time to settle in and make sure it's worked.

! Notice Laura says, 'it's worked'.

Mark: OK ... so what time shall we say Laura has her angry six or seven minutes?

Skill note

It is important to persist. If the therapist gives up, the family will not take it as an important task.

Laura:	Maybe about 20 past.
16:50 Mark:	20 past...so 5:20...OK, right, so how about that as a task for the next week. Sounds a bit daft, doesn't it, but try it out ... OK ... so for ten minutes you can be as angry as you want to and everybody has to listen. OK? Then (turns to Laura) for six or seven minutes

you can be as angry as you want to and everybody has to listen. They don't respond, like Mum said earlier, people listening to what the anger's saying. They don't have to say anything ... they just listen ... OK? You got me? So they don't argue back. We are just going to practice seeing if those special minutes can give you the chance to communicate what you're trying to communicate ... OK? So that's your task for the next week, and I'm really looking forward to hearing what happens.

? If Mark has chosen to work on 'unhappiness', how might the conversation have gone? What reframes could he have used? What tasks might have helped?

Summary

In this film, Mark has used the family language to introduce a reframe when Joel volunteers that his anger has two aspects. This allows Mark to define anger as a form of communication so that the family doesn't have an anger problem but a communication problem! This is much easier to solve than the former. In therapy with families, if the reframe makes sense to them, they will not only go along with it, but will embellish it and use it themselves. If the use of it improves family life, they will persist and set up a virtuous cycle of problem resolution. Reframing can be an instant activity like changing 'sad' to 'angry'. But in this section, you can see that it also might take time. The therapist might go through a number of 'phases' like in a game of football or rugby. After all, it is highly unusual for a goal or try to be scored from the first kick of the ball! In this process words are changed slowly, contexts are altered, conversations are built upon and eventually a very different description emerges. Here the assumption that Joel is 'angry' is changed to the family needing to learn to communicate. This gradual change of meaning is like the word play game that changes the word 'Mum' to 'Dad' in four changes by substituting one letter at a time. See if you can do it.

References

Aesop (1994). *Aesop's fables*. London: Wordsworth Editions.

Bateson, G. (1972). *Steps to an ecology of mind*. New York: Ballantine.

Berger, M. (1978) (Ed). *Beyond the double bind*. New York: Brunner/Mazel.

Cooperrider, D. and Whitney, D. (2005). *Appreciative enquiry*. San Francisco: Berrett-Koehler.

Crenshaw, W. and Barnum, D. (2001). What makes it strategic? In Zeig, J. (Ed) *Changing directives*. Phoenix: Milton Erickson Foundation, pp. 101–118.

Dahl, R. (2016). *Fantastic Mr Fox.* London: Puffin.

Erdoes, R. and Ortiz, A. (1999). *American Indian trickster tales.* New York: Penguin.

Fisch, R. (2004). So what have you done recently? MRI brief therapy. *Journal of Systemic Therapies,* 23: 4–10.

Fisch, R., Weakland, J. and Segal, L. (1982). *The tactics of change.* San Francisco: Jossey Bass.

Grove, D. and Haley, J. (1993). *Conversations on therapy.* New York: Norton.

Hale, D. and Frusha, C. (2016) MRI brief therapy. *Journal of Systemic Therapies,* 35: 14-24.

Haley, J. (1973). *Uncommon therapy.* New York: Norton & Co.

Haley, J. (1976). *Problem solving therapy.* San Francisco: Jossey Bass.

Haley, J. (1984). *Ordeal therapy.* San Francisco: Jossey Bass.

Haley, J. (1993). *Jay Haley on Milton H. Erickson.* New York: Brunner/Mazel.

Horigian, V., Suarez-Morales, L., Robbins, M., Zarate, M., Mayorga, C., Mitrani, V. and Szapocznik, J. (2005). Brief strategic family therapy for adolescents with behaviour problems. In Lebow, J. (Ed) *Handbook of clinical family therapy.* New Jersey: Wiley & Sons: 73–102.

Kuipers, E., Leff, J. and Lam, D. (2002). *Family work for schizophrenia.* London: Gaskell.

Laing, R. (1976). *The politics of the family.* Harmondsworth: Penguin.

Madanes, C. (1981). *Strategic family therapy.* San Francisco: Jossey-Bass.

Madanes, C. (1984). *Behind the one way mirror: advances in the practice of strategic therapy.* San Francisco: Jossey-Bass.

Madanes, C. (1990). Sex, love and violence: strategies for transformation. New York: Norton & Co.

Madanes, C. (1995). *The violence of men.* San Francisco: Jossey-Bass.

Marshall, E. (2012). *Anansi's journey.* Jamaica: University of West Indies Press.

Mazza, J. (2001). Haleyisms. In Zeig, J. (2001)(Ed) *Changing directives: the strategic therapy of Jay Haley.* Phoenix, AZ: Milton Erickson Foundation Press, pp. 252–255.

Miller, W. and Rollnick, S. (2002). *Motivational interviewing.* New York: Guilford.

Minuchin, S. (2001). Walking with Jay. In Zeig, J. (Ed) *Changing directives: the strategic therapy of Jay Haley.* Phoenix, AZ: Milton Erickson Foundation Press, pp. 3–11.

O'Hanlon, B. (1987). *Tap roots: underlying principles of Milton Erickson's therapy and hypnosis.* New York: Norton & Co.

Sexton, T. (2011). *Functional family therapy in clinical practice.* New York: Routledge.

Shah, I. (1968). *The pleasantries of the incredible Mulla Nasrudin.* London: Jonathan Cape.

Watzlawick, P., Beavin, J. and Jackson, D. (1967). *The pragmatics of human communication.* New York: Norton.

Watzlawick, P., Weakland, J. and Fisch, R. (1974). *Change.* New York: Norton.

Weinstein, D. (2013). *The pathological family.* Ithaca: Cornell University Press.

Zeig, J. (2001)(Ed). *Changing directives.* Phoenix, AZ: Milton Erickson Foundation Press.

Chapter 7

The Milan and Post-Milan approach

Changing rules and meanings in family life

Key points

- The ideas from the original Milan Associates underlie much of contemporary family therapy practice.
- They established a model for conducting a family therapy session and designed ways of encouraging a systemic perspective to emerge in family thinking.
- The main focus in this approach is on the rules of behaviour within relationships and the meaning of this behaviour within family life.
- The Milan Associates first used the one-way mirror as a technique in therapy because it provided the team with a different perspective.
- Many Postmodern or social constructionist practices developed out of the Milan approach.

Introduction

If we imagine that family therapy is a building, then the contribution of the four clinicians known as the 'Milan Associates' provides the very cement that binds the bricks together. Unfortunately, such a metaphor implies that their contribution is static and 'solid'. This is in fact far from the case. The Milan Associates' ideas, collectively and individually, have continued to change and adapt from the 1970s through to the contemporary world of family therapy. Indeed, many of the therapists that they trained continue to provide significant insights into the process of therapy, and thus continue their influence (Bertrando, 2007; Ugazio, 2013). These factors make it extremely hard to either isolate the Milan approach to family therapy, or to faithfully record all their contributions. To bring some clarity to the description of the Milan approach, this chapter will adopt a largely historical structure, beginning with the 'early' ideas and gradually covering the more contemporary 'Post-Milan' ideas.

The Milan Associates

The founder of the Milan approach has always been credited as Mara Selvini Palazzoli. As a psychoanalyst and psychiatrist in Milan in the 1960s, she developed interventions for young people with anorexia (Selvini Palazzoli, 1963). However, as her early work developed, she gradually moved from 'the intra psychic to the transpersonal' and gathered a group of like-minded psychiatrists to join her on this journey. By 1971, the 'Milan Associates' had formed the Institute for Family Studies in Milan where the team began to use the ideas of Watzlawick (Watzlawick *et al.*, 1967) to inform their family interventions. The four associates were: Mara Selvini Palazzoli, Luigi Boscolo, Giuliana Prata and Selvini Palazzoli herself (see Figure 7.1a and Figure 7.1b). Their first book, *Paradox and counter-paradox* (1978), was largely influenced by the Palo Alto (strategic) ideas of Waltzlawick *et al.*, (1967). Later, they drew upon Bateson's (1972) ideas and once more shifted their practice.

Figure 7.1a Gianfranco Cecchin and Giuliana Prata. From the archive of Giulia Prata with the help of Laura Fruggeri.

Figure 7.1b Mara Selvini Palazzoli. From the archive of Matteo Selvini, School of Psychotherapy, Milan, Italy.

The team then began a decade of creative collaboration out of which came some of the most impressive techniques that have been adopted by family therapists around the world. Martin (1985: 11) states that:

> [O]ut of this prolonged incubation based on the 'marriage' of psychoanalytic and Batesonian ideas came not only a clear, brilliant application of Bateson's circular epistemology … but also … a detailed, precisely described technique … for interviewing and intervening with families.

The team published their first book in English in 1978 (Selvini Palazzoli et al., 1978) and followed this with a series of influential articles published in a range of journals (Selvini Palazzoli et al., 1980a; 1980b).

The context in which the Milan team worked is often understated, but it is highly relevant to the way their work developed. First, the psychoanalytical (all four team members were trained as psychoanalysts) roots of their thinking permeate the early writing. There is a dispassionate and objective 'feel' to how they describe their therapy. An example of this is that in psychoanalytical therapy, the therapist sits behind the client. In 'classic' Milan family therapy, the therapists sit behind a one-way screen. Second, this era in Milan was the era when the large psychiatric institutions were being closed in a movement spearheaded by Basaglia (Foot, 2015; Rogers and Pilgrim, 2001). It is almost inconceivable to imagine how powerful this movement was and Milan became a symbol of worldwide opposition to the way psychiatry was practiced. In this context, treatments that provided family-based solutions to psychiatric problems were favoured. In other words, there could not have been a better context for the Milan team to promote the treatment of the family for conditions like schizophrenia and anorexia.

Fact box

Basaglia was a politically active psychiatrist who revolutionised the treatment of detained mentally ill patients in Italy during the 1970s.

However, almost by the time their later works had been published, the Milan Associates had split into two groups. Selvini Palazzoli and Prata largely stayed within the model that they had created, seeking to vary only some of their practices whilst applying them to new contexts (Selvini Palazzoli et al., 1986; Selvini Palazzoli et al., 1989; Prata 2002). Although these contributions are not insignificant, it is those of the other two Associates, Boscolo and Cecchin, that have had a wider impact on family therapy practice across the globe. The term 'Post-Milan' was developed to encapsulate their approach. The following sections will therefore concentrate upon these two eras of Milan family therapy. After we have outlined their main ideas, we will summarise how the Milan practices have become part and parcel of everyday family therapy practice, including some aspects of 'collaborative' and 'Postmodern' practice.

Early Milan: key concepts

Much to the annoyance of many other schools of family therapy, the Milan team adopted the term 'systemic family therapy' for their approach. Although this seems to imply that other forms of family therapy are not systemic, it certainly does establish that the practice of the Milan team was. They began *Paradox and counter-paradox* (1978) with the following:

> The family is a self-regulating system which controls itself according to rules formed over a period of time ... [which] ... comes to exist ... through a series of transactions and corrective feedbacks ... [which determine] what is permitted and what is not permitted in the relationship ... these rules have the quality of communication.
>
> (Selvini Palazzoli *et al.*, 1978: 3)

Further, "families, in which one or more members present behaviours traditionally diagnosed as 'pathological', are held together by transactions and therefore by rules that are peculiar to the pathology" (1978: 4). In many ways, this summarises the Milan team's ideas perfectly. They adopted the Batesonian concepts of systems and of the importance of feedback loops in maintaining and changing systems. Unlike Minuchin, their focus of attention was on the 'rules' of behaviour within interactions rather than the structure in which relationships were embedded. They understood that problems in family life were rooted in rules of behaviour that had built up over time, and in the meanings that behaviour was given within family life. They encapsulated this in the following claim: "the power is only in the rules of the game which cannot be changed by the people involved in it" (1978: 6). The method that they created centred, not surprisingly, on changing the rules that dominated family life. The method owed a great deal to the Palo Alto or strategic approach to family therapy (Chapter 6) although it certainly grew larger than that.

With this theoretical concept came a practical method for conducting family therapy sessions. This model was called 'the five-phase session'. This meant that the session began with the team preparing for meeting the family. They would examine the referral information, or review what had happened in the previous session and elaborate on directions for the therapy to take. The session would then be conducted with a co-therapy team of a male and female therapist (the interviewing team), while another two sat behind a one-way screen or mirror observing the session (the consulting team). After about 45 minutes, the therapists would leave the family and have a consultation with the team behind the screen. During this third phase, the equipment would be switched off, and the family left in privacy. During the consultation, the consulting team would propose interventions, which the interviewing team would take back into the family session (the fourth phase). Typically, this phase would be short, and largely consist of a message for the family. Again, usually, this message would be a request for them to behave in a certain way until the next session. Once the family had left, the therapist team would reform, review the effect of the message and plan for the next session. This highly formalised, perhaps ritualised, way of working may owe something to the psychoanalytical training of the four Milan Associates. Its function seems to have been to mark out the therapy as 'out of the ordinary' and thus make it more likely that the family would be engaged and respond to the message of the team.

This method of conducting family therapy sessions, although now rather 'old fashioned', has nevertheless continued in a number of variations through the last 40 years. But it is the key techniques that the Milan team used that have been more practically influential. In the following section, we will outline the main techniques adopted by the Milan team.

Early Milan: key techniques

Although *Paradox and counter-paradox* (Palazzoli *et al.*, 1978) had a major impact on the practice of family therapy, it was probably their 1980 (Palazzoli *et al.*, 1980a) article that laid out a method, which could be followed more easily. In this paper, they described three 'guidelines for the conductor of the session'. We will outline these in order.

I. Hypothesising

Although there is no doubt that family therapists from other approaches were making hypotheses and formulations about the aim of their work, the Milan team were the first to introduce a formal description of what this meant to family therapy. They state

> the hypothesis establishes a starting point for [his] investigation … if it is proved false, the therapist must find a second hypothesis.
>
> (1980a: 3)

In the Milan team's practice, the hypothesis is an attempt to gather what information the therapist has gained to make a coherent systemic description of what is happening in the family. In the same paper, it is stated: "A fundamental point to emphasise is that every hypothesis must be systemic, must therefore include all components of the family and must furnish us with a supposition concerning the total relational functioning" (Selvini Palazzoli, 1980a: 6).

As the concept of hypothesising developed (often outside of the Milan team's writing), various aspects of it, as a practice, became significant. One was that the hypothesis needed to be built on the information gained in the interview or from the referral information. The second was that multiple hypotheses were valued. The reasons for this were that the therapist and the team were encouraged not to 'fall in love' or 'get married' to any particular hypothesis because *it might limit the direction of therapy.* Burbatti and Formenti (1988) explain this also from a philosophical perspective. They repeat Bateson's adage that 'the map is not the territory', therefore therapists need to guard against assuming that their hypothesis is a 'true' picture of what is happening in the family. Because of this, teams influenced by Milan will create a variety of hypotheses and 'test' them out during the therapy with the family: multiple hypotheses guard against believing any particular one is 'true' (Jones, 1993).

So, the hypotheses are created by the therapeutic team as a way of generating ideas about what could be happening within the family.

Task I

Note: the tasks in this chapter relate directly to Joel and his family and the skills and techniques are demonstrated in the film – Milan/post-Milan schools - Circular questions. We have chosen to adopt this model in this chapter because Milan techniques can be more subtle than those of other schools.

Think about and generate several hypotheses that can explain why Joel is depressed or why he is angry with his parents.

Remember: the hypotheses have to be systemic and relational.

Example 1: 'Joel is depressed because he misses his biological father' is not a systemic hypothesis because it concentrates upon Joel alone.

Example 2: 'Joel's depression functions as a way of maintaining the family pattern of distance in the relationship between Maria and Nick; and it prevents Nick addressing his limitations as a father'. This is a systemic hypothesis because it involves at least three family members and is not 'linear'.

The third quality of a hypothesis is that it directs the intervention of the therapist. So, if the therapist thought that it would be helpful to explore how Joel's depression maintained family patterns, she or he might begin to ask the family to think about how they would interact *if he wasn't depressed*. At first, such a line of approach may seem strange to the family. But the intention of using hypotheses like this is to gradually help the family realise that changing Joel's depression can only be achieved if they change how they behave and think as well.

Fact box

Relational here means the thoughts, feelings or behaviour of an individual, which are related to their relationships with others.

Task 2

Consider other hypotheses that might apply to Joel's family.

Example 3: 'Joel's family are unable to name their disappointments with each other. If they did, it might end up destroying their relationships. So, it is easier for Joel to "behave" depressed, so that they cannot think about these other issues'.

This hypothesis explores the 'rules of the game' that determine how family members behave. If the therapist pursued this hypothesis, she or he could begin to explore how Maria and Nick know that Joel is depressed instead of just angry for instance.

A further quality of the hypothesising process for the Milan team was that because the therapists are constantly creating hypotheses, they retain their neutrality (discussed later in the chapter) and are more able to be alert to ways in which the family are encouraging them to think.

For example, working with Joel's family, it would be easy for the therapist to 'assume' that the family's description is correct, e.g. the 'problem' is Joel's depression. But by formulating different hypotheses, the therapist can maintain a systemic perspective while working with the family (Campbell *et al*, 1989).

2. Circularity

The concept of 'circularity' was first introduced in the 1980 paper. Later we will talk about how this concept led to a particular kind of questioning, but as it was initially described, it was about helping the therapist respond to feedback:

> By circularity, we mean the capacity of the therapist to conduct his investigation on the basis of feedback from the family in response to the information he elicits about relationships and therefore difference and change.
>
> (Selvini Palazzoli, 1980a: 8)

In this sense, circularity matched Bateson's ideas, who emphasised it in at least two ways. First, it asks the therapist to conduct the therapeutic interview as if there are 'no things', only relationships. By maintaining a circular process of information gaining and responding, the therapist is entering a world in which she or he only sees patterns. Furthermore, she or he communicates this way of viewing family life *to the family*. The second aspect of the concept that derives is that it proposes that:

> Information is difference. Difference is a relationship (or a change in the relationship).
>
> (Selvini Palazzoli, 1980a: 8)

It is proposed that human systems only notice something if there is a *difference* to notice. This difference may be in thoughts, behaviours or feelings. The therapist should conduct the session so that difference emerges between family members and this difference should help them learn something new about their situation.

The Milan team laid out a particular way of eliciting this kind of difference through the use of what they called 'triadic questions' and which we now know as 'circular questions', which we will discuss later.

3. Neutrality

This is the third recommendation from that original paper (Selvini Palazzoli, 1980a). It directs the therapist to not be 'on anyone's side' in the session. Again, we might wonder if this neutrality had its origins in the psychoanalytic method. The team wrote:

> The end result of the successive alliances is that the therapist is allied with everyone and no one at the same time.
>
> (1980a: 9)

Fact box

Meta-level here describes holding a meaning or understanding which is beyond or different to that of the family.

Jones (1993: 16) explains that neutrality was designed to help the therapist "occupy a 'meta-level' in relation to the family". Moreover, this helps the therapist have a "point of view different from that of the family and its individual members". Jones states that only by having a meta-level view can the therapist be of any use to the family: e.g. agreeing or believing that the family's ideas about the problem can discourage therapeutic change. Burbatti and Formenti (1988) comment that so often families expect the therapist to be one of a "saviour", a "witch doctor" or a "judge". But accepting these roles limits the therapy. Instead:

> The therapist avoids accepting the obvious and stable definitions of the prob-lem ... avoids accepting a more or less thin proposal for coalition with one of its members ... avoids blaming the patient's parents as the cause of the problem ... to establish consistency with the systemic model.
>
> (Burbatti and Formenti, 1988: 88)

The idea that the therapist should be 'neutral' was criticised in later years as it implied a lack of care, a lack of awareness of situations where a family member was being abused and ignorant of the impact of the therapist's presence upon the family. Accordingly, in Post-Milan practice, it was renamed and re-described.

Early Milan: some key practices

So far, we have outlined the initial ideas presented to the world of family therapy by the Milan team. Out of these came a number of clinical practices.

Circular questioning

In the first paper, the Milan team used the phrase 'triadic questions' but very soon afterwards the term 'circular questions' was adopted. If family therapy has given any gift to the world of psychotherapy, it is these types of questions. Put simply, a circular question is one that asks a family member to think about how they are related or connected to another family member, either by behaviour, feelings or thoughts. For instance: "When your Dad does that, what does it have you doing?" is a circular question. This line of enquiry then leads into a truly 'circular' direction when the therapist asks: "OK, and when you do that, what does your Dad do?" What the therapist has established is:

- What one family member does affects other family members.
- There is often a circular pattern between family members.
- Thus, the pattern can be changed if one or both family members do something differently.

These two examples are not, of course, 'triadic' because there is not (yet) a third family member in the description. An example of a triadic question would be: "What does your brother do when he sees you and your Dad interacting in this way?" In their 1980 paper, the Milan team explain the value of these kinds of questions:

> This technique [initiates] a vortex of responses in the family that greatly illuminate the various triadic relationships. In fact, by formally inviting one member of the family to meta-communicate about the relationship of two others, *in their presence*, we are not only breaking one of the ubiquitous rules of dysfunctional families, but we are also conforming to the first axiom of the pragmatics of human communication: in a situation of interaction, the various participants … cannot avoid communicating.
>
> (Selvini-Palazzoli *et al.*, 1980: 4)

In the same paper, the Milan team further describe using these 'triadic' questions to track sequences of behaviour and thinking within families. The intention is to introduce *difference* into the way the family understands what is happening between them. Thus, in the example given, the therapist will explore how the brother's behaviour perhaps maintains the pattern between the father and his

Table 7.1 Categories of circular questions

Name of the type of question	Example	What effect might the question have?
Relationship tracking questions/ Sequence of interaction questions.	'When x does that what does y do?' or 'When they do that, what do you experience?'	These questions elicit information but emphasise the interconnection of family members. These kinds of questions can cross the three time zones: past, present and future.
Comparison questions/ Ranking questions.	'Who is most concerned about what is happening for x?' or 'Who is closest to whom in the family?'	These questions create a context in which all family members are aware about how they influence each other. They can often help the 'unspoken' be spoken. But they also help name the differences in family members' experiences.
Hypothetical questions.	'If you were to do x rather than y, what do you think your dad would do differently?'	These questions 'seed' change in quite a concrete way. They show that if one piece of behaviour/ feelings/understanding changes in one family member, then others may change too.
Temporal questions.	'Did things change in your relationship after your dad lost his job?' or 'If things didn't change, what would happen to your relationships in two years' time or when you leave for University?'	These questions provide a 'challenge for change' and link changes in relationships to events.
Contextual questions.	'When you think she "wants to get attention", how does your reaction influence what she does?' or 'How is the way you are as a parent influenced by how your parents' were with you?'	These questions evoke connections between two contexts. They help families see how behaviour in one context means different things in a different context.
Reflexive questions.	'When your Dad lost his job, how did that change what you thought about him and your relationship with him?' or 'If you changed how you understood why she did this, how would that change what you thought about her?'	These questions are designed to stimulate an understanding of 'self in relationship' so that families can change how they behave/think/ feel. The therapist *does not know how the family will respond to these questions.*

brother: 'How does what your brother does contribute to this interaction between you and your Dad?'

The adoption of circular questions within family therapy blossomed almost as soon as the 1980 paper was published. Various authors began to systematise how they could be used, and then to create typologies of 'kinds' of circular questions. Tomm (1984a) initially emphasised that circular questions were designed to highlight *differences* within the family system: "many therapists intuitively ask difference questions but often do not recognise the notion of difference as a heuristic stem in the question" (Tomm 1984a: 259). He then went on to provide possibly the most coherent typology of the use of questions in therapy (Tomm, 1987; 1988). Although this typology is only one among a number of models (Penn, 1982; Brown, 1997; Nelson *et al.*, 1986; Tomm, 1985). Indeed, the creativity of individual clinicians is often demonstrated in the variety and inventive kinds of questions they use. Table 7.1 provides at least some of the infinite variety of circular questions, and although it draws on the literature, it is in no way exhaustive.

It is impossible to provide examples of every category of circular questions. We would recommend that readers look at the literature we reference here. However, before moving on, there are a couple of practice points that are important to note. One is that circular questions need to be spaced out with 'normal' conversation; otherwise they can become monotonous. However, if the therapist is asking an important question, they should learn to persevere. One of the common clinical failures in learning to use circular questions is to give up after the first question 'bombs'. Another is that some family therapists create too complex circular questions (this happens in the film) and sometimes need to be reminded that they should be brief, simple and parsimonious. They have been described as 'gossiping in the presence of others', which certainly, in British culture, is seen as 'rude'.

It is, however, also important to realise that they are designed to achieve something: a relational understanding amongst family members. So, although they may feel clunky at first to training therapists and to families alike, the therapist should persevere. Trainee therapists often ask how will they know which questions to use? The answer is that usually your questions will be linked to your hypotheses (see Table 7.2 for additional Milan Associate practices).

Task 3

Have a look at the questions described in Table 7.1 and consider which hypothesis about family patterns they might be connected to.

Table 7.2 Other significant Milan Associate practices

Name of technique	Purpose	Examples that could have been used in the film 'Milan and Post-Milan'
Positive connotation.	This is a particular kind of reframing (see Chapter 6). The view by the Milan team was that people did not change when they were being criticised. So, they always found a positive explanation for whatever behaviour was exhibited.	*'It is really important that Joel continues to show you, his parents, that he is depressed. This makes sure that you are able to express your concern for him and prevents you worrying about your own worries'.*
Use of paradox.	The Milan team believed that many family difficulties were maintained because of communication that perpetuated *double binds* (see Chapter 6). They thus created paradoxes (and counter paradoxes) to challenge these communications.	*'Not only should Joel continue to show you his depression. We are convinced that any attempt by him to stop being depressed would cause a family disaster.'*
Final intervention.	In the fourth phase of the session, the team almost always came back with a message or 'prescription' of behaviour that they wanted the family to undertake before their next session. This was designed to perturb the pattern that the family had adopted.	*'We think it is really important that Joel continues to keep his parents' focus on him by showing even more evidence of depression in the next two weeks'.*

Post-Milan ideas and techniques

At the start of the chapter we explained that in the 1980s, the Milan team went through a divorce of sorts. This meant that Cecchin and Boscolo established a new version of the Milan school, which came to be called 'Post-Milan'. Cecchin (1987) began this new phase by arguing that 'neutrality' needed to be understood as 'curiosity'. His explanation relied on the thinking of the biologists Maturana and Varela (1988), who said that reality is constructed by each individual and therefore the therapist was not able to make a judgement between 'better' and 'less good' ways of being within family life. Accordingly, curiosity was the most useful therapeutic stance. Cecchin commented, "Curiosity leads to exploration and invention of alternative views" (1987: 406).

Further, this perspective, "Celebrates the complexity of interactions and invites a polyphonic orientation to the description and explanation of interaction" (1987: 406).

He also noted:

> We only know what has happened in the past; we do not know what future cultural patterns will be. Therefore, we cannot teach, a parent how to be a parent, a child how to be a son or daughter.

As a result, Post-Milan family therapy practice dispensed with that final 'message' to the family and sought to help the family re-think their lives throughout the course of the session. The therapist's adoption of a curious stance was seen as helpful in stimulating change without in any way 'prescribing' what should be done. This approach was fuelled by *uncertainty*, which was an integral part of the curiosity of the therapist: in other words, curiosity was not a technique as such, rather a state of therapeutic mind.

Fact box

Lynn Hoffman is an American social worker turned family therapist who has worked with many of family therapy's influential thinkers including the Milan team.

A second feature of Post-Milan practices was a belief in *second-order cybernetics* (Hoffman, 1985). These had already been implicit in Bateson's ideas but were foregrounded by the Post-Milan therapists. First order cybernetics assumes that an outsider can describe a family system (e.g. how it works and why it works that way). But Second order cybernetics maintains that what is seen is determined by the prejudices, orientation, etc. of the observer. In other words, it is impossible to describe a human system without taking into account what the observer thinks she or he sees. The system is, in effect, in the *eye of the beholder.*

Fact box

Harry Goolishan was a family therapist pioneer who developed the Postmodern approach known as 'collaborative therapy' with Harlene Anderson who is an American psychologist.

A third contribution to Post-Milan practice, came from the work of Anderson and Goolishian (1988) who suggested that 'systems' actually only existed in the realm of *language.* Because of this (i.e. talking about a pattern *creates the reality* of the pattern), they argued that family therapy was about a 'conversation' not about 'making things change'. This idea gave therapists the option to focus on words and explore their meaning to each family member and then to the wider culture in which the family is embedded. This approach falls within a *social constructionist* understanding of therapy (McNamee and Gergen, 1992).

Although most of these theoretical ideas emerged before the concept of *Postmodernism* entered the family therapy vocabulary, they largely indicated what was to come. Overall, they created a gentler, and skilful collaborative set of practices (see Table 7.3 for Post-Milan practices).

Table 7.3 Common practices of Post-Milan family therapists

Name of practice	Purpose of practice	Example
Curiosity.	By taking a curious stance, the therapist evokes curiosity within the family.	"I am really interested in why you interpret this behaviour as anger. Could you just help me understand this a little more, please?"
Seeking multiple descriptions of behaviour. ('multi-versal thinking').	To explore alternative views which can provide variety of options.	"So, Nick sees this behaviour as anger. Maria sees it as sadness. Which is most useful, do you think?"
Concentration on the meanings of words.	To help the family explore alternatives and decide if they are more helpful to resolving their difficulties.	"I wonder if you think other people may understand depression in a different way?""If they did see it as a 'way of growing up', would that be more helpful to you as a family?"
Collaboration.	To emphasise that the therapist does not have the answers but the family have the solutions: they just need help uncovering them.	"Of all the ideas, we have talked about today, which ones do you think you would like to try, which ones would make the most difference to your lives?"
Increasing use of reflexive questions.	The focus is still on helping family members appreciate their inter-connection but moves more to a continuous way of intervening and focus upon family members reaching their own understandings, not the therapist's understanding.	"What have you learnt from this session?""Have we talked about the right things about your family today?"

The legacy of Milan: from Post-Milan to contemporary practice

In our opening section, we noted that the Milan team's ideas continue to provide the cement in the house of family therapy. As can be seen in the 'family therapy' family tree (see Chapter 2), the ideas of the Milan team have continued to grow and develop and much of contemporary practice is influenced by their work. There are a number of significant practice changes that have flowed from the Milan and Post-Milan schools, which we will describe as part of their legacy. First, it is important to note that the whole structure of family therapy sessions has evolved from the Milan school. Most family therapists will spend some time reflecting on the information they have about a family or on the last session with the family before they begin the session. This would normally be a space where ideas about what patterns were influencing the 'problem', what meanings about family life had emerged and how the therapist can influence these processes would be considered. The session would then often include a break (even if the therapist does not have a team) for further reflection. Finally, a session would end with some sort of summing up and possibly a task for the family.

Second, the Milan team taught family therapists how 'team work' can encourage creativity and be a valuable resource for families and therapists alike (Selvini and Selvini-Palazzoli *et al.*, 1991). There is some research that shows that having more than one therapist gives families a diverse perspective on their problems and the solutions to those problems. It also reassures them that their concerns are being taken seriously. From a therapeutic position, team work helps family therapists respect multiple perspectives and helps them stay in a reflective 'systemic' space. On one level, this has enshrined 'humility' (as well as curiosity) into the practice of family therapists and this is no bad thing.

Fact box

Tom Andersen was a Norwegian family therapist who is mostly remembered for his development work on 'the reflecting team'.

Indeed, perhaps the most influential changes to family therapy practice in the last 20 years have been changes to how the team works. In 1991, a Norwegian family therapist called Tom Andersen (1991) published a paper that argued for the Post-Milan 'multiple perspective' concept to be centred on how teams work. He introduced what he called 'the reflecting team'. This practice involves the team talking about their ideas in front of the family *and* the therapist, rather than keeping their thoughts 'private' and 'behind the one-way screen'. His argument was that as therapy (from a Post-Milan perspective) was about finding new descriptions of problems, making the team conversation transparent allowed families to hear more 'news of difference' (notice how Bateson's ideas remain important). This itself made the way the team worked more open and collaborative. Reflecting team models have been hugely influential across Europe and the UK, though less so in the private practice dominated USA. Once more, there is some research confirming that families appreciate this way of working (Willott *et al.*, 2012).

A number of other significant contemporary family therapists were also trained by the Milan school. In Chapter 9 we will refer to Bertrando's ways of working systemically with individuals (2007), but he has also embraced 'dialoguism' (see later in the chapter) and also integrated narrative ideas into the Milan 'house'. Ugazio (2013) has taken the emphasis on meanings into a new phase by exploring how meanings are often constructed with opposites in mind (again see later in the chapter). Fruggeri (Davolo and Fruggeri, 2016) has continued to explore the intricacies of Post-Milan practice within cultural contexts.

These are what we might call the 'direct legacy' of the Milan and Post-Milan schools. There are, however, some significant indirect legacies. Because the Post-Milan approach embedded reflexivity and uncertainty (Mason, 1993) within its model, of all the schools of family therapy, it was the most prepared for what we might call the 'Postmodern' or 'social constructionist' revolution in therapeutic thinking (McNamee and Gergen, 1992; Gergen, 1999). Interestingly, White, for instance, one of the founders of narrative family therapy, was initially a 'Milan-style' therapist (White, 1983).

Fact box

Postmodernism is a philosophical movement that asserts that there are no certainties: that 'knowledge' is local not universal. It is sceptical about any 'grand narrative'.

There were a number of developments in Post-Milan family therapy that prepared it for what could almost be called the 'spring' growth that came after family therapists took on board Postmodern ideas. These developments (almost 'bridges' between one phase and another) included the ideas from biologists Varela and Maturana (1988), and the communication theories of Cronen and Pearce (1985).

Fact box

Cronen and Pearce (1985) proposed a hierarchy of contexts in which all communication was embedded. This model became called 'The coordinated management of meaning' (CMM). This placed language within a wider societal and cultural context.

Fact box

Varela and Maturana (1988) argued that it was not possible to determine how an outside process would change a biological organism. They therefore said that therapists should 'give up' on the idea that they can 'change' a human system.

The result of these changes in theory led, as we have said, to a proliferation of practices many of which 'came from' the Post-Milan school but gradually diverged significantly. It is impossible to summarise all these, but we provide examples in Table 7.4.

Table 7.4 Varieties of Post-modern family therapies (not including Narrative and Solution Focused)

Originator/Name of model	Primary ideas	Practice examples
Semantic Polarities (Campbell and Groenbaek, 2006; Ugazio, 2013).	Within organisations and families, one view inevitably leads to its opposite and people take up 'positions' in relationship to this polarity.	A parent may assert that children should behave. Someone will therefore take up to opposite view: that they should be encouraged to be individuals. The therapist will explore these polarities and help members take up new positions.
Collaborative enquiry (Anderson and Gehart, 2007).	Therapy is a collaborative enquiry between two people. The therapist does not draw on any particular knowledge except in how to manage a helpful conversation.	Anderson talks about being 'with' a client and approaching the conversation as a host/hostess does inviting people into their home.
Open Dialogue and dialogic approaches (Seikkula et al., 2012; 2006).	These therapists draw on the ideas of Bakhtin and Vygotsky who argued that language is a social phenomenon which draws out a response that changes perceptions and experiences.	Seikkula has applied this method to network meetings where an individual is experiencing what is called a 'psychotic episode' (Seikula and Arnkil, 2006). By hosting an open conversation about the experience of the person and their family, psychiatric admissions have been reduced (Seikkula, 2002).
Humanistic, ethical 'just talk' approaches (Bird, 2000; Pearce, 2012).	This group of therapists emphasise the way language can be used by therapists to create connections for clients. They use a range of techniques including ones from Narrative, Milan and feminism.	Bird uses what she calls 'relational externalising' to evoke hope and healing for those who have experienced abuse in relationships.
Systemic therapy as a transformative practice (McCarthy and Simon, 2016).	Systemic therapy has a unique outlook on the social context of private/ family problems. If these conversations are creatively stimulated, therapy can take part in the transformation of context/society.	Afuape (2016) outlines how her approach within a group work context for survivors of sexual abuse contributed to them being empowered to find a form of personal and social 'liberation'.

Fact box

Vygotsky was a Russian developmental psychologist who emphasised that the significance of words was not within their actual 'meanings' but in the sense they are given within the context of a conversation. This led him to examine the interactional processes that 'surround' language. He became interested in how talk constructs meanings (see Seikkula, 1993; 2003).

Fact box

Bakhtin, also a Russian psychologist, was more concerned with meanings and the multitude of meanings that are evoked in conversations. Because language is a social phenomenon that helps 'create' selves, Bakhtin suggested that human beings live in a 'polyphonic' world: their selves are multiple and constructed by the different language used in different contexts. (see Seikkula, 1993; 2003).

There are a number of common practice approaches that seem to have been adopted by most of these Postmodern and Post-Milan schools of family therapy. Theoretically, some of them reject systems theory as their source (Lowe, 2004), although many of the skills they use have evolved from the systemic world. Many of them draw on other philosophical and theoretical sources such as 'everyday conversational' theories as developed by Shotter (1993). First, almost all of them place a great premium on 'collaboration' that, in their use of the term, implies that the therapist works very hard at reducing any power differentials between therapist and client. Second, many focus upon the *conversational* aspects of therapy. Again, this means they attend to words very closely and seek to explore the 'language of problems' to help clients develop new attitudes to their 'problems'. Third, the therapist is encouraged to shun the 'change' intention: the conversation is designed to move the way the client leads, not the way the therapist determines. These trends in contemporary family therapy have had their critics (Rivett and Street, 2003). Minuchin (1998) (see Chapter 5), for instance, argued that these approaches had 'lost' the vibrancy of working with families as many of them have become solely focused on individual therapy. Flaskas (2002) and Pocock (1995) have also argued that some 'grand narratives', or at least a more nuanced approach to them, are useful to therapists.

What the last 20 years have shown is that the influence of the Milan Associates continues to mushroom and grow within systemic practices that are often far from the initial constructions of the team. Yet the fundamental glue of the building, the cement, holds up the possibility of almost endless experimentation. We would recommend that readers use this chapter to explore these experimentations while rooting their practice within the circular, curious and humble attitudes that are the heir of the four Milan Associates.

Please access the film using the eResources tab on the webpage for the book, which can be found on the Routledge website: www.routledge.com/9781138831438

Watch film: Milan and Post-Milan schools – circular questions

Introduction to film

In this film, you will see Mark (the family therapist) meeting with Maria, Nick and Joel. Mark uses techniques from the Milan and Post-Milan schools to help the family members unpick the description of being a teenager, conflict, unhappiness, sadness and anger.

00:44 Mark: Welcome back, nice to see you again. I'd like to spend this time thinking in a little bit more depth about Joel's unhappiness, and I'm going to ask you a few questions about that unhappiness and some of the questions might be a bit complicated, but the reason we ask these kind of questions is we are trying to help people think about how they connect to each other and how one thing and one person's ideas connect to another person's behaviour.

Skill note

Here the therapist ensures that the family understands the 'types' of questions that are going to be asked.

Mark: So, I guess a good place to start would be who first noticed in the family that Joel seemed to be going through an unhappy phase?

Skill note

This is a typical first circular question. It invites family members to think about the 'act' of noticing that something is wrong with another family member. Often what emerges is a difference of views or responses and understandings. Notice also that Mark avoids ascribing 'depression' to Joel's experience. Again, this is very much in line with the Milan Associates methods. Mark is keen to see if family members did use the concept of depression for his experience.

01:26 Maria: I think that would be me … well, he stayed in his room a lot *(she ascribes this behaviour as being significant).* As it went on, I heard him crying one night, so I asked him what was the matter … and he said nothing. And then I just thought I should take him to the doctors.

Skill note

There may be many reasons why Joel said 'nothing'. Mark does not unpick these at this point but another therapist might. Also, it is interesting that Maria 'takes Joel to the doctor's'. This response to distress is very culturally orientated.

Mark: OK … did you say to Joel, 'I think you are unhappy'? Did Joel say, 'I am unhappy'? … What language did you use …?

Skill note

Mark is keen to hear how the family describes the experience.

Maria: I wasn't quite sure myself then … I thought it was hormones … growing up and getting angry.

Skill note

This description suggests that Joel's experience is a passing phase, also a 'normal one' for boys. From Joel's perspective, this might have felt like his experience wasn't being 'heard' by his mother.

02:46 Mark: Did you share that with Nick … it was the average ups and downs of teenage-hood?

Skill note

Here Mark is seeking to find out whether this definition was a shared one or contested within the family.

02:58 Nick: Yes, just that general moodiness when you become a teenager.

Mark: And when did that change? When did you decide … it wasn't hormones, it wasn't moodiness of teenagers, it was sadness, it was unhappiness, something different?

Skill note

Here Mark is asking a transitional question which implies that the previous definition may have been wrong!

03:19 Maria: I think when the two of them started arguing more and more and … Nick thought it was that Joel was rude to him because he's not his real dad.

03:44 Mark: So Nick increased the problems …

Maria: I don't want to say Nick increased the problem but his feeling that he's just a stepdad … so I think he was very unhappy about that, he got upset about that …

Skill note

The conversation has shifted slightly. Maria has said that when things got worse between Nick and Joel, she began to think it was not general moodiness. This was an important change to notice.

04:23 Mark: Joel … she thinks that the conflict with Nick made your unhappiness worse. Could you just help us think about that a little bit … does conflict with Nick make you more unhappy?

Skill note

Mark is carefully unpicking the description that has been offered and is at times emphasising certain phrases and ideas rather than others. This is called punctuation.

Joel: Well yes. I don't want to get into arguments. It's not a nice feeling. If you're feeling bad and then you get into an argument, the whole thing escalates.

05:48 Mark: Sometimes when those things happen, you feel better being angry with someone else than you are sad with yourself. Is that one of those things that happens for you?

Joel: I guess ... yeah, to a degree.

Mark: So somehow the angry helps you deal with the sadness?

Skill note

Mark is exploring the cycle: sadness leads to conflict, then the conflict takes over and obscures the sadness. This is a cycle between Nick and Joel. We might ask if it works for both parties: both are 'sad' but feel angry when it gets going.

Joel: Yes, I guess.

06:29 Mark: What do you think would have made a difference then so your Mum heard you crying ... what would have had to happen for you to have felt that your unhappiness was being dealt with by your family. What would they have to have done?

Joel: I don't know ... coming in the room and asking what was wrong might have made it worse ...

Skill note

This obviously isn't what the family therapist wants to hear! As alluded to previously, there may be very good reasons for Joel's uncertainty. Rather than 'going for a solution' the therapist needs to help family members understand why coming into the room wouldn't have helped.

Joel: Maybe ... whenever ... I don't know.

Skill note

The therapist notices that Joel almost says something. He probably has got something to say but can't say it yet or now. The therapist could guess what he might have wanted to say. In family therapy, the therapist might ask family members what they think he might want to say. Instead, Mark has decided to move the conversation down a different avenue: Joel isn't ready to say anything yet, so Mark has to go back to understandings and processes.

07:41 Mark: Nick, when Maria senses that Joel is unhappy, he's sad, what does she do?

Skill note

In the flow of the conversation, Mark has learnt that relying on Joel is not successful nor are the more complex questions about how other family members should proceed. So, he has returned to the parental relationship. Notice the long silence as Nick thinks. Mark has asked a reflexive question.

08:03 Nick: I suppose she says, 'what have you done to upset Joel?'
Mark: OK, so do you think that she therefore interprets Joel's sadness as something to do with his relationship with you?

Skill note

This is crucial. If this is so, then Mark can encourage other ideas to emerge: maybe the sadness is to do with his relationship with Maria or his biological father or other young people.

08:22 Nick: Maybe not all the time, but it feels like I'm to blame.
Mark: What could she do that would be different that would stop making you feel you were to blame?
Nick: Perhaps she just ought to say, 'Joel is upset … perhaps we could talk to him'… sort of include me in it …

Skill note

At this point, Mark could have asked Maria what stops her doing this. But, interestingly, Mark moves into another avenue of direction. We may not know why he does this. One of the important skills to learn in using circular questions is to stay with the theme and explore it fully. Instead of doing this, Mark chooses to 'widen the frame' and look at relationships elsewhere in the family. It is possible that he has decided in the session that too much concentration on the parental relationship may not be advisable.

Mark: Nick, when Maria notices that Joel's unhappy, do you think that affects her relationship with Laura?
Nick: I'm sure it does … Laura is the youngest and just gets pushed out, a bit left out.

Skill note

This information allows Mark to comment that the unhappiness affects people in the family differently. Again, at this point he could have externalised the unhappiness (see Chapter 7). In Milan therapy, this would be unlikely: it would be more usual to map how different people in the family relate to the unhappiness differently. Again here Mark choses to stay with other family members' unhappiness.

09:42 Mark: Who notices when other people in the house are unhappy? When you're unhappy, Maria, who do you think notices that you're unhappy?

Maria: I would say all of them as I quite often start to cry and they all can see (Nick nods in agreement). But the most sympathy I get is from Joel.

Skill note

This is really interesting information. It almost constitutes news of difference because it confirms the mother–son relationship and by definition excludes Nick, her husband. We would be interested to know why this happens and whether he in some way encourages it.

Maria: Laura is too upset ... I think she may go to her room and cries as well but she probably wouldn't want me to see her ... Nick it makes him really uncomfortable ... I think it's Joel.

10:50 Mark: When you're unhappy, Maria, and Joel helps you with your unhappiness, do you think that makes a difference to his unhappiness?

Maria: For the short term it helps him to forget about his unhappiness and he tries to comfort me, but I think at the end of the day it makes it even worse for him ... Because he has his own problems ... I think it's even harder for him ...

11:43 Mark: So Joel, do you think it is harder for the rest of your family to cope with your unhappiness or ... with your Mum's unhappiness?

Skill note

This is a reflexive question: Mark does not know how Joel will answer, even if he will answer. But he does.

Joel:	I feel like it is probably easier to deal with Mum's …
12:26 Mark:	Do you have an idea about what it is about mum that makes it easier for people to deal with her unhappiness better than yours?
Joel:	She shows that she's unhappy.
12:44 Mark:	Does Nick ever show that he's unhappy?

Skill note

The Milan team tried hard not to label people. So, notice that Mark is not talking about a family member being unhappy but rather about family members showing unhappiness.

Joel:	I rarely notice that he's unhappy. I don't think I've ever seen him unhappy.
13:05 Mark:	OK, shall we ask Mum. Maria, do you ever see Nick unhappy?
Maria:	Well of course.
Mark:	You do? OK, what do you notice about Nick when he's unhappy?

Skill note

This conversation is using circular questions to stimulate an awareness in the family that there are many ways of showing unhappiness and that many members of the family are unhappy, i.e. Joel is not on his own!

13:21 Maria:	Well, he would close himself inside, close himself, even more … he would shut himself inside and he wouldn't want to talk than before, not wanting to talk … he would just say I'm fine … I can sense it's not.
Mark:	Is Maria right, Nick?
Nick:	Maybe, yeah maybe, my stuff is a bit more inside. I think I feel anger because of it as well.
Mark:	So, it is a bit like Joel … the sadness and the anger are somehow connected?
Nick:	Yes, I think so, seeing people moping, unhappiness, it is hard to tolerate sometimes.
Mark:	So, do you find yourself getting more angry when Maria is sad?

Skill note

The conversation has taken a turn towards the dichotomy of sadness and anger. But it has also begun to connect Nick's anger with sadness.

Nick:	Well, I hate to see her sad so it does trigger something in me, so yeah.
Mark:	OK, and then, so do you think Maria sees your anger rather than your sympathy for her sadness?
Nick:	I think so, yes, that would make sense.
Mark:	Do you think that is the same for Joel? That he sees people's anger rather than their sympathy for his sadness?
Nick:	Yes, I reckon that is yeah, yeah …
Mark:	If everybody in the family was able to see the sadness rather than the anger … who would find it hardest to see the sadness rather than the anger?
15:15 Nick:	I think Joel …
15:39 Mark:	Is he right?
Joel:	Maybe …

(Mark sums up the conversation.)

Mark: I think what we have been seeing is that you all share sadness and you all share different ways of being sad, but it's hard for each of you to recognise when people are sad. Sounds like there is a connection there and it sounds like we have heard also that sadness and anger are connected and sometimes one gets blurred with the other. Does that make sense? Maybe we will come back to this next time.

Summary

In this film Mark uses reflexive and circular questions to highlight how the family members are connected to each other through the experience of expressing their feelings. At the end of the session Mark summarises the message that he wishes the family to take away: that it is not only Joel that has feelings. Family members appear to share feelings, which are related, and this connects the family members to each other in a disruptive way that warrants further exploration.

References

Afuape, T. (2016). A 'fifth wave' systemic practice punctuating liberation. In McCarthy, I. and Simon, G. (Eds) *Systemic therapy as transformative practice.* Farnhill: Everything is Connected Press, pp. 43–61.

Andersen, T. (1991). *The reflecting team: dialogues and dialogues about the dialogues.* New York: Norton.

Anderson, H. and Gehart, D. (2007). *Collaborative therapy.* New York: Routledge.

Anderson, H. and Goolishian, H. (1988). Human systems and linguistic systems. *Family Process*, 27: 371–393.

Bateson, G. (1972). *Steps to an ecology of mind.* Chicago, IL: University of Chicago Press.

Bertrando, P. (2007). *The dialogical therapist.* London: Karnac.

Bird, J. (2000). *The heart's narrative.* Auckland, NZ: Edge Press.

Brown, J. (1997). Circular questioning: an introductory guide. *Australian and New Zealand Journal of Family Therapy*, 18: 109–114.

Burbatti, G. and Formenti, L. (1988). *The Milan approach to family therapy.* New Jersey: Aronson.

Campbell, D., Draper, R. and Huffington, C. (1989). *Second thoughts on the theory and practice of the Milan approach to family therapy.* London: Karnac.

Campbell, D. and Groenbaek, M. (2006). *Taking positions in the organisation.* London: Karnac.

Cecchin, G. (1987). Hypothesizing, circularity and neutrality revisited: an invitation to curiosity. *Family Process*, 28: 405–413.

Cronen, V. and Pearce, B. (1985). Toward an explanation of how the Milan method works: an invitation to a systemic epistemology and the evolution of family systems. In Campbell, D. and Draper, R. (Eds) *Applications of systemic family therapy: the Milan approach.* London: Grune and Stratton: 69–84.

Davolo, A. and Frugeri, L. (2016). A systemic-dialogical perspective for dealing with cultural differences in psychotherapy. In McCarthy, I. and Simon, G. (Eds) *Systemic therapy as transformative practice.* Farnhill: Everything is Connected Press, pp. 111–124.

Flaskas, C. (2002). *Family therapy: beyond postmodernism.* Hove: Brunner-Routledge.

Foot, J. (2015). *The man who closed the institutions.* London: Verso.

Gergen, K. (1999). *An invitation to social construction.* London: Sage.

Hoffman, L. (1985). Beyond power and control: toward a 'second order' family systems therapy. *Family Systems Medicine*, 3: 381–396.

Jones, E. (1993). *Family systems therapy.* Chichester: Wiley and Sons.

Lowe, R. (2004). *Family therapy: a constructive framework.* London: Sage.

McCarthy, I. and Simon, G. (2016) (Eds). *Systemic therapy as transformative practice.* Farnhill: Everything is Connected Press.

McNamee, S. and Gergen, K. (1992). *Therapy as social construction.* London: Sage.

Martin, F. (1985). The development of systemic family therapy and its place in the field. In Campbell, D. and Draper, R. (Eds) *Applications of systemic family therapy: the Milan approach.* London: Grune and Stratton.

Mason, B. (1993). Towards positions of safe uncertainty. *Human Systems* 4, 181–200.

Maturana, H. and Varela, F. (1988). *The tree of knowledge: the biological roots of human understanding.* Boston: Shambala.

Minuchin, S. (1998). Where is the family in narrative family therapy? *Journal of Marital and Family Therapy*, 24: 397–403.

Nelson, T., Fleuridas, C. and Rosenthal, D. (1986). The evolution of circular questions: training family therapists. *Journal of Marital and Family Therapy*, 12: 113–127.

Pearce, K. (2012). *Compassionate communicating.* Oracle, AZ: CMM Institute for Personal and Social Evolution.

Penn, P. (1982). Circular questioning. *Family Process*, 21: 267–280.

Pocock, D. (1995). Searching for a better story: harnessing modern and postmodern positions in family therapy. *Journal of Family Therapy*, 17: 149–173.

Prata, G. (2002). *A systemic harpoon into family games.* London: Routledge.

Rivett, M. and Street, E. (2003). *Family therapy in focus.* London: Sage.

Rogers, A. and Pilgrim, D. (2001). *Mental health policy in Britain.* Basingstoke: Palgrave.

Seikkula, J. (1993). The aim of therapy is to generate dialogue: Bakhtin and Vygotsky in family session. *Human Systems*, 4: 33–48.

Seikkula, J. (2002). Open dialogues with good and poor outcomes for psychotic crises: examples from families with violence. *Journal of Marital and Family Therapy*, 28: 263–274.

Seikkula, J. (2003). Dialogue is the change: understanding psychotherapy as a semiotic process of Bakhtin, Voloshinov and Vygotsky. *Human Systems*, 14: 83–94.

Seikkula, J. and Arnkil, T. (2006). *Dialogical meetings in social networks.* London: Karnac.

Seikkula, J., Laitila, A. and Rober, P. (2012). Making sense of multi-actor dialogues in family therapy and network meetings. *Journal of Marital and Family Therapy*, 38: 667–687.

Selvini, M. and Selvini Palazzoli, M. (1991). Team consultation: an indispensable tool for the progress of knowledge. *Journal of Family Therapy*, 13: 31–52.

Selvini-Palazzoli, M. (1963). *Self starvation.* London: Human Context Books.

Selvini-Palazzoli, M. (1986). *The hidden games of organisations.* New York: Pantheon.

Selvini-Palazzoli, M., Boscolo, L., Cecchin, G. and Giuliana Prata (1978). *Paradox and counter-paradox.* New Jersey: Jason Aronson.

Selvini-Palazzoli, M., Boscolo, L., Cecchin, G. and Giuliana Prata (1980a). Hypothesizing, circularity, neutrality: three guidelines for the conductor of the session. *Family Process*, 19: 3–12.

Selvini-Palazzoli, M., Boscolo, L., Cecchin, G. and Giuliana Prata (1980b). The problem of the referring person. *Journal of Marital and Family Therapy*, 6: 3–9.

Selvini-Palazzoli, M., Cirillo, S., Selvini, M. and Sorrentino, A. (1989). *Family games.* London: Karnac.

Shotter, J. (1993). *The cultural politics of everyday life.* Toronto: University of Toronto Press.

Tomm, K. (1984a). One perspective on the Milan systemic approach: Part 1. Overview of development of theory and practice. *Journal of Marital and Family Therapy*, 10: 113–125.

Tomm, K. (1984b). One perspective on the Milan systemic approach: Part II. Description of session format, interviewing style and interventions. *Journal of Marital and Family Therapy*, 10: 253–271.

Tomm, K. (1985). Circular interviewing. In Campbell, D. and Draper, R. (Eds) *Applications of systemic family therapy.* London: Grune and Stratton.

Tomm, K. (1987). Interventive interviewing: Part II: reflexive questioning as a means to self-healing. *Family Process*, 26: 167–183.

Tomm, K. (1988). Interventive interviewing: Part III: intending to ask lineal, circular, strategic or reflexive questions? *Family Process*, 27: 1–15.

Ugazio, V. (2013). *Semantic polarities and psychopathologies in the family.* New York: Routledge.

Watzlawick, P., Beavin, J. and Jackson, D. (1967). *Pragmatics of human communication.* New York: Norton.

White, M. (1983). Anorexia nervosa: a transgenerational system perspective. *Family Process*, 22.

Willott, S., Hatton, T. and Oyebode, J. (2012). Reflecting team processes in family therapy: a search for research. *Journal of Family Therapy*, 34: 180–203.

Chapter 8

Narrative therapy

Interpreting the story

Key points

- The core narrative belief is that our realities are organised and maintained by the stories we and other people tell about us.
- Narrative therapists hold a series of assumptions that steer their approach to their work and these assumptions are connected to a number of techniques or interventions that the therapist uses with the person who consults them.
- The narrative therapist seeks to uncover the skills of the person who has the problem to enable them to manage change in a different way.
- These techniques have been integrated into the work of non-narrative therapists and other helping professionals.

Do you remember the last time you bought a new book? Did you choose it because the cover design caught your eye? Was it the author's name that drew your interest? Was it a classic novel, crime fiction, or non-fiction? Whatever the genre, the author's aim when you opened the first page was to transport you to another place or another experience, or maybe help you learn a new skill. However, it was you, the reader, that interpreted the words and made sense of the narrative as you turned over each new page. Interpretation of language is the essence of the narrative approach. Narrative therapists believe that words are powerful and have the power to change the life experience of those who read them or listen to them. This change can be negative or positive, helpful or unhelpful, depending on how they are selected and used. This might sound obvious but when narrative therapy emerged as a school of family therapy in the late 1980s/early 1990s, it was a different approach, which later became an established stand-alone, Postmodern therapeutic model. Considered to be social constructionist, with various origins from philosophers such as Foucault and Derrida, anthropologists such as Bateson and Geertz, as well a number of family therapists, all have influenced the narrative school. But it is Michael White and David Epston (Figures 8.1 and 8.2, respectively) who, since 1981, have been credited with developing this therapy as we know it today. It is helpful to think about their backgrounds and how they were led to the narrative approach.

Michael White (1948–2008) was born in Adelaide, Australia. He originally worked as a probation officer and later trained as a social worker. Subsequently, he practised as a family therapist at the Dulwich Centre, Adelaide, which he founded in the 1980s. Initially trained in the Milan school of family therapy, White later felt restricted by general systems theory. He was drawn to focus on how people understand their life experiences, how they respond to the problems in their lives and the possible alternative ways of understanding these problems.

Figure 8.1 Michael White.
Image source: © Dulwich Centre

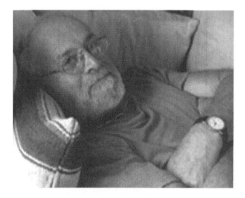

Figure 8.2 David Epston.
Image source: © Rebekah Jensen

White worked with Aboriginal communities but is especially known for his work around schizophrenia and anorexia and with children and young people. He wrote extensively about this practice and the narrative approach until he unfortunately died from a heart attack at 59 years of age whilst on a teaching tour in San Diego.

It could be said that White co-created an alternative family therapy narrative, which veered away from the historical systemic focus. His co-creator, David Epston (whom Michael considered to be his 'blood brother'), collaborated on many publications, including their major work *Narrative means to therapeutic ends* (1990). David was born in 1944 in Canada but travelled to Auckland, New Zealand, in his late teens where he studied anthropology and sociology before travelling to Britain to study community work and then social work. Social work led to him to becoming a family therapist in the late 1970s, and family therapy led him back to Auckland where he co-founded his practice, The Family Therapy Centre, during the 1980s. Both White and Epston had interesting eclectic early professional lives and the richness of these experiences is apparent in their therapeutic thinking.

The combination of their life experience and trainings in community and social work undoubtedly impacted and informed the fundamental principles of narrative work. It is a collaborative approach between client and therapist, focused on an interest in life stories and the empowerment of the disempowered. Evidence of such principles can be seen in their work with people struggling with schizophrenia and domestic violence. Since White's death, Epston has continued to write, practice and teach the narrative approach.

It is claimed that narrative therapy is organised around a narrative metaphor not a systems metaphor, i.e. the core belief is that our realities are organised and maintained by the stories we and others tell about ourselves rather than by the influence and experience of our relationships. However, on examination some narrative ideas look somewhat systemic (see Table 8.1).

In narrative therapy, stories are defined as interpretations of life events and are thought of as being linked, sequentially across time, within a plot (Morgan, 2000). But there are other similarities between the models: both systems and narrative

Table 8.1 Similarities between systemically informed family therapy and narrative family therapy

Narrative idea	Systemic element
Problems are constructed within cultural contexts.	People are influenced by the beliefs/rules of the culture of which they are part.
Mapping the influence of the problem.	An exploration of how the 'problem' impacts the person's relationships with others.
Landscape of action questions.	These types of questions seek to help identify how the 'problem' has influenced the actions of the person and the actions of any other persons present.
There is no 'one' objective truth; there are only multiple 'truths'.	Related to the coordinated management of meaning model (Pearce and Cronen, 1980) where meaning/truth is co-created with others and is ever evolving.

approaches suggest that our understanding of life experiences and life problems is influenced by others as well as culture. Both seek to unravel this influence and explore alternative understanding. The narrative therapist seeks to uncover the skills of the person who has the problem, which will enable them to manage change in a different way (narrative therapists usually call those who consult them people and not clients). The new way of managing change may be behavioural, emotional or cognitive. Systemic therapists also seek to facilitate change but seek change through the system of relationships rather than through the individual's re-construction and understanding of their identity.

Morgan (2000) suggests that narrative therapists hold a series of assumptions that steer their approach to their work:

1. The problem is the problem; the person is not the problem.
2. Problems are never present 100 per cent of the time.
3. Our understanding of life experiences changes over time.
4. Problems are constructed within cultural contexts.
5. There is no 'one' objective truth; there are only multiple 'truths'.
6. People are the experts in their own lives and have skills/beliefs/values and abilities to help them with problems.
7. The therapist should take up a non-expert position.
8. The use of therapeutic documentation and ritual is a valuable resource to sustain change.

These assumptions are connected to a number of techniques/interventions that the narrative therapist seeks to explore with the person who consults them, some of which are illustrated later in the chapter. Narrative therapy uses numerous labels to identify and explain the techniques used (some of which are shown here in **bold**). These labels can be confusing and so we have summarised them in Table. 8.2.

Table 8.2 Narrative terms and techniques

Narrative technique/concept	Description
Alternative story (aka Preferred Futures).	Life stories that do not support the dominant story and indicate new possibilities for future life.
Deconstruction.	Interpreting the beliefs, ideas and experiences of the person and others that underpin the story of the problem.
Dominant story.	Fixed beliefs about the person that affect their past, present and future understanding of themselves, e.g. "I am the pretty sister not the brainy sister", "I am hopeless with money".
Externalisation.	The objectification of the problem in order to separate it from the person.
Externalising conversations.	The use of questions to develop the externalisation of the problem and establish its personality, e.g. "What does Guilt take away from your friendships?"

Table 8.2 Continued

Narrative technique/concept	Description
Exploring the effects of the problem (aka Mapping the influence of the problem).	Uncovering how the problem has influenced every aspect of life. From the way the person thinks and feels about themselves and others and how they behave to whether this is helpful or unhelpful (see Figure 8.3).
Landscape of action questions.	Seek to establish what the problem has the person doing and the consequences/details of their acts, e.g. "Were you with anyone else when The Monster appeared? What did they do?"
Landscape of identity questions.	Seek to establish what the problem has the person thinking or knowing about themselves, e.g. "What does it say about you that you could do that?"
Naming the alternative story.	A label for a different way of living outside of the problem (derived from the words and ideas of the person).
Naming the problem.	A label is used as a form of externalisation to further distinguish the problem from the person (derived from the words and ideas of the person).
Outsider-witnesses group.	A staged ritual where two or more people, known or unknown to the person (who may have life experience relevant to the person's situation), are invited to listen to and give reflections to the person, as they talk about their story and their preferred future.
Problem-saturated story.	A dominant story that organises a person/family, preventing it from changing or finding alternative stories.
Re-authoring conversations (aka Re-storying conversations).	The therapist aims to link up events over time into a story that is meaningful for the person who brings the problem.
Remembering conversations.	Exploration of relationships that have been helpful in the past and the present (whether animals, objects, places or people). Used to establish the alternative story.
Scaffolding.	An incremental process of moving a person from a story which is known and familiar to one that is unfamiliar.
Statement of position map.	Through the process of naming the problem, exploring the history of the problem and subsequent effects of the problem, the position of the problem in the person's life is established.
Thin description.	Descriptions which exclude other meanings, e.g. attention seeker, pessimist, failure, etc.
Thickening the story.	Expanding and engaging with the details and content of a person's life and lives of those around them which reinforces the alternative story.
Unique outcomes (aka Sparkling Events or Moments).	Occasions where the problem has not been present, which are contradictory to the experience of the problem.

1.   The problem is the problem; the person is not the problem.

Externalisation is the narrative response to the idea that people are socialised to believe that 'problems' reside within people. Externalising has been described as the personification/objectification of the oppressive problem that the person experiences. It is a process whereby the problem is ascribed an identity of its own, separate to the identity of the person or relationship that was previously ascribed the problem. This allows for a refocus, away from the person and onto their relationship with the problem: an idea rooted in the Strategic Family Therapy school. Externalisation opens up possibilities for action against the problem that were inaccessible before. It can be helpful for people and their families to establish distance from the problem and subsequently change their judgements and attributions of the person.

White famously used externalisation in his work with a young boy plagued by faecal soiling, which was externalised and named 'Sneaky Poo' (White, 1984). **Naming the problem** is a part of the externalising process and helps to further separate the problem from the person. The problem is known as 'it' until a suitable name is identified; this is done in close collaboration between the person and the therapist as it is vital that the therapist does not use their own language. The therapist tunes into the language used by the person to describe the problem and reflects it back, e.g. 'the laziness', 'the nightmare', 'the fright of your life'. Alternatively, the therapist tentatively offers an appropriate name, for example, anorexia could become known as 'Ani': as an abbreviation of both the girl's name 'Annie' and 'anorexia'. Tantrums may become 'The Monster'. Notice the use of capital letters, which identifies the problem as a proper noun and externalises it further. A name can be used alongside a drawing of the problem made by the person, or an animal or an object can be selected to represent it, e.g. a tiger, a sports car, etc.

Narrative therapists suggest that all problems can be externalised: problems in relationships, e.g. arguing, mistrust, feelings, sadness, anger, and cultural practices such as racism, discrimination. However, therapists should be careful to explore the wider context of people's lives when using externalisation if they are to avoid reinforcing the dominant ideas behind the problem itself, i.e. issues of power and oppression.

Externalisation *should not* be used when working with violence and sexual abuse. There is a risk that the victim could interpret the externalisation process to mean that the perpetrator is not responsible for their actions. Therefore, the therapist could unintentionally reinforce the abuse. However, attitudes and beliefs that support the abuse or violence of the abuser could be externalised, e.g. the belief that the way a woman dresses can provoke a sexual assault.

Externalisation takes place within the context of **externalising conversations**, where open questions are used to investigate the problem and build a personality profile. Where the Milan team used curiosity (see Chapter 5), narrative therapists use externalising conversations to focus upon the behaviour, values, beliefs, plans, thoughts, motives and actions of the presenting problem. It is as if narrative therapists behave as detectives, investigating a crime scene asking questions such as:

'So, what did Ani have you thinking about yourself when you ate your breakfast?'

'What did you do when Ani wanted you to hide the food from your mum?'

'What did Ani think about your idea of having a rest after your snack?'

'What does Ani have planned for you over the Christmas holidays?'

Task 1

Think about something you enjoyed doing as a child, e.g. a hobby, a subject at school, etc. and have an externalising conversation with yourself about this. Ask yourself, "When did football first enter your life?"; "What did playing the piano have you thinking about yourself?" Notice how you feel about yourself as you ask these questions.

In this way, externalising conversations are used to **explore the effects of the problem** (or **map the influence of the problem**). By exploring the effects of the problem, the full impact on all aspects of the person's life is revealed both to the therapist and to the person bringing the problem (see Figure 8.3). Without this exploration, it may appear that the therapist does not fully appreciate the severity of the problem and the person may feel misunderstood. Such exploration will potentially highlight skills and competencies that the person has been using, and so thickens the **alternative story**.

Figure 8.3 Exploring the effects of the problem.

Task 2

Think about a significant event that happened in your family whilst you were growing up, e.g. the birth of a new baby, a house move, change of school, etc., and consider the impact this had upon you using the headings in Figure 8.1.

---

2.   Problems are never present 100 per cent of the time.

There are occasions when the person has overcome the problem. These are revealed during **deconstruction** conversations and are considered to be **unique outcomes**: events that contradict the dominant **problem saturated story**, where the person has successfully resisted the problem (Morgan, 2000).

Unique outcomes, also known as '**sparkling events**', are events that stand out as different to the problem and which would have been difficult to achieve given the history of the problem. The therapist will need to listen out for what they consider to be a unique outcome; it may present as an action, a thought, feeling, belief or an event, either in the past or the present. However, only the person consulting the therapist can determine what constitutes a unique outcome. The therapist should avoid persuading the person but can ask direct questions to help the process, e.g. "When do you notice Ani is not as strong as usual?"; "How did you stop Ani preventing you from taking the holiday with your sister?"

3.   Understanding of life experiences changes over time; and
4.   Problems are constructed within cultural contexts.

Culture has a strong influence over the way we understand our lives and which stories are dominant or subjugated. Gender, class, race, ability, age, etc., provide a background 'noise' in which we make meaning of life both in the past and the present and this meaning can change over time. The narrative perspective is that problems grow when supported by larger cultural ideas and beliefs, e.g. racism is supported by ideas of white privilege and power, which perpetuates the social-economic and political domination of non-white ethnic groups; the sexual objectification of women and also men has historically been supported through the promotion of the 'Page 3 Girl and Page 5 Fella' (female and male models are selected to have their semi-naked photographs published daily in a British tabloid newspaper). Through narrative deconstruction of the broader cultural beliefs, the roots of problems can be uncovered, helping people to challenge them and chose a preferred future.

Narrative therapists use deconstruction conversations to decipher the cultural beliefs; practices and concepts that assist the problem and help the person view the problem differently. Cultural beliefs that have assisted the problem in the past and beliefs that sustain the problem in the present are of particular interest and are examined in detail through the use of questions that seek to capture the meaning of the problem to the person who struggles with it. 'Un-spoken' truths, e.g. 'women are naturally maternal' or 'men struggle to express their feelings' are questioned and evaluated as to whether they are helpful for the person in their quest to change the problem, or whether they are supporting the problem or are a source *of the* problem. Cultural beliefs, which have been somehow helpful in the past may, when examined, prove to be unhelpful in the present. The person is helped to recognise this change over time and to take up a different perspective. The idea that our interpretation of life events and the subsequent narrative we tell ourselves and tell others changes over time and is not fixed, is closely related to the next assumption.

5.   There is no 'one' objective truth; there are only multiple 'truths'.

Like systemic therapists, narrative therapists also suggest that there are multiple 'truths' that provide multiple interpretations and multiple solutions. Epston and White articulated the idea that logical positivism (a belief that only information derived from the sciences is valid knowledge and is therefore the 'truth') was behind the mental health problems of members of Western society. They explained that the people that consulted them were socialised to accept being pathologised by others (i.e. medical professionals) and to pathologise themselves, e.g. 'I am depressed', 'I am psychotic', 'I am bi-polar'. This pathology became an internalised Self-description, which obscured other 'lived experiences' (White and Epston, 1990). Such pathologies prevented professionals and the people who consulted them, from searching for alternative stories. Consequently the alternative stories become buried and subjugated along with opportunities for alternative understanding and possibility of change. They suggested that there are many different stories occurring in our lives simultaneously, which we interpret according to dominant explanations and context of the time. For example, a mother might describe her family as being warm, self-sufficient and close; a teacher may describe the same family as disorganised and dysfunctional, and a social worker may understand the family as being impoverished and underprivileged. The teacher subjugates the story of 'closeness' and instead privileges the story of 'dysfunction', the social worker privileges the story of 'impoverished' over the story of 'self-sufficiency', and the parent privileges 'warmth' over the story of 'poverty'. All these multiple interpretations are the 'truths' of the people who hold them, and although all are valid (for the time that these people hold them), none are 'the' truth.

6.   People are the experts in their own lives and have skills/beliefs/values and abilities to help them with problems.

This assumption is a crucial underpinning of the narrative approach and of other third-generation or Postmodern approaches. Here the therapist is seen as a participant–observer who collaborates in a reciprocal process, helping the person to identify and value their own experiences and indirectly proposing that they resist deferring to the dominant view imposed by another person, establishment or culture. Narrative therapists draw upon the tools of their trade to establish this proposition within the therapy sessions. Externalisation is a first step and seeks to empower the person to see the problem as separate to their skills and abilities. Once the problem is externalised, the person is elevated from a position of victim *of the* problem towards expert *on the* problem. From this position they are asked questions: questions which map the effects of the problem, deconstruct the problem and highlight sparkling moments. Sparkling moments are particularly important in the process of helping the person increase their belief in their skills and abilities to re-author their own life, as they are examples of their skills in action. However, acknowledging this involves moving from a place of familiar problem-saturated ideas of incompetence, to a place of unfamiliar, problem-solving competence and traversing the gap in between. Narrative therapists help to bridge this gap through the process of **scaffolding** questions. Scaffolding questions introduce ideas that are not so different from the person's self-concept that they are rejected out of hand, but are just different enough to provoke food for thought. They act as a support of the familiar ideas, whilst at the same time provide an opportunity for reassessment of past events and reconnection with skills that might otherwise be overlooked. The therapist seeks to engage the person's curiosity and imagination to thicken their beliefs about their skills and build their confidence. Hopefully an increase in confidence progresses into the identification of an **alternative preferred future**.

Task 3

Think back to your school reports and bring to mind comments from teachers which were negative, e.g. 'chatterbox', 'fidget', 'easily distracted', etc. (And if, reader, you were fortunate enough not to have experienced this, think of something that could have been written!) Think about externalising this comment, think of occasions when this comment was not true and think of the skills this comment suggests.

---

7.   The therapist should take up a non-expert position.

When people attend therapy, it is likely that the solutions that they have previously attempted have served to perpetuate the problems they intended to solve. It is the narrative therapist's job to facilitate conversations rather than come up with solutions and answers. The decentring of the narrative therapist is different from the strategic and structural idea that the therapist 'knows' what needs to change, towards *consultation* on the client's interpretation. However, that is not to say that the therapist will not keep a strategic focus to the externalising conversation. After all, people come to therapy to be helped to change problems they have been unable to change on their own. The narrative therapist facilitates conversations from a curious, respectful position to allow the person(s) consulting them to tell their story. The therapist carefully reflects the person's language and checks out his understanding: the therapist does not assume a shared common understanding. The person is the primary 'author' of the conversations, but the therapist has the task of making the power of language and sociocultural influences explicit. Decentred does not mean disengaged and neither does it mean non-influential and passive. The therapist is influential, not through structuring interventions but through their use of questioning.

As highlighted previously in Table 8.2, questions within conversations are the main tool of the narrative therapist: **externalising conversations, re-authoring conversations, remembering conversations, landscape of identity questions** and **landscape of action questions**. White turned the use of therapeutic questions and formulation of questions into an art form, using questions to build narratives and scaffold the person's or family's challenge to their problems. Narrative questions make direct reference to the person's language, and when watching session recordings of White working with families, you may notice his careful note taking and repetitive use of the language the person who is consulting him uses. Narrative therapists (because of their social constructionist thinking) are less interested in the original *cause* of the problem and more interested in its *effect* in the here and now and its legacy from the past. They ask questions to generate stories about life experiences, not information, only asking questions that they do not know the answer to.

8.   The use of therapeutic documentation and ritual is a valuable resource to sustain change.

Epston is credited with developing the use of letters and documents in therapeutic work (Epston and White, 1992). Epston wrote letters to people after therapy sessions as summaries of the main ideas from the session and as part of the collaboration between himself and the person(s). Epston (1994) claimed that letters extended the therapeutic conversation "The words in a letter don't fade and disappear the way a conversation does ... A client can hold a letter in hand, reading and re-reading it days, months and years after the session". There are many classifications of letters with many different functions (Morgan, 2000); they are largely used alongside other documentation to summarise knowledge, reiterate goals and capture progress and change in the therapeutic work. The language used in the letters and documents is selected to reinforce and continue the externalisation process and encourage the person or family in their endeavours between sessions and on completion of therapy. They can be used as part of the direct therapy process to thicken the alternative story or used as the entire therapy process (where direct work is impossible). They can take the form of contracts between different people, which they each sign as a symbol of their commitment to change. They can also be letters from the therapist to family members or other professionals, which record therapeutic change or which request the support of a significant person to help with change. Family members can be encouraged to contribute to the change process by replying to the letter, and letter-writing campaigns can follow (Madigan, 2011).

Documents can take the form of certificates or awards to celebrate sparkling events such as 'Battles won in the fight against Ani', 'The completion of operation "Move Ani Out of My Life"'. An example of a certificate is shown in Figure 8.4.

Task 4

Referring to the comments made about you at school in Task 3, create a therapeutic letter or certificate to the 'younger you', which celebrates your success in overcoming this alleged character deficit.

Rituals and celebrations, both formal and informal, are used to mark significant points in the therapeutic process. They are used to commemorate the process of moving away from the problem-saturated story towards the preferred future and act as a reinforcing parallel of this process. They are personalised and specific to the person involved. At celebrations, invitations to significant people are issued, an agenda set and people are invited to speak about their observations of the progress of the person being celebrated. The therapist might take part or may not even be present. Food might be shared and certificates issued. Rituals and ceremonies do not necessarily involve celebration but are also used to remember an event such as a loss, trauma or an episode that is incomplete in some way. The narrative group process **outsider-witness** (developed from the work of Myerhoff, 1986) is a four-part definitional ceremony. White developed an

Figure 8.4 Example of a therapeutic certificate.

'alumni' directory of outsider-witnesses made up of people who had consulted him in the past. The alumni would be called upon if they had shared similar experiences to the person currently in therapy. They would attend an organised ritual to listen to and comment on the story told by the person in therapy. White believed that the outsider witness benefitted as much from the process as the person that they were witnessing and this formed part of their own re-authoring process. Myerhoff's idea lives on within the family therapy clinic 'reflecting team' (Andersen, 1991) which, although traditionally made up of multi-disci-plinary skilled-helper professionals, could alternatively be likened to a group of outsider-witnesses (see Chapter 10).

Legacy

Narrative therapy is a collaborative approach between therapist and the person(s) consulting them. Together they construct a new story through the use of tech-niques: some of which are rooted in systemic practice. Having said this, narrative therapists suggest that there are other competencies beyond learning these tech-niques and do not wish to be seen as using a 'cook-book' type therapy. Morgan (2000) describes narrative as an "attitude and orientation", not just a "skill or tech-nique". Stating that the philosophies of feminism, anthropology, a commitment to social justice and a belief in social constructionist ideology underpin narrative therapy. However, it is the narrative skills and unique therapeutic tools of change that attract therapists from other trainings who wish to work with people within such a creative, collaborative approach. It is possible for non-narrative therapists to learn these therapeutic tools. Indeed, ideas from narrative therapy have been successfully integrated into systemic family therapy practice and the larger psy-chotherapy field. The use of externalisation in the family therapy treatment of eating disorders is an example of this (see Chapter 4).

Please access the film using the eResources tab on the webpage for the book, which can be found on the Routledge website: www.routledge.com/9781138831438

Watch film: Narrative school – Externalisation

Introduction to film

This is the first session of family therapy for Jess (who is the identified patient) and her mother, Susie, and grandmother, Pat, and they are meeting Jo, their family therapist, for the first time. Jess does not meet the criteria for an anorexic diagnosis at this time but is struggling to maintain a healthy eating pattern. In this session you will see Jo begin the process of 'joining' and building a therapeutic alliance. She uses externalisation to help the family think differently about their current difficulties and externalises a problem related to the disordered eating: 'Tension' as this seems to be more important for the family at that time both in the therapy room and at home. However, the process would be the same whether Jo had externalised anorexia or any other problem affecting the family.

01:10 Jo:	So Abbie is nearly 19, is that right, she's at University in Hull and unfortunately can't be with us? Is there anybody who needs to be on here that isn't on here?
Pat:	No, that is everyone.
Jo:	That's everyone? OK, well thank you for your introductions and thank you for helping me with your genogram. Now, whilst we were talking a number of issues came up, one of which was the return of Jess having eating problems again, but I was wondering, of all the issues we discussed what should we talk about first?
Susie:	Well, what's brought us here is Jess's anorexia …
Jess:	Well and what caused it: you and your drinking.
Susie:	Jess, it is not my fault that I've…
Jo:	You know, I would agree and we do need to think about anorexia and how it has returned to the family because this is really concerning, but I am interested in all your ideas and I was wondering, you know, if Abbie was here, it's a funny thing to ask you, but if Abbie was here, what do you think she would say?

Skill note

Jo uses a circular question to incorporate all family members' views. Abbie may hold an **alternative story** about the problem that has brought the family to therapy; this is part of the **deconstruction process**.

Jess:	How are we supposed to know what Abbie would say? She's not here is she?
Jo:	Unfortunately she can't be with us, Jess, and that's a shame, because she is up in Hull, but if she was here and I know it is a weird question to ask you, but you know, if she was here what do you think she might say?
Pat:	Well, what I think what she'd say, it is so tense at home that she was just glad to be away, and there were arguments and rows and worries and …
Jo:	And the tension, is this the type of tension she doesn't like?

Skill note

Jo picks up on the language used by the family to begin the process of **naming the problem** and **exploring the effects of the problem.**

Susie:	Well, I don't like it either ... none of us do ...
Pat:	No ...
Jo:	None of you like the tension, is that right? Has Susie got that right, Pat?
Pat:	Absolutely, yes, it is arguments, there's silences, we tread on eggshells, it is terrible.
Susie:	Yeah, it is tension you can feel it as soon as you get in the front door.
Jo:	So the name for it is Tension, I've got that right, it's not arguing, no, that's the right word for it?

Skill note

Jo tentatively checks out her understanding of the problem and names it as 'Tension' (**therapist takes a non-expert position**).

Notice the use of capitalised 'T' in Tension as Jo seeks to separate to Jess and her family from the identity of the problem (**externalisation/the problem is the problem**).

Jo:	Jess, do you recognise that Tension has appeared in your family?"
Jess:	Suppose so ...
Jo:	Can anyone tell me, when it first appeared?
03:29 Susie:	I don't know, I think it first appeared around the time that Jess went to secondary school, she was about 11, she seemed worried about something, but I couldn't really work out what she was worried about ...

Skill note

Conversation continues with a focus upon Susie and the history of her alcohol misuse.

05:02 Jo:	And Pat, I can see that it's difficult for you too, that you are really concerned about Susie and when she was drinking in the past, and Susie, I can see that it really affects you when your mum talks about it here and it will be important for us to talk about that, but I wondered if we could just park that for a minute and just think a little bit more about Tension, would you be interested in that? Jess, Susie? Yeah OK?

Skill note

Jo attempts to focus the conversation away from **the problem-saturated story**, which identifies Susie as the problem; instead she seeks to further identify **the problem as the problem**, i.e. Tension.

Jo: So, Susie, it sounds like you first noticed Tension had entered the family and that was when Jess started her new school. Can you tell me what Tension had you doing at that time?

Skill note

Through the use of externalising conversation, Jo seeks to explore the **effects of the problem** through the use of **landscape of action questions**.

Susie: What it had me doing? That's a weird question …
Jo: It is a weird question.

Skill note

Discussion continues to explore the background to the arrival of 'Tension' and then focuses upon an **alternative story** of the relationship between Pat and Susie, where Pat appears to accept that Susie cares for her wellbeing. Notice that Jess appears unhappy during this conversation. Jo could have drawn attention to this to bring Jess back into the conversation, but she sticks with the dialogue between Susie and Pat. What would you have done?

07:46 Jo: So, how do people puts things right in the family, you know, when you're not talking to each other? How do things get put right when they go wrong?
Jess: No one knows how to put things right in this family …
Jo: No, and do you think if Abbie was here, Jess, would she say that or would she say something different?
Jess: She'd agree with me and gran.
Jo: Does she always agree with you and gran?

Skill note

Jo seeks to uncover **alternative stories**.

Jess:	No, sometimes she agrees with mum.
Jo:	OK, Susie, do you remember a time when Abbie agreed with you?
Susie:	Yeah, when she's home from Uni she, she backs me up when it all gets too tense around Jess and her eating.
Jo:	So, Abbie is good at backing you up against the Tension, is that right?
Susie:	Yeah, you could say that, yeah, yeah, I mean just sometimes it gets on top of me and I just need some support.
Jo:	Yeah, and what does 'support' mean to you, Susie?
Susie:	Well, I mean in the past it would have probably meant drinking, but now I do try and use other methods of coping, you know, I might watch TV or read a magazine or something.
Jo:	And when Tension gets too much for you, Jess, what do you do?

Skill note

Jo seeks to **thicken the story** through the use of a **landscape of action question**.

Jess:	I go upstairs, put on a film or just listen to my music.
Jo:	You do, do you ever watch anything together as a family?
Jess:	We used to, when Abbie was home …
Pat:	Yeah, we used to have really good nights, didn't we? Do you remember we used to get a film usually on a Saturday and we'd buy popcorn or chocolate or something and we'd all curl in the chairs and bring quilts and it was just girlies' night wasn't it, and it was lovely?
Susie:	Yeah, I remember that, I mean, it was good 'cos you used to watch as well.
Jo:	It sounds like you really enjoyed that time together.

Skill note

Jo seeks to **identify the alternative story** by highlighting a **sparkling moment**.

Pat:	Yeah, do you remember that?
Jess:	Yep.
Pat:	It was good, wasn't it?
09:42 Jo:	So I wonder where Tension was then?

Skill note

Jo highlights the concept that **'problems are never present 100% of the time'**.

Pat: There wasn't any, was there? Not really then …
Jess: I never really noticed it …
Jo: No? Maybe you just had some everyday problems that families have?

Skill note

Jo highlights an **alternative story:** it is normal for families to have problems sometimes.

Susie: Well, really yeah, they were just everyday problems, just like normal families.
Jo: So I was wondering where was Tension and where is Tension now, if we think about now, and where is it when it's mealtime?

Skill note

Having externalised 'Tension', Jo is able to switch back to the reason for referral: anorexia and further the **exploration of the problem.**

Susie & Pat: It's everywhere!
Jo: Sounds like it takes full advantage of mealtimes, is that right? What does Tension have you doing, Jess?

Skill note

Another **landscape of action question** will help the family to understand the connection between the **dominant stories** of Tension and anorexia and also the connection to other family issues including Susie's alcohol use and parenting. The externalising conversation continues.

13:53 Jo: Do you think that there might be … I just had this idea do you think that there might be a connection between Jess feeling left out, Jess not eating and the Tension? Are they connected in some way?
Susie: Yeah, I think they are definitely connected, I mean, I worry when I see that Jess isn't eating so then I try and get her to eat. You might call it nagging, but I try and get her to eat and then she gets tense 'cos I am trying to get her to eat and then it all just snowballs and then we have an argument and then no one ends up eating anything anyway.
Jo: And Tension has its way and wins! Do you know, I wonder what Tension has in store for this family?

Skill note

Jo continues to map the influence of the problem through continuing the externalising conversation.

14:39 Susie: Another weird question … Umm … just to make us more miserable I suppose … Oh, that bloody Tension, I just, I'd really like to give it a piece of my mind, umm, I could strangle it, or bloody shoot it!

Jo: Do you know, I just had a mad idea, Susie, that Tension was sat here in this chair What would you say to it?

Skill note

As part of the **externalising conversation**, Jo seeks to strengthen the fight back against 'Tension' through the use of a role play exercise. This exercise can be utilised when working with individuals as well as family groups.

15:54 Jo: What would have to happen for Tension to get back into this family, do you think?

Skill note

This is a **scaffolding question**, which seeks to put the family into an **expert position** and encourage them to think about an **alternative future**.

Susie: I think if mum started on at me again, that would bring it back.
Pat: Yeah, but you have to talk to me.
Susie: Well I do, well I try …
Jess: Or if mum started drinking again, that would definitely bring it back.
Susie: Oh … stop going on about it!

Skill note

Discussion progresses around Susie's past use of alcohol (**problem-saturated story**). Jo acknowledges the family concerns about Susie's alcohol use but chooses to continue to seek out an **alternative story/preferred future.**

19:38 Susie:	I do want things to be different now.
Jo:	I wonder if another thing you all want to be different is the way anorexia has returned to your lives? Because what we know about anorexia is that it impacts everybody in the family in different ways. Jess, can you tell me some of the ways that anorexia has impacted you? Is it the same as before or is it different this time?

Skill note

Jo returns to the reason for the referral: anorexia and asks more questions in order to **deconstruct** the problem and construct a **statement of position map**.

Summary

In this film excerpt, you saw the therapist, Jo, turning 'Tension' into a proper noun and establishing it as separate to Jess and her family in order to unite them in a battle against Tension rather than battle against each other.

Having addressed the issue of tension, both within the room and in family life using externalisation, it is possible to use the same narrative skill to explore 'anorexia' and build up a picture of its influence on Jess and her family. Notice that Jo first uses the description 'eating problem' so as not to introduce language alien to the family, but picks up the work 'anorexia' after Susie uses it. Even though eating problems – anorexia – is the main reason for Jess's referral, it is sometimes necessary to first pay attention to other issues which are impacting family relationships and are significant to the family; however, anorexia is obviously a very serious issue and would be challenged throughout the family work.

References

Andersen, T. (1991). *The reflecting team: dialogues and dialogues about dialogues.* New York: Norton.

Epston, D. (1994). Extending the conversation. *The Family Therapy Networker,* 18(6): 30–37, 62–63.

Epston, D. and White, M. (1992). *Experience, contradiction, narrative and imagination: selected papers of David Epston and Michael White, 1989–1991.* Adelaide: Dulwich Centre Publications.

Madigan, S. (2011). *Narrative therapy.* Washington DC: American Psychological Association.

Morgan, A. (2000). *What is narrative therapy?* Adelaide: Dulwich Centre Publications.

Myerhoff, B. (1986). Life not death in Venice: its second life. In Turner, V. and Bruner, E. (Eds) *The Anthropology of Experience.* Chicago: University of Illinois Press.

Pearce, W. and Cronen, V. (1980). *Communication, action, and meaning: the creation of social realities.* Praeger.

White, M. (1984). Pseudoencopresis: from avalanche to victory, from vicious to virtuous circles. *Family Systems Medicine,* 2: 150–160.

White, M. and Epston, D. (1990). *Narrative means to therapeutic ends.* New York: W. W. Norton & Company.

Chapter 9

Working systemically with individuals
Opening up a different view

Key points

- Working systemically with individual clients is established within the schools of family therapy.
- It is possible to adapt family therapy skills when working with individual family members.
- Therapy with individuals calls upon the creativity of the therapist to be systemic.
- The therapist working with individuals needs to develop a level of systemic self-awareness.
- The use of action methods can help individuals to gain a different view upon their presenting problems and enable them to take up a different position in their relationships and in relation to their social identity.

Introduction

When therapists work with individual clients systemically, it is as if they are opening a window between the client and their significant relationships and life experiences. Through this open window there is a possibility that the client will be able to see a clearer, different view to the current one. They may be able to recognise that the 'problem' that brought them to therapy, which they believed was located internally is actually linked to another external 'problem' and vice versa. That is to say that rather than being separate individuals with separate problems, they are linked to other individuals with connected problems even if they are the sole person presenting in the therapy room. This is important because if this is ignored and the window remains closed, the possibility for understanding and a potential source for change could also be closed. If, as therapists, we agree that generally people seek therapy to change or improve their wellbeing in some way and that engagement with the world and connection to others through healthy relationships is a factor in improvement of wellbeing and happiness (Vaillant, 2012;

Fowler and Christakis, 2008), wouldn't we be myopic therapists not to push the window wide open?

Before thinking about ways of working systemically with individuals, we must first think about why we would do this and what the different schools of family therapy tell us. There is a lack of dedicated literature concerning this therapeutic way of working and therefore there are few key figures in this field (Boscolo and Bertrando, 1996; Hedges, 2005; Breunlin and Jacobsen, 2014). It is interesting to note that many family therapists spend much of their time working therapeutically with individual clients. This might be due to the reluctance of family members to join in with family sessions, the reality of the 'therapy market', e.g. it is mostly individuals that ask for therapy, or it may be due to family therapists choosing a less challenging task than working with whole families – for example, due to the financing of private health care in the USA, family therapists work with individuals and with couples as well as with families. Szapocznik *et al.*, (1983) even argued that there was some evidence that family therapy was better conducted when one member of the family was seen on their own. Similarly psychiatrists Boscolo and Bertrando (1986) described a type of individual systemic therapy as the treatment of choice for some clients (Figure 9.1).

Underlying the whole debate about systemic work with individuals are two versions of 'what the self is' (for an extended discussion see Rivett and Street, 2003). In one version, the self is an integrated experience similar to that suggested by other psychotherapies. If this is accepted, then systemic work with

Figure 9.1 Here on left and right, Luigi Boscolo and Paolo Bertrando.

Thank you to Paolo Bertrando for supplying these images.

individuals will tend to be similar to that undertaken by psychoanalysts and coun-sellors. Another version suggests that the self is more 'systemic' and fluid. Here systemic work with an individual takes on quite a different practice: exploring relationships, different perspectives and 'internal others'. The third-generation social constructionists have proposed a more complex model of the self that to some degree synthesizes these two views. In social constructionist terms peo-ple are defined by their relationships, conversations with others and from their positions and differences in relation to other people (Larner, 1998). However, within this version, social constructionists such as Harré (1995) describe 'a per-sonal mode of being' where individuals have a personal sense of themselves. This sense is often said to emerge from 'inside' the mind of the person through the process of an internal 'conversation' with the outside world. Dutch psycholo-gist Hermans (2004) describes this as the 'dialogical self', an idea where internal processes or thoughts (self) merge with meaning derived from external dialogue in social conversation within a recursive pattern. He explains that the internal self is both influenced by, and has an influence upon, dialogue with others. Hence, it is understandable that from a theoretical point of view, social constructionist practice may also often involve work with individuals although this may be more *relational* than *systemic*.

Whichever ideas about the 'self' most interest the therapist, what will be of equal concern is Larner's link between self and the idea of personal agency or autonomy as it is this that is at the heart of choice and change and the core of therapy. Larner (1998) comments upon an individual's autonomy being 'con-strained by the circumstances of their own lived narrative', that is to say, that the stories that are told to a person by others and the stories they tell themselves limit the opportunities for them to embody a different personhood. However, Larner also comments upon the capacity of such an individual to be self-reflec-tive. It is this ability for self-reflection that the therapist working systemically with the individual must engage with. It is here that the spotlighting of the dialogical self of the individual opens an opportunity for a deeper exploration, which may not be possible when working with a whole family group, where the family therapist is juggling to share and build a therapeutic alliance with multi-family members.

Task 1

Think back to your primary school reports and any statements made about you, e.g. 'chatterbox', 'creative', 'disruptive', 'good sportswoman', 'impul-sive', 'talented musician', etc. How have these descriptions influenced you? Why do you think some descriptions have influenced you whilst oth-ers have not?

Historical development

Breunlin and Jacobsen (2014) have explained why they think individual work began to expand in family therapy. They propose that Strategic Family Therapy (Chapter 6) argued that systemic change could occur when one element of a system changed. It was therefore no longer necessary to work with the whole system in the room as previously argued by family therapists (such as Minuchin). Boscolo and Bertrando (1986) have a more positive view about this expansion. They explain that the development of systemic work with individuals arose during the 1980s when some individual therapists began to take notice of family and couple therapy. Simultaneously, some systemic family therapists began to recognise family members as individuals. They suggest that there were two contrasting theoretical therapeutic schools of thought at this time: one that explored the client's presenting problem and focused upon finding a solution, which included Milan and Solution Focused Brief Therapy (SFBT), alongside another that included models that explored the client's inner world and focused on changing their 'world view', e.g. psychodynamic and psychoanalysis. Boscolo and Bertrando introduced a new model: 'Brief/Long-term Therapy', which integrated both. Combining ideas from psychoanalysis and Gestalt with those from the strategic and narrative schools, it is adaptable depending upon what is most useful for the presenting client and prioritises therapist self-reflexivity throughout. The quality of the therapeutic alliance and empathy are also considered essential. The ability to establish a strong therapeutic alliance and convey empathy is somewhat dependent upon the self-reflexivity of the therapist. Self-reflexivity of the therapist is particularly important when therapists are working individually with individual clients, i.e. without the benefit of a co-therapist or a reflecting team. These companions help guard against unhelpful coalitions between the therapist and client and any countertransference responses (Carr, 1986). We will return to this later in Chapter 10 and consider reflexivity in the context of systemic self-awareness (Rivett and Woodcock, 2015).

What have other systemic therapists said about working with individuals? Family therapists Betty Carter and Monica McGoldrick (1999) warned against losing a systemic focus and highlighted a common pitfall to:

> Compartmentalize theorizing about family separately from theorizing about the individual…to shift to psychodynamic or psychoanalytic thinking. (1999: xvi)

Family therapists Carl Whitaker and Augustus Napier (1978) proposed that individual therapy be used as the final part of the family therapy process if requested by an individual family member, suggesting this should happen when they had individuated from the family system. Similarly Breunlin and Jacobsen (2014) suggest that family therapy work should begin with 'whole family therapy' and move to 'relational family therapy', where the therapist works through a systemic lens with a family subsystem or individual family member.

As already discussed, family therapy theory proposes that problems which affect individuals are effects of problems within relationships and are best considered and treated within the context in which they arise, i.e. the family group, the couple, the organisation, etc. These relationships are generally considered a resource for change. This leaves a dilemma for the therapist working with one part of a relationship system: can they recreate the context and relationships of their individual client in a systemically meaningful way within the therapeutic space? In some ways this is exactly what a systemic therapist undertakes even when working with more than one individual, as it would be impractical and physically impossible to work in the presence of all the figures from all the client's relationships, inside and outside their family.

So, how do therapists work systemically with only one part of a family or organisational system? Our proposed approach to working with individuals in this way is an integrative one, and therefore the content of this chapter expands on some concepts, which are referenced elsewhere in the text. This is done in the hope of making the reading experience more fluid and less disjointed at the risk of being repetitious. Our focus here is upon solo-therapists working with an individual client.

Key concepts

What does it mean to 'work systemically with individuals'? It means that the therapist's goal is to help the client think about themselves systemically, i.e. as part of a system upon which he or she both impacts and is impacted by. In practice

Figure 9.2 Aspects of the relational self.

this means helping the client to explore the different aspects of this system including their relationships, family structure, their personal and public personas, their social identity and belief systems (see Figure 9.2). We will explore each dimension separately, and although our focus is on the individual, the reader will recognise the validity of the ideas for joint family work also.

1. Social identity

Clients bring to therapy issues they wish to change in some way. These issues may be related to the way they relate to society, their culture and/or their place within it. The therapist brings to the role of therapist their own culture and social experiences which impacts their practice. This makes for a complex interactional space. However, if the therapist is to be helpful to the individual client, they will aim to explore these experiences and the meanings that the client has constructed from such experiences. John Burnham and Alison Roper-Hall have developed a framework (Burnham, 1992, 1993; Roper-Hall, 1998; Burnham, 2012), which aids the therapist in such a task. It is a list of social differences known by the mnemonic 'Social GGRRAAACCEEESSS' (an acronym for gender, geography, race, religion, age, ability, appearance, class, culture, ethnicity, education, employment, sexuality, sexual orientation and spirituality; see Figure 9.3).

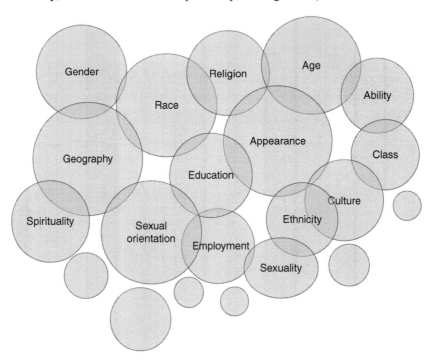

Figure 9.3 Intersections of self.

(Adapted from Burnham, 2012, by permission of the author.)

The Social GGRRAAACCEEESSS (SG) model has been used in systemic training to encourage reflexivity, systemic self-awareness and cultural competence (Burnham, 1993, 2012; Roper-Hall, 1998). It also has a use as an aide-memoire for practitioners working systemically with individuals. It can be used outside of the therapy room to help the therapist plan future sessions around areas of enquiry that they are curious about and inside the therapy room to highlight differences and similarities both within the family of origin and the extended family group. For example, conflicting family of origin beliefs and values within couple relationships can be discussed and the impact examined. Discussion around the domains of the GGRRAAACCEEESSS is likely to expose transgenerational differences as well as transgenerational convergence when used in conjunction with a genogram. Burnham (2012) highlights the fact that some aspects of SG are 'visible and voiced' and others are 'invisible and unvoiced', which leaves the practitioner the dilemma of how to avoid overlooking the visible aspects, which might hold valuable content for the client, whilst not over-focusing on the unvoiced aspects, which may well be less valuable and less helpful for the client. Burnham suggests that practitioners may also consider what invisible aspects of SG they will disclose of themselves, e.g. religious and spiritual beliefs, sexuality, etc., and how this may or may not serve the client and the therapeutic alliance.

2. The family/individual lifecycles

As already stated, Carter and McGoldrick (1999) describe the family as an evolving system moving through time in a lifecycle and, alongside this, each individual family member has a lifecycle within the family system. Carter and McGoldrick identified six stages that a family reaches as it develops over a life span, shown in Figure 9.4. Each stage is accompanied by a series of emotional and structural hurdles. The description of family used is a traditionally historical form: marriage, having children, children leaving home, etc. However, Carter and McGoldrick acknowledge that not all families are identical and that contemporary life is much more complex. They also acknowledge that the cultural context of the family brings stressors including social, economic, political and spiritual, and these have a reciprocal impact on the family, the individual and on society at a wider level (see Chapter 2).

When the therapist helps the individual client think about the current stage of their family and individual system, they are able to reflect upon the different stages that they have transitioned. Transitions are considered times of opportunity and also times of challenge across cultures. However, different cultures will place different importance upon different transitions. Transitions between the different stages can be stressful and problematic for all family members, especially when individuals do not adapt and achieve the expected development between stages for whatever reason. For example, a death during the 'family with adolescents stage' can become problematic, as the bereavement will call upon the family to become closer, which will conflict with the adolescent task of separation. The

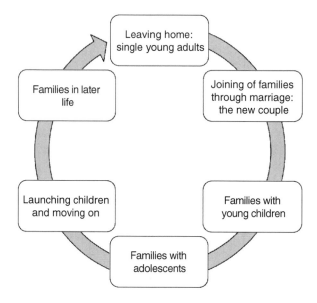

Figure 9.4 Life cycle stages.

family lifecycle model offers a helpful framework in which therapists can help individual clients organise and make sense of memories, thoughts and emotions from the past, present and into the future. This could also be a useful framework for the practitioner or helper in which to develop their own self-reflexivity of the personal transition experiences that their clients will encounter. This will help bolster their systemic self-awareness (see Chapter 10) which, as has already been said, holds even greater importance for the sole therapist working with individuals without the benefit of a co-therapist or reflecting team. Carter and McGoldrick have not ignored the individual in their family model and have incorporated a model of nine stages and individual lifecycle tasks. These are complimentary to the family lifecycle and represent the 'self in context'. The life tasks range from talking and developing empathy during infancy through to caring for self and nurturing others during early adulthood to accepting dependence and death during the aging stage (Carter and McGoldrick, 1999).

3. Values and beliefs

In Carter and McGoldrick's stages and life tasks model (1999), awareness around self-management and moral and philosophical thinking begin during adolescence. This could be seen as part of a search for identity and differentiation within the family and wider peer group, which Bowen (see Chapter 2) describes in his *Family systems theory* (1978). Bowen explains the process of the differentiated self and the achievement of an individual 'solid self', which is able to separate emotional and intellectual functioning and is able to hold beliefs, values and opinions despite relational or cultural influence or pressure. The 'pseudo self' is described as the opposite, where individuality is lost and one person is fused to another. Differentiation is supported through the process of 'coaching', which in this context, is understood to be the therapeutic guidance of an individual client to change their interactions with family members in the hope that the family members will, in reply, undergo change. Therefore, family therapy is not confined or defined by the number of family members in the therapy room and the individual client completes homework tasks with their family members, outside the therapy sessions itself. It could be said that an important factor in working with an individual is to assist their differentiation and to help them understand where their values and beliefs come from. Some clients choose therapy as they find themselves pursuing life styles which are unfulfilling. This can lead to discontentment and a desire for change when they realise that they are following a lifestyle, which they have not consciously chosen.

Fact box

Differentiation used here is similar to the Jungian concept of individuation. This is a process by which an individual consciously develops an identity and personality with a set of beliefs and values.

Circular questions (Chapter 6) are a useful tool to help individual clients understand where their beliefs and values differentiate from those of other family members. The therapist can use circular questions to explore the origins of the client's values and beliefs. Exploring how these ideas are connected or not connected to those of others and how they may be involved in the development and/or maintenance of the problem the client is seeking help with. The construction of a genogram could also be useful in this task. As already stated, genograms (McGoldrick, Gerson and Petry, 2008) are frequently used by family therapists and other professionals and are a useful tool for assessment (Chapter 3). Genograms can aid the clarification of family belief patterns and widen the understanding of the family development process and the individual client's place within it. Genograms are particularly useful when working systemically with individuals as they bring other family members into the room (if only in pictorial form) and therefore bring the family tree to life.

Task 2

Draw up a genogram (see Chapter 2), which is focused upon your career path. Think about the influences upon your choices and the internal and external stressors that have or have not had an impact upon these choices.

4. Relationships with others

The importance of understanding the client's relationships with others, especially family members, is a core belief held by systemic family therapists. It could also be said that individual clients often present with linear ideas that they are the 'problem' or that someone else is the 'problem'. Either way this is material for systemic exploration. Circular questions are a helpful tool: 'How did they discover that they were the problem and what else was happening at that time?' , 'Who else supports this idea and who would disagree?', 'What did they notice that led them to believe that someone else was to blame for the problem?', 'What is happening when they notice the person being part of the solution and not the problem?' Circular questions connect relationships with the thinking and feeling experienced within them.

A logical way of exploring the individual client's relationship with others would be to invite the 'other' into the therapy room. And even in individual work this can be possible and desirable. The physical presence of others, particularly non-family members, in therapy sessions, is a practice of narrative therapy (Chapter 8) and an idea that can be utilised when working systemically with individuals. Michael White and David Epston (1990) used the concept of the 'outsider-witness' (Myerhoff, 1986) and developed the practice of introducing non-family members as expert visitors in the therapy room. These experts have previously experienced the 'problem' the client is struggling with. The idea of interviewing and listening to an independent person links with another narrative therapy idea of the 'alternative story'. As already stated there is power held in the stories we construct about ourselves throughout our life events and the meanings we and others attribute to these life events. By inviting non-family members into the therapy room to listen and comment upon the 'story' that the client tells about themselves and their problem, the client can benefit from the recognition of their struggle by a third party. They might also be helped to see possibilities of a way forward into their own preferred future when listening to the outsider-witness's story. This concept can be further developed by the therapist working systemically with an individual through the invitation of 'significant others' to therapy sessions. 'Significant-other' visitors could be family members or friends or colleagues. As already stated, clients commonly present for individual therapy with a 'problem/issue' that they believe is situated within themselves and is therefore unrelated to their relationships. During the initial sessions, whilst the therapist explores the individual client's presenting issues, it can become apparent to the client that the 'problem' may not, after all, be intrapersonal and may in fact be interpersonal/relational and therefore it would be sensible to invite the other(s) to a therapy session. It could be said that this change in thinking about 'the problem' is a fundamental 'transformative event' (Sluzki, 1992) in the therapy process and other systemic thinkers agree (Coulehan et al., 1998). This may prove to be the most powerful shift in understanding that the therapist working systemically with an individual client achieves. The ethics of inviting outsider-witnesses and significant-others to sessions needs to be thoroughly discussed and agreed both with the individual client but also with the 'visitors'. All parties should be clear about expectations and the limits of the session to enable informed consent to be given. Whereas 'outsider-witnesses' bring their personal experience of a similar transition or issue to that of the client, 'significant-other' visitors can be utilised in therapeutic conversations about the client's past and present. It can be possible for them to share their memories and thinking about the client, which can expand the client's story and allow a different story to be heard.

5. The inner and the outer worlds

The concept of inner and outer worlds is traditionally a psychodynamic idea. Boscolo records his early struggle to integrate systemic ideas into his psychodynamic practice with individuals (Boscolo and Bertando, 1996), finding the two theories to be profoundly different. Over the years, some family therapists have questioned the possibility that an inner unconscious world could be acknowledged and could be of interest to systemic therapists (Larner, 1994; Pocock, 1995). However, our clients don't tend to make a distinction between their inner and outer worlds, and their emotional inner world can be very present in the therapy room. Bertrando (2012) describes emotions as being immediate and spontaneous communication. It could be said that all therapists regardless of their modality will empathise with this. However, usually empathy alone is not enough for change to be made. If the therapist first works empathically with this emotional communication, they can help the client find alternative ways of having conversations about their emotions and also about the root cause of the emotion. This different process may resolve the problem that they have been unable to resolve through only experiencing their emotions alone.

Narrative therapists seek to help clients find an alternative way to understand themselves and the 'problems' they seek to solve through the concepts of 'alternative stories' and the use of 're-membering' conversations (Myerhoff, 1982). Narrative therapists aim to help this process further through the use of externalisation and externalising conversations (Chapter 8). White held the view that by taking the problem from within the person and separating it to be something outside of the person, new options could emerge. When working systemically with individuals, the therapist has to put effort into bringing the client's relationships from their outer world into the room and also to make tangible their inner world. Action methods from the world of psychodrama offer a way of doing just this and have been adopted by family therapists over time.

Fact box

Action methods have been defined as 'visual and role-based approaches to individual and group work' (British Psychodrama Association, 2015).

Psychodramatist Williams (1995) states that visual and action methods allow for externalisation and facilitate a system to be redefined, and new responses to the system to be triggered. When working systemically with individuals there are different ways to externalise the problems that our clients bring. Action methods such as enactment (Minuchin, 1974; White, 2007), internalised other interviewing (Tomm *et al.*, 1998) and sculpting (Papp *et al.*, 1973; Cohen, 2006) have historically been used by family therapists to bring externalisation into their work (Chimera, 2013). An example of an enactment is shown in the structural school film and described fully in Chapter 5.

Action methods have origins in psychodrama, a method conceived by psychiatrist Jacob Moreno (1889–1974). Psychodrama creatively brings together cognitions, emotions and physical action. Action methods are a tool in this process. Williams (1995) suggests that the kind of knowing one requires in therapy cannot always be expressed in words, yet talking therapies have neglected 'seeing and doing' and have been almost exclusively based on spoken language. Sometimes clients benefit from 'doing something in action' within the therapeutic space rather than 'talking about a reaction' outside of it, and sometimes they benefit from doing both.

Action methods are experiential and Williams (1989: 16) described them as having "The ability to get quickly to the emotional and interactional 'heart of the matter'".

The action methods described here can be powerful experiences, and we suggest that you are guided by your own sense of competency and training when practising them with clients. The action method 'small world' or 'miniature sculpt' provides an opportunity for the client to experience a sense of unfamiliarity and difference in a situation that they may feel very familiar and even 'stuck' with. The concept of 'small world' originates from a number of sources including drama therapy and play therapy. Small world objects such as toy figures, miniature animals, buttons, etc., can be chosen by the client to symbolically represent aspects of the presenting problem, whether arising from their internal or external worlds, for example, depression, anxiety, relationships, work issues, conflict with family members, etc. This creates 'aesthetic distance' between the client and the presenting problem. Chesner (2008) defines this as achieving psychological separation from a person or situation and one's own sense of self and reality. The experience of temporarily separating from the reality of their problem can create opportunities for the client to view the problem differently and obtain new understanding. This could be described as 'action insight': "an insight gained by something more than a verbal process" (Sherbersky, 2014: 94).

Task 3

Think about a benign situation in your life that is causing you some difficulty. Use any objects that you have around you, e.g. paper clips, loose change, etc., to represent the people or significant features involved in the problem. Notice what happens when you move objects in and out of view.

Another action method, 'internalized other interviewing' (IOI), derives from the work of Karl Tomm (1998) and can be defined as: "A method to explore, enhance, and/or modify a client's inner experience of another person's inner experience, and potentially alter the virtual and lived relationships between the client and the other person" (Common Language for Psychotherapy (CLP), 2014). IOI calls upon the client to 'embody' the 'other' and experience another 'way of being' and can offer the therapist an opportunity to engage the client in new dialogues around familiar 'stuck' patterns of behaviour and responses. It was originally conceived to be practised in the presence of the actual 'other' to allow for live feedback from the person not being interviewed. Recognised as a method for increasing empathy between people (Burnham, 2000), IOI can be used to interview other 'subjects' such as the presenting problem, an emotion, a belief, etc. Tomm suggests that IOI has the ability to bypass a client's established defences and increase understanding when used to explore conflict in relationships. But it can be difficult for clients to answer questions as another person or problem, therefore, it should be carried out with care and compassion. It can be equally as difficult for the therapist to keep the interviewee in role and keep in mind who they are interviewing. (A demonstration of an IOI is shown in the accompanying film for this chapter.)

Another tool for this work is the theory of circular causality or circularity, which is an idea from systems theory, used to describe the process of how a system (e.g. a family) uses its own behaviour to determine what the next behaviour should be (Street, 1997). An example of circularity is shown is Figure 9.5.

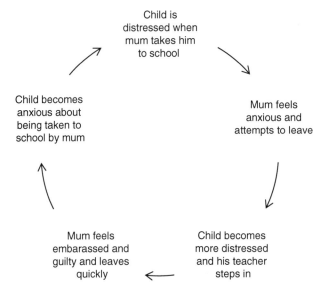

Figure 9.5 Exploration of circular processes.

From Figure 9.5, we could surmise that the next time the child is taken to school he will be significantly more distressed and cling onto his mother and refuse to let her leave, leaving her feeling significantly more upset and guilty. It can be noted that the child's behaviour influences the actions of the parent and the actions of the parent influence the subsequent child behaviours. This is mutual causality: where the behaviour of one person connects to the behaviour of another in a pattern (Chapter 2). Circularities tend to be repetitive in nature (Watzlawick *et al.*, 1967) and maintain behaviours through the process of feedback loops (Chapter 2). Therefore, they can hold useful information and it can be helpful to understand circularities more fully by tracking them with the client. When tracking circularity with an individual client, the therapist should include all others who play a part in the circularity and enquire about thoughts and emotions as well as actions (Reibstein and Sherbersky, 2012). This can be done verbally but has more impact if the therapist (or client) draws the circularity onto paper as this externalises the process and creates some objectivity between the process and the client. Once the circularity has been drawn or discussed, the therapist can help the client to identify any changes that can be made at any point in the circularity, which may lead to a different outcome. By drawing the circularity, as shown in Figure 9.5, it may be possible for the parent to identify potentially different options, e.g. the parent may need support from a teacher to enable them to leave their child or it may be decided that the child is taken to school by another family member.

Task 4

Think about a routine that you do regularly that you wish to change, e.g. a drive to work, an exercise routine, etc. and plot the steps of this from beginning to end. Remember to involve all people who play a part in it and notice your thoughts and feelings. Identify one step that you could change – what is the impact of this change?

Legacy

Working systemically with individuals requires that the therapist make a pseudo therapeutic connection with people they will (most likely) never meet for the benefit of the client they meet with. In this chapter, you have read about some different ways systemic models can be adapted to work with individuals. We have thought about systemic development in this field. The influence of social constructionist thinkers has contributed to this way of working, and because family therapists have shown an ability to undertake this kind of work, their influence in other models of psychotherapy has grown. Breunlin and Jacobsen (2014) claim that increasingly in the USA there is a focus away from whole family therapy practice on family therapy training programmes and suggest that a ratio of 1 in 20 sessions convened by family therapists are conducted with individuals. They predict this will increase, citing the difficulties in arranging whole family sessions due to the busy nature of modern family life and the cultural belief in individuality and individuation. Therefore, with this growing trend in mind it could be said that systemic work with individuals will become a more common occurrence in the UK and Europe in the years ahead.

Please access the film using the eResources tab on the webpage for the book, which can be found on the Routledge website: www.routledge.com/9781138831438

Watch film: working systemically with individuals – internalised other interview

Introduction to film

Pat is meeting alone with the therapist (Jo) in this session. You will see Jo use internalised other interviewing (IOI) in the hope that the exercise will enable Pat to be more empathic and understanding towards her daughter, Susie. This is especially important as Pat is judgemental of Susie and blames her for neglecting her granddaughters' care through drinking alcohol in the past, but is not able to see that Susie's depression impacts her ability to parent and that she drank to self-medicate.

At the start, you will notice Jo clarify that she would like to share some of the information from the individual session with the other family members, this is especially important when balancing working with individuals alongside parallel joint family work.

Jo:	Hello, Pat.
Pat:	Hi.
Jo:	Thanks for coming along on your own today to help me think about Susie and Jess. We'll need to have some time at the end to think about what we're going to share with them about the session because I think that might help them.
Pat:	Yeah I'll do anything actually because it's really starting to get me down as well.
Jo:	Susie having depression is getting you down?
Pat:	Yes, it is, I just think she needs to snap out of it because the girls are suffering,
Jo:	In what ways do you think the girls are the suffering?

Pat: Well, Susie hasn't really been there for them and she's missed out on being a mum and they've missed out on having her as a mum, seeing them growing up being able to do things with them, missed the nice times really.

Jo: So they've missed Susie being around and they've missed out on having a mum? Is there anyone else whose missed out on having Susie around?

Pat: I missed her company, we used to have, we used to have a lot of fun, we used to take the girls out, we used to go to the park with them, we used to cook with them together, you know, when they were little.

Jo: Mmm, it sounds like you really enjoyed those days,

Pat: Well, I did 'cos Susie was good company and she was funny. She had a wicked sense of humour and we used to watch … we used to like the same TV programmes, we used to watch EastEnders together, but we haven't done very much for a long time now and actually I feel like I've run out of steam,

Jo: So it sounds like you had more energy back then, is that right? Can you say why?

Pat: Well, I was younger I suppose that was part of it, and then I was ill which didn't help. But when I was younger I seemed to have more energy; I used to read with the girls, I used to listen to them, I used to spend more time with them and now I just feel flat …

Jo: And I remember you talking about having periods when you felt flat when Susie was a little girl. Is it the same as then or is it different now?

Pat: I think it's worse now, I do, yeah I think it's worse. I think it feels bigger and I kinda feel that I just need to snap out of it.

Jo: A bit like Susie with her depression?

Pat: I suppose it is, I don't know, I suppose the only way we'd know that is if we asked Susie.

Jo: Well, if Susie was here, do you think she would say that the depression is similar to your tired flat feelings or do you think she'd say something else?

Pat: I don't know, I don't know, you'd have to ask Susie. I wish I could get inside her head, I've tried often enough,

Jo: Yeah, I know it's a hard question, isn't it? It's really hard to know for sure. Do you know I just had a thought, I wonder if you might be up to doing an experiment with me?

Pat: An experiment, like what?

Skill note

When an action method like IOI is introduced as an experiment, it removes expectation of success or failure.

Jo: Yeah, it sounds weird, doesn't it? Well, I just have this idea that you might be able to talk as if you were Susie, so I could ask you some questions, a bit like an interview and you could answer as if you were Susie. How does that sound?

Pat: So you want me to pretend to be Susie?

Jo: Well yes…

Pat: Well, I'm not an actress.

Jo: No, and it's not so much about acting, Pat, it's more about you answering questions as if you were her. So, I would ask you to sit in a chair, in that chair there, the spare chair and think about what it might be like for Susie, what do you think?

Pat: Well, I can try; I don't know that I'll be any good at it, but I'll try. What do you want me to do, move there?

Jo: Yeah OK, if you're willing to give it a go, but before you move though, I just wanted to ask you a few questions to get you in the role of Susie, and then when you move I'll ask you the questions as if you were Susie. So how do you think Susie would sit in the chair?

Skill note

Jo asks questions to encourage Pat to embody Susie to get her into role.

Pat: Umm, I suppose it depends whether she was here or at home. I guess if she were at home she would slouch, but if she were here she is quite tense so she would probably be sitting up.

Jo: OK, so she'd sit up like that, and what do you think she would be wearing?

Pat: Again, if she were at home probably jeans and a sweatshirt or something like that …

Jo: OK, so I am going to ask you to move in a moment, and I just want you to bring Susie to mind and consider what she might be thinking and feeling and answer as you imagine she would answer.

Pat: OK, I'll try … right … oh gosh, this is hard … I am Susie…

Jo: Hello again, Susie, thanks for agreeing to meet today. I know we have met before, but can you just remind me a bit about yourself?

Skill note

These questions are asked to help Pat further with enrolling, to help her to think and feel as if she were Susie.

Pat: My name is Susanna, I'm 40 and I live in Bristol, and I'm a single mum with two girls. I've got Abbie who is 19 who is at university and I've got Jess who is 17 who is living at home, and I split with their father not long after Jess was born and I'm on my own now.

Jo: OK, and what do you do with your spare time? Do you, have you got any hobbies?

Pat: I used to have, used to have, but I haven't really got any hobbies now.

Jo: So what did you used to do when you did have hobbies?

Pat: Well, I suppose it depends on how old I was, I mean well after I left school, I suppose it wasn't a hobby, I worked, I worked in an estate agents and I loved that job I did. But then Susie also used to ride horses, she was brilliant when she was riding horses, she worked at the local …

Jo: So, Susie, it sounds like you enjoyed horse riding.

Pat: Sorry…

Jo: Were you a good horse rider, Susie?

Skill note

When clients are taking part in an internalised other interview, they can slip out of role. Jo notices this and gently redirects Pat back into the mind of Susie.

Pat: Umm … yes I was, yes, I was very good actually, well I was told I was good, I wasn't terribly sure, but I worked at the local livery yard and they used to let me ride some of the competition horses and I was actually doing really well and I used to compete with them and I loved it, I absolutely loved it and I even thought that it might be a way of a profession for me in the future. But as I say, well, I ended up working in the estate agents, part of that was that I found out … I got together with the girls' dad and next thing is I found out I was pregnant and you can't really compete on horses when you're pregnant so I had to give it up … yeah …

Jo: So it sounds like you had to give up something you were good at and you enjoyed. What was that like for you?

Pat: Well, I sort of lost my hopes and my dreams really. I had, yeah, I had done well and I had been … and I won quite a few competitions and I had some cups that mum put on the mantelpiece and was really proud of me, but life got in the way really …

Jo: So, I wonder what happened to your dreams?

Pat: I had to abandon them and then I had Abbie and then I had Jess and then I drank … and you know about that …

Jo: And I do know about that but I was also thinking, what did Susie's drinking do to the people around her?

Skill note

Referring to Susie in the third person could have potentially confused Pat but *she* seems to accept it. IOI can be as confusing for the therapist as it is for the client!

Pat:	It upset my mum and it upset the girls and I wasn't there for them, so I wasn't even a good mum to my girls,
Jo:	What does being a good mum mean to you?
Pat:	Being there for them, listening to them, doing things with them, yeah and for my mum to notice that I was being a good mum to my girls.
Jo:	Do you think she notices you being a good mum?
Pat:	I suppose she probably did, probably, but not recently.
Jo:	And what would it be like if she did notice more often?
Pat:	Well, I would like her to notice and I'd like her to think well of me.
Jo:	What would need to change for your mum to think well of you?
Pat:	I suppose I need to carry on not drinking and I need to keep having support yeah, I think that's probably ... I need to go on accepting support too, don't I? And I need to keep helping Jess.
Jo:	Look we're coming to the end of talking like this together but there was just one thing that I wanted to ask you first – do you think your mum can forget about the past and forget about you letting people down, is that possible?

Skill note

Jo introduces the description 'letting people down', which has not been used by the client, Pat appears to accept this, but it would have been more sensitive and attuned for Jo to reflect the client's language throughout.

Pat:	I think she could but what I need to do is to carry on accepting support, and I need to carry on helping Jess, I need to do that.
Jo:	OK, so we are at the end now, is there anything you want to say just before we finish, Susie?
Pat:	I know that mum wants me to be happy, I know she does ...
Jo:	OK, so that's the end of the experiment so if you could, you could return back to your seat, Pat.
Pat:	OK, that was very strange,
Jo:	It is very strange, so Pat, and you are Pat, aren't you? I just want to check you are Pat and not Susie?

Skill note

Jo is careful to de-role Pat once she has returned to her chair.

Pat: I am Pat and I can't believe it wasn't that difficult to be in her head. I never thought I could do that.

Jo: Were you surprised by anything you thought or anything you felt?

Pat: Yeah, I suppose I had forgotten how disappointed she must have been with her life, she's given up so much and I hadn't really thought about it 'cos she was good at her job.

JO: And it sounded like she showed great talent at horse riding, and I was thinking you must have been so proud of her?

Pat: I was, and the cups on the mantelpiece, we've still got them and I look at them, and do you know actually I hadn't looked at them? I had forgotten that they were there, you know they'd just become part of the furniture really. And yeah it was, she lost her horses, she lost her job because of the drinking, and then she was pregnant and then she was pregnant again and then she lost her husband, and it all caught up with her but it caught up with me too.

Jo: You've been through a lot as a family, haven't you? Jess has had problems with eating, Susie lost her dad, you lost your partner, the girls missed out on having their mum around and it was almost like alcohol saw its opportunity and jumped in.

Skill note

Jo utilises another form of externalisation around 'alcohol'.

Pat: Alcohol has got a lot to answer for.

Jo: It sounds like at some point Susie thought alcohol was the answer.

Pat: I think you're right.

Jo: Is there anything that you will take away from that experience?

Pat: Yeah, I had forgotten life before Pete really and how well Susie coped with the toddlers on her own and how she did a better job at being a mum than I ever did and was full of energy, whereas I was just tired and flat, you know when she was growing up so …

Summary

In the film clip, Pat is asked to take on the role of Susie whilst Jo asks her questions about herself-as-Susie. First, Jo helps Pat to get into role and embody Susie before interviewing her about her past and present family relationships. A hope for the exercise was to help Pat empathise with Susie's situation and hopefully soften her critical position towards Susie. Pat seems to remember and accept the difficulties that Susie has managed in the past. The IOI was supported through the therapist's use of externalisation and personification of Susie's 'problem': alcohol. Externalisation is not used here to take any responsibility away from Susie but to help Pat focus her criticism upon alcohol rather than Susie. De-rolling is a vital aspect of this method of working and is as important as the initial enrolling.

References

Bertrando, P. (2012). Cultural and systemic ethos in systemic therapy. In Krause, I (Ed), *Culture & reflexivity in systemic psychotherapy*. London: Karnac, pp. 115–137.

Boscolo, L and Bertrando, P. (1996). *Systemic therapy with individuals*. London: Karnac.

Bowen, M. (1978). *Family therapy in clinical practice*. New York: Jason Aronson.

Breunlin, D. and Jacobsen, E. (2014). Putting the family back into family therapy. *Family Process*, 53: 462–475.

British Psychodrama Association www.psychodrama.org.uk/what_are_action_methods. php. Accessed 02.01.15.

Burnham, J. (1992). Approach – method – technique: making distinctions and creating connections. *Human Systems*, 3: 3–27.

Burnham, J. (1993). Systemic supervision: the evolution of reflexivity in the context of the supervisory relationship. *Human Systems*, 4: 349–381.

Burnham, J. (2000). Internalized other interviewing: evaluating and enhancing empathy. *Clinical Psychology Forum*, 140: 16–20.

Burnham, J. (2012). Developments in Social GGRRAAACCEEESSS: visible-invisible and voiced-unvoiced. In Krause, I (Ed) *Culture & reflexivity in systemic psychotherapy*. London: Karnac, pp. 139–160.

Carr, A. (1986). Three techniques for the solo family therapist. *Journal of Family Therapy* 8: 373–382.

Carter, B. and McGoldrick M. (1999). *The expanded family life cycle, individual, family and social perspectives*, 3rd Ed. Boston, MA: Allyn & Bacon.

Chesner, A. (2008). A passion for action and non-action. In Shohet, R. (Ed) *Passionate Supervision*. London: Jessica Kingsley.

Chimera, C. (2013). Editorial - a hidden history of action in family therapy. *Context*, 125, April: 39–41.

CLP Common Language for Psychotherapy www.commonlanguagepsychotherapy.org/file-admin/user_upload/Accepted_procedures/internalizedotherinterv.pdf. Accessed 18.01.15.

Cohen, D. (2006). "Family Constellations": An innovative systemic phenomenological group process from Germany. *The Family Journal: Counseling and Therapy for Couples and Families*, 14: 226–233.

Coulehan, R., Friedlander, M. and Heathrington, L. (1998). A change in constructivist family therapy. *Family Process*, 37: 17–33.

Fowler, J. and Christakis, N. A. (2008). Dynamic spread of happiness in a large social network: longitudinal analysis over 20 years in the Framingham Heart Study. *BMJ*, 337: a2338.

Harré, R. (1995). The necessity of personhood as embodied being. *Theory and Psychology*, 5(3): 369–373.

Hedges, F. (2005). *An introduction to systemic therapy with individuals, a social constructionist approach.* England: Palgrave Macmillan.

Hermans, H. J. M. and Dimaggio, G. (2004). *The dialogical self in psychotherapy.* New York: Brunner & Routledge.

Larner, G. (1994). Para-modern family therapy: deconstructing postmodernism. *Australian and New Zealand Journal of Family Therapy*, 15: 11–16.

Larner, G. (1998). Through a glass darkly: narrative as destiny. *Theory and Psychology*, 1998, 8: 549–572.

McGoldrick, M., Gerson, R. and Petry S. (2008). *Genograms: assessment and intervention*, (3rd Ed). New York: W. W. W. Norton & Company.

Minuchin, S. (1974). *Families and family therapy.* London: Harvard University Press.

Myerhoff, B. (1982). Life history among the elderly: performance, visibility and re-membering. In Ruby, J. (Ed) *A crack in the mirror. Reflective perspectives in anthropology.* Philadelphia: University of Pennsylvania Press.

Myerhoff, B. (1986). Life not death in Venice: its second life. In Turner, V. and Bruner, E. (Eds) *The anthropology of experience.* Chicago: University of Illinois.

Napier, A. and Whitaker, C. (1978). *The family crucible, the intense experience of family therapy.* New York: Harper Row.

Papp, P., Silverstein, O. and Carter, E. (1973). Family sculpting in preventative work with 'well families'. *Family Process*, 12: 197–212.

Pocock, D. (1995). Searching for a better story: harnessing modern and postmodern positions in family therapy. *Journal of Family Therapy*, 17: 149–174.

Reibstein, J. and Sherbersky, H. (2012). Behavioural and empathic elements of systemic couple therapy: the Exeter Model and a case study of depression. *Journal of Family Therapy* 34: 271–283.

Rivett, M. and Street, E. (2003). *Family therapy in focus.* London: Sage.

Rivett, M. and Woodcock, J. (2015). Étapes vers la connaissance systémique du Soi dans la formation des thérapeutes de la famille. In Ackermams, A. and Canevaro, A. (Eds) *la naissance d'un thérapeute familial.* Toulouse: Éditions: 279–302.

Roper-Hall, A. (1998). Working systemically with older people and their families who have 'come to grief'. In Sutcliffe, G. Tufnell and U. Cornish (Eds) *Working with the dying & bereaved: systemic approaches to therapeutic work.* London: MacMillan, pp. 117–206.

Sherbersky, H. (2014). Integrating creative approaches within family therapy supervision. In Chesner, A. and Zografou, L. (Eds) *Creative Supervision across Modalities.* London: Jessica Kingsley Publishers, pp. 89–108.

Sluzki, C. (1992). Transformations: a blueprint for narrative changes in therapy. *Family Process*, 31: 217–230.

Street, E. (1997). Family counselling. In McMahon, G. and Palmer, S. (Eds) *Handbook of counselling*, 2nd Ed. London: Routledge, pp. 75–93.

Szapocznik, J., Kurtines, W. M., Foote, F. H., Perez-Vidal, A. and Harvis, O. (1983). Conjoint versus one-person family therapy: some evidence for the effectiveness of conducting family therapy through one person. *Journal of Consulting & Clinical Psychology*, 51: 889–899.

Tomm, K., Hoyt, M. and Madigan, S. (1998). Honoring our internalised others and the ethics of caring: a conversation with Karl Tomm. In M. Hoyt (Ed) *The handbook of constructive therapies.* Philadelphia: Brunner Routledge: 198–218.

Vaillant, G. E. (2012). *Triumphs of experience. The men of the Harvard Grant study.* Belknap Press: World.

Watzlawick, P., Beavin Bavelas, J. and Jackson, D. (1967). *Pragmatics of human communication a study of interactional patterns, pathologies and paradoxes.* New York: W. W. W. Norton & Company.

White, M. (1988/9). The externalising of the problem and the re-authoring of lives and relationships. *Dulwich Centre Newsletter*, Summer: 5–28.

White, M. (2007). *Maps of narrative practice.* New York & London: W. W. W. Norton & Company.

White, M. and Epston, D. (1990). *Narrative means to therapeutic ends.* New York & London: W. W. W. Norton & Company.

Williams, A. (1989). *The passionate technique*, New York & London: Tavistock/Routledge.

Williams, A. (1995). *Visual and active supervision: roles, focus, technique.* New York & London: W.W. W. Norton & Company.

Chapter 10

Systemic supervision
Reflective practice to enhance outcomes

Key points

- Supervision is a requirement of many professional bodies, both inside and outside of the psychological therapies.
- Systemic supervision calls upon the supervisor to be both reflective and reflexive.
- Systemic supervision has developed from different theories and methods devised by systemic thinkers over time.
- Systemic supervision can be 'live' where the supervisor is part of a therapy team or can be retrospective (as shown in the accompanying self-reflexivity film).
- Cultivation of a 'systemic mind' and 'systemic self-awareness' is a discipline, which can be developed and enhanced through supervision.
- Systemic self-awareness encourages the therapist to develop a sense of themselves in relationship to others and how this influences their practice.

Supervision within the psychotherapies has often been compared to looking into a mirror (Burck and Daniel, 2010). The idea is that by viewing your practice in a looking glass you will be able to ensure against *doing harm, recognise why you are not progressing with some families and improve outcomes for all of the people you work with.* Of course, because family therapists use a one-way screen, the mirror metaphor has a more powerful and pertinent twist. Thus, when a family therapist places their practice before a mirror, they see not only what they do and the way the families react to what they do, but also the reflection of 'ghosts' of their own experience reflected back at them. As systemic thinkers, family therapists should also look out for the 'ghosts' that influence the family's behaviour and recognise how all these different presences affect what is happening within the process of the therapy. In other words, supervision should illuminate a multitude of possibilities for understanding and intervention.

Figure 10.1 © Emily Kear. Reprinted with her kind permission.

Fact box

A reflecting team are an additional person(s) who observe the therapy session and then share their thoughts/feelings/ideas with the family and lead therapist. See Chapter 7.

Within systemic supervision, the mirror also brings with it a *three-dimensional* quality. This has something of an *Alice through the looking glass* (Carroll, 2007) experience of life. For instance, in family therapy, the supervisor may actually be 'in another world' behind the screen. The inhabitants of the 'behind the glass' world might physically enter the therapy room (as part of a reflecting team in front of the mirror), but even when they don't, they are present in the mind of the therapist in the room with the family. This process evokes not just a *reflective* approach to therapy, e.g. reflecting on what is happening, but a *reflexive* one in which the attention of the therapist comes full circle to understand how they influence what is said and done, how the systems they are embedded in influence what is said and done and how being in supervision influences what is said and done (see Figure 10.1).

This chapter provides an overview of systemic supervision based upon the accompanying film. It seeks to explore how the process of reflection and reflexive practice can improve how a family therapist works with a family. In doing this, the chapter will demonstrate what is *unique* about systemic supervision.

Seeing your reflection: making practice more conscious

One of the central purposes of the theory and techniques used by family therapists was to help the therapist remain *outside* the family system that they were working with. Systems theory, in its 'first generation' incarnation, argued that to change the system, the therapist had to observe it first. An example of this practice would be the way the Milan group used the team (Chapter 7) during the therapy session. Within our metaphor, these techniques helped the therapist observe the family as if *they* were in a mirror. This was important because, as the therapist works with the family, she or he is *inducted* into thinking like the family. She or he gets too close to be able to see 'the wood for the trees' and more subtly, she or he may even begin to *think* like the family. Family therapists have used various ideas to help the therapist avoid this process. They talk about having a 'meta-perspective', which means a perspective 'outside' or 'above' the perspective(s) that are emerging in the therapy room. Indeed, there used to be a phrase 'caring is sharing but Meta is better'. Although 'second-order' family therapy doubted that 'meta' was better, reflective ideas still maintained that the therapist needed to develop the ability to hold multiple perspectives in mind. Supervision, therefore, is fundamentally a way in which family therapists are helped to maintain this perspective.

Family therapists, like other psychotherapists, have always reflected on their work (see Johns, 1995, approach for nursing; Yelloly and Henkel, 1995, for social work; and Gibbs, 1988, for educational theory). The literature is full of case studies, analyses and theoretical debates. But they have not always had a theory about what reflection means. Schön (1983) is perhaps the most significant theorist in this area and Hoffman (2002) brought his ideas into the family therapy world. Schön (1983) argued that practices like supervision were a form of 'reflection on action' that helped the professional learn how to improve what they do. However, the purpose of this kind of reflection was to enable the professional to achieve 'reflection in action' so that *in the moment* of practice, something different could be done. Schön's ideas have tremendous similarities to both systemic theories about feedback loops and change, but also echo Bateson's ideas about finding a *difference that makes a difference*. Because family therapists were often trained in a live supervision format (with either a supervisor inside the therapy room or behind the mirror as mentioned before), 'reflection in action' was a common phenomenon anyway. Burch (see https://en.wikipedia.org/wiki/Four_stages_of_competence) proposed that trainees move from a position of unconscious incompetence to unconscious competence through the process of reflection.

Task I

Imagine what you would see if you held a mirror up when you meet a friend. Would you both exude an equal amount of interest in each other? Would you want to talk about the same things? Would you smile as much as each other? Who would talk most? What might you learn about your relationship with your friend from watching this exchange?

From these ideas, family therapists have taken a number of key practices that help them cultivate an awareness while they are working that helps them see themselves 'in the mirror', some of which they share with other psychotherapies. For instance, they aim to bring the experience of practice back to the theory, in this case the theory of systems and family functioning. It would not be unusual for a therapist to be asked in a supervision session 'what their formulation or hypothesis was'. It is very common for theory to be forgotten when therapists are 'stuck into a session'. Another common practice would be to ask the therapist to start with what their 'dilemma' or 'challenge' is when working with the family. This technique is used in the film that accompanies this chapter. The question functions as a way of bringing the therapist's awareness to their experience and encourages 'reflection on action'.

There are also practices that have emerged specifically from the systemic field which are key to how systemic supervision works. The first is simply the cultivation of a *systemic mind* within the therapist. Bateson (1972: 434) wrote that:

> The curious twist in the systemic nature of the individual [man] is that consciousness is, almost of necessity, blinded to the systemic nature of the [man] himself.

What he is arguing in this crucial statement (and throughout his work) is that holding a systemic mind is a discipline. Further, it is a discipline that should be guarded, protected and enhanced through the process of supervision.

Fact box

A linear explanation refers to the idea that problems originate from a sequential cause & effect process. Systemic thinkers believe that problems are complex, multi-faceted and therefore not straightforward in origin.

Task 2

How easy do you find 'holding a systemic mind'? Think about how often you think about yourself 'in isolation'; think about how often you might 'blame' an individual for what happens to them or those around them; think about people you have helped and how easy it is to assume there is a 'linear' explanation for what is going wrong.

Try to give yourself a score out of ten for your 'systemic quotient'. Are you happy with your score? How might your family, friends, colleagues score you? What would help you increase this score?

In a systemic supervision session, therefore, the supervisor will work hard to maintain the 'systemic mind' while inviting the therapist to activate theirs. This will be encouraged through questions about the 'whole', about 'patterns' and about 'systems'. This is shown in the film clip that accompanies this chapter.

Further reflecting practices

The way family therapists understand 'reflection' underwent a revolution when a Norwegian called Tom Andersen (1991) (see Figure 10.2) began to adapt what, initially, was a traditional Milan style form of family therapy.

Figure 10.2 Tom Andersen.
Source: mastersworks.com

Taking his cue from the developments in Post-Milan family therapy (Anderson and Goolishian, 1988; Anderson and Gehart, 2007) and the contribution of the biologists who influenced Post-Milan therapy (Maturana and Varela, 1988) (Chapter 7), Andersen (Andersen, 1991; Friedman, 1995) focused on the process of listening, speaking and hearing as the way 'difference' was introduced within family therapy. He therefore began the emphasis on *dialogue* rather than *monologue* as the process by which family therapy worked. This later became a fundamental concept in social constructionist family therapy (Chapter 2). He writes:

> When each of those engaged [in therapy] holds meanings that are somewhat different from the meanings of the others, new meanings might emerge if the meanings are exchanged during conversations. If conversations do not exist, the meanings tend to stand still.
>
> (Anderson,1991: 37)

Andersen also suggested that listening led to thinking, which also led to change. The technique (he would argue it was more a philosophy of practice than a technique) he developed to achieve this was called 'the reflecting team'. In his sessions, rather than the therapist talking to his or her team in the middle of the session, the team would come into the room where the therapist sat with the family, and the team would talk about what they had been thinking while they listened to the session. Andersen (1991, 40) says:

> This procedure gives ... a possibility to have an inner dialogue as they listen to the versions the team presents.

Task 3

Think about a time when someone said something to you that had a profound effect on how you thought, felt or behaved. How did that happen?
Can you remember how the words kept going through your mind? Or
sparked other words?

Andersen's respectful, ritualised use of 'turn taking' in listening and speaking
ensures that systemic supervision also functions as a place where supervisor and
therapist enter a conversational space (see Burck and Daniel, 2010) in which various ideas can be spoken about and heard. The reflecting team concept also rein-
forces the idea that just the process of talking can evoke useful change: it implies
a *faith* in the process of gradually uncovering different thoughts and feelings.
Metaphorically, the reflecting team is like the power of water: gently wearing
away at rocks and so exposing quartz or fossils. Systemic supervision has inher-
ited this approach to 'talking about cases' and although there is much more going
on as well, the emphasis on reflecting is central.

What might we see in the mirror of supervision?

When a family therapist looks at himself or herself in the mirror of supervision,
there are a few aspects of the 'self' that she or he is likely to notice first. The
most obvious one is their socially assigned sex. The biological body offers some
information, although for non-binary and transgendered individuals this might
have a different significance (Bigner and Wetchler, 2012). The second might be
race. Again, there is a rich systemic literature exploring how race influences both
therapy and the supervision of therapy (Krause, 2012). For instance, when a white
supervisor is supervising a black therapist, there are inevitably issues of power
and history between them. Equally, when a white therapist is working with a black
family, processes will be present even if they are not 'voiced' (Boyd-Franklin,
1989). Systemic authors have commented on the fact that there are pressures *not*
to voice these processes: discussion about race and ethnicity in supervision and
therapy are rife with shame, guilt and fears about 'getting it wrong' (Vecchio,
2008). Supervision's task is to explore these factors and help the therapist understand what they are 'ignoring' or finding hard to discuss with the family. It is also
part of supervision to help the therapist unpick the consequences for these families
of their own cultural, ethnic and other biases. As we have implied there are other
differences which are less visible such as sexual orientation, gender, cultural position, religious attitudes, class position and physical or mental ability. In Chapter
2, we explained the way that family therapy woke up to these influences in the
1980s (McGoldrick *et al.*, 2005), and we discussed how they changed the way
therapists understood families, society at large and their own theory (McGoldrick

and Hardy, 2008). In contemporary practice, it is an ethical responsibility for family therapists to reach a level of cultural competence (O'Hagan, 2001) in their clinical work. Supervision is a significant forum in which this can be explored. Burnham (2012) has provided a succinct way for family therapists to explore these differences and he has put them on axes that orientate therapists. He suggests that these 'Social GGRRAAACCEEESSS' (an acronym for: gender, geography, race, religion, age, ability, appearance, class, culture, ethnicity, education, employment, sexuality, sexual orientation and spirituality: see Chapter 9) fall between ones that are visible or invisible, voiced or unvoiced. Other systemic psychotherapists have argued that supervision is a crucial place where these dynamics can be explored and developed (Boyd, 2010; Ayo, 2010; Bond, 2010; Hernández-Wolfe and McDowell, 2014; McIntosh, 1998). It is therefore incumbent on the supervisor to help the therapist think both about any diversity issues that may be present but not spoken about in the therapy with the family. But this also should come full circle and address such issues between the supervisor and the therapist.

Task 4

Look at the film from the previous chapter and write a list of all the diversity issues that are present. These should cover language, culture, class background, educational background, age, gender, etc.

If Mark had been the supervisee in the clip that accompanies this chapter and Jo had been supervising him, how might Jo have brought these issues out within the supervision session? How might you have approached them? Which ones are visible and which ones have already been voiced? Are the invisible and unvoiced ones more numerous than the voiced and visible?

Reflexive processes in supervision

In our opening paragraphs, we noted that family therapists are uniquely able to do more than 'reflect' on their practice. Because they have a systemic orientation, they also think reflexively. What this means is that they see what happens in the mirror of supervision but they also think about what has influenced them to behave, think or feel in the way they have with that particular family. If we stay with the mirror metaphor, family therapists can *go behind the mirror* and observe what lies in that *Alice through the looking glass world.* This is called 'self-reflexivity'. Burnham (2005: 3) defines this:

> I think of self-reflexivity as a process in which a therapist makes, takes, or grasps an opportunity to observe, listen to, and question the effects of their practice, then use their responses to their observation/listening to decide 'how to go on' in … the work.

Hedges (2010: 3) states further that:

> Reflexivity is a stance that we take towards the patterns we are co-creating when we communicate.

She also notes that working with others, as many family therapists do, or receiving supervision helps this reflexive process.

There are a number of components of self-reflexivity. One has been discussed regularly by family therapists over the course of their history and has recently been called 'systemic self-awareness' (Rivett and Woodcock, 2015). Rivett and Woodcock argue that for family therapists to invite families into the relational way of thinking, they must themselves have a consciousness of themselves as relational creatures. Within this way of thinking, supervision has a function to help the therapist understand what is influencing their practice from their own family background. An example of this is the idea that there will be 'trigger' families (McGoldrick, 1982) that will bring out within the therapist some script from their own background. Other psychotherapies train their students by exposing them to regular therapy for them to develop this deep self-understanding. Very few family therapy courses do this (Williams *et al.*, 2015; Woodcock and Rivett, 2007), although Bowen influenced family therapists to set 'family homework' tasks for their students (Bregman and White, 2011; Bowen, 1972; Lieberman, 1987).

Fact box

Dr. Murray Bowen (see Figure 10.3) was an early family therapy researcher who studied family interactions by bringing whole families into a hospital setting (Weinstein, 2013). His ideas are more influential in the USA than in Europe. One of his central ideas is that family therapy is about helping individuals separate themselves from the patterns that constrain them within their family of origin.

Of course, a supervisor is not the supervisee's therapist: it is not ethical for the supervisor to create a *dual relationship* (e.g. one where a supervisor is both a therapist and an evaluator of the supervisee) with the supervisee (Lee and Nelson, 2014). However, there are ways in which the supervisor can invite the supervisee to consider why they react, behave and think in the way they do with particular families in relation to their own family experience.

Fact box

Haber and Hawley (2004) encourage students of family therapy to bring their own families into the supervision session if they experience issues with certain kinds of families. Their own families hear what their dilemmas are and then provide consultation to them about how to proceed.

Figure 10.3 Dr. Murray Bowen.
Source: courtesy of the Bowen Center

Another process that sometimes emerges in supervision is called *parallel process*. Here, the way the family respond is projected onto the therapeutic system and each system parallels the other. An example would be where a family is in conflict and the family therapy team finds itself replicating this conflict in some way. The supervisor needs to help the team or therapist reach an understanding of how they have enacted this process and encourage them to find another way of relating to the family. Again, this might be the result of their own experiences. One technique employed in team supervision is to review each team member's family tree (Rivett *et al.*, 1997). This makes conscious the kinds of dynamics that may influence the team when they are working.

Another helpful concept that contributes to family therapists becoming reflexive about their practice is that of *relational reflexivity* (Burnham, 2005). Burnham used this idea to help family therapists focus on their relationship with the *family*. He encouraged therapists to ask the family how they thought their relationship was going. He writes:

> When the therapist explicitly engages the client(s) in the process [of thinking about the conversation they are having] it becomes relationally reflexive.
>
> (Burnham, 2005: 5)

If we pick up the metaphor that we have used in this chapter, Burnham is suggesting that the therapist asks the family what *they* see in the mirror. More specifically, he is asking them what they see in terms of their relationship to the therapist. Such a method has two aims. The first is to directly create an atmosphere of collaboration, of emphasising that the therapist can listen and learn alongside the family and therefore can improve the therapeutic alliance. But it also invites the family into the 'systemic mind' that we talked about earlier. By doing this, it will hopefully increase their motivation, commitment and responsibility taking for change.

To help therapists develop this reflexive *and* systemic mind, supervisors might use relational reflexivity within their supervision practices.

Task 5

Relational reflexivity is a method used in supervision as well as in therapy. In the film, how might Mark have invited Jo into a relationally reflexive position?

He might have asked her how their interaction was going from her point of view. He might have suggested they talk about the gender dynamics of an older male supervising a younger female. What else might he have asked?

All these are tools that systemic supervisors might use to help family therapists both improve their practice *and* help families get better outcomes from therapy. Often supervisees bring cases to supervisors because they have reached what they call 'a stuck place'. All the techniques, or tools, outlined earlier in the chapter will be used by the supervisor to help the therapist find a different way through the complexities of working with families. Sometimes they will bring on an 'a-ha!' moment when the therapist grasps a way forward. Sometimes the supervisor will need to take the therapist back to the original formulation (assessment) and sometimes review the family's ability or willingness to change. Rober (1999), however, argues that these stuck moments are as much to do with the therapist as with the family. He suggests that therapy gets stalled because the therapist has lost either their courage or their optimism. Systemic supervision will evoke these experiences and help the therapist review which it is and how to progress.

Conclusion

In this chapter, we have used the metaphor of a mirror to highlight the ways that systemic ideas influence how supervision is managed within the family therapy field. We have shown how complex such a model of supervision can be and we have demonstrated in the film some of these complexities. As we have said in other chapters, this is only one of the ways that family therapists approach supervision. The literature on supervision in family or systemic psychotherapy is as varied and fulsome as within other modalities (Burck and Daniel, 2010; Campbell and Mason, 2002; Gorrell Barnes *et al.*, 2000; Todd and Storm, 2014; Lee and

Nelson, 2014). We would recommend that readers approach some of this literature to deepen their understanding of systemic supervision.

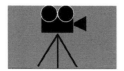

Please access the film using the eResources tab on the webpage for the book, which can
be found on the Routledge website: www.routledge.com/9781138831438

Watch film: Self-reflexivity supervision

Introduction to film

Jo has worked with Jess' family for a number of sessions. Mark, Jo's supervisor, has
observed some of these. This supervision session is designed to help Jo reflect on
her work and find 'better' ways of working with them. All family therapy practice
raises dilemmas and uncertainties and the following transcript selectively highlights
these. Mark's task is to help Jo name these and then find ways of overcoming them.

Mark: The first area to address is the issue of safety and risk.

Skill note

All supervision occurs within the context of people's lives and the dangers
that psychological problems and family relationships may cause. It is essential that therapists are aware of these factors and take them seriously and act
in a professional way around them.

Jo: There are signs of a relapse but not yet needing a more formal intervention.
Mark: So you are reasonably confident that the eating disorder is not needing
action but how about safeguarding as I have heard there are alcohol issues
in the family.
Jo: These were issues in the past but not now.

Skill note

In these conversations, the supervisor needs to be alert to the process in
which safeguarding and risk can be lost within the therapeutic relationship.
Sometimes, the supervisor will need to challenge the therapist more by asking
questions such as "what might you have missed?" or "have you noticed that
the work and the relationship you have built up prevents you thinking about
risk or safety?" Since this is a training tape, Mark does not pursue this issue.

Mark: So, I like to start supervision by asking what dilemma is uppermost in your mind when working with this family?

Skill note

Here like many supervisees, Jo names a 'balance' but it is not immediately obvious what balance she refers to. Again, close working with families means that the therapist often does not reflect and think about what is going on so the language they use makes sense to them but not to others.

Jo: I want to think about getting the balance right in working with the family. There are many complex issues: eating disorder, alcohol misuse, depression in the female line of the family.

Mark: I guess I am interested in hearing what patterns you see as maintaining these issues.

Skill note

Here Mark is seeking to help Jo get some clarity on the family dynamics that are involved in the problems: either causative or maintaining.

Jo: When I think of this family, I think of a couple of triangles really. Between Pat, Abbie and Jess, because Pat had to pick up the parenting when Susie was drinking. Also between Susie, Pat and Jess.

Mark: I recognise that … what relationship pattern does the triangle solve? How does it help this family cope?

Jo: There seems to be a history of someone always having to be on the outside … Now it is Abbie … I don't know, but there is a culture here about being single parent families.

Skill note

The supervision process evolves by encouraging the supervisee to gradually think things through. Often the supervisee answers a different question to the one they have been asked. So, Jo has not yet answered Mark's question but she is working it out!

Jo: Maybe it is a family that can only be twos ...

Mark: Is it something about exclusivity? That it is hard to have closeness with more than one person. They struggle to split loyalties. What this brings to mind is that if that is the process in the family, what do you experience as happening in the room? So, as the therapist in the room, who is working the hardest to make you build an alliance with them?

Skill note

Systemic supervision centres on the multiple levels of influence and the way different systems interact. There is a long history in family therapy of the idea of parallel process, e.g. that what happens in one system often also happens in another if the systems meet. Almost a repetition by exposure: by osmosis.

Jo: (Stops and thinks) As you were talking, I was thinking about me feeling a bit drawn towards Susie because at times it feels as if Pat and Jess gang up on Susie ... because of what she has done or failed to do in the past. But also, I feel quite drawn to Jess. I help her speak and she is 17 and has had an eating disorder and is a vulnerable girl.

Skill note

These kinds of processes can aid and destroy the therapy! If we remember the discussion in Chapter 2 about the alliance, Mark is helping Jo think through how she may unwittingly be being drawn into alliances that may potentially cause problems.

Mark: So, we now see that you are part of this triangulated family! At times you get pulled in to support Susie, at times Jess.

Skill note

What has now emerged is indeed a parallel process. Mark spells this out. Parallel process might not be a bad thing! Mark explores:

Mark: Do you think this pattern in the room is helpful? Is it replicative or corrective? So, is it repeating that idea that family members have to split each other up and not hold loyalties to more than one person, or is this pattern helping them learn something else?

Skill note

Mark is drawing on Byng-Hall's ideas about how family scripts work within families. He is also seeing if Jo can enact difference in the therapy.

Jo: I think it is a bit of both.

Skill note

This may well be true, but the point of supervision is to help the therapist offer more alternatives to the family. Mark does not choose to highlight this. Rather he decides to help Jo work out what is happening in the sessions so that she can make a choice! In this supervisory parallel process, if the therapist demonstrates the ability to choose a way of behaving, then the family are going to get the message that they can chose as well.

Mark: So as the flow of the session progresses, do you notice when it is one or other?

Jo: I am alert to it and this comes back to the balance I talked about when we started. I have had a session with Pat on her own to try and not let her feel left out. I am aware that being drawn to Jess and Susie, where does that leave Pat?

Skill note

Jo has acted in a way that prevents her alliance with Susie and Jess excluding Pat. This is again a fundamental systemic idea: powerful family member's needs need to be included somehow or they may prevent therapy achieving its goals.

Mark: I am interested while you are in the room, are you able to think … 'Now I am going to show them that I can have a relationship with two family members and not push someone out?' Are you aware of this *(agency)* or are you aware of being constantly pulled into one alliance or another alliance?

Jo: I think I have tried to be fair and fair handed *(notice how Jo interprets the question)* but probably no. In the sessions I have had so far, Susie has drawn me in.

Mark: Do you have an idea about what you can do or say in the room, which says to Susie that it is possible to be close to more than one person?

Jo: Well, I could use structural techniques, move my position; I might just notice it out loud.

Skill note

Supervision is also about extending skills: so often therapists get 'stuck' in doing what they have always done. Here Mark is stimulating a wider repertoire of skills to increase Jo's ability to help the family.

Mark: So Jo, we know these patterns happen in families and we know that the therapist gets drawn into some of them. As therapists, we often seem to be available to be drawn into certain relationships and not others. I am wondering if you as a therapist can understand why you seem to be more drawn into a relationship with Susie, a Mum labelled as alcoholic, or Jess, a vulnerable young woman?

Skill note

Supervision is not therapy and the idea that supervisors should avoid 'dual relationships' has a long tradition in family therapy. But of course there are elements of supervision that connect to therapy. Mark chooses to allow Jo to think about the question respectfully because he does not want to draw Jo into a therapeutic relationship! However, clearly there may be places where he would ask for more details. If Jo was drawn into relationships with her clients that seriously affected their problems, e.g. the therapist became part of their problems, then Mark would have a duty of care to the family to inform Jo that she should stop working with them. He may even have to make representations to the accrediting body for family therapists.

Jo: I have wondered because I do feel a bit irritated by Pat in the room. She's like a dog with a bone with the drinking. So, I am probably falling into unwittingly bolstering Susie up against these accusations. I'm not sure about Jess. I'd have to think more about that.

Mark: I thought your language there was interesting and I wonder if you have had a parent or a partner who has been a 'dog with a bone'. But I will leave that for you to think about. To go back to the opening question. Has this conversation helped you review if you have got the balance right?

Jo: I started out thinking I did have the balance right, but now I think it is too much weighted towards Susie.

Summary

Like therapy, supervision is about change. However, again like therapy, this can be challenging for the supervisee. In this film clip, Mark has encouraged Jo to think about the 'dilemma' she brought to the session. He has also helped her connect to professional responsibilities about safety and respect for all family members. Supervision therefore is a complex process with many roles and levels, but it is also a journey of discovery. The 'aim' of the journey is to create curiosity and reflexivity within the therapeutic system.

References

Anderson, H. and Gehart, D. (2007). *Collaborative therapy.* New York: Routledge.

Anderson, H. and Goolishian, H. (1988). Human systems as linguistic systems. *Family Process*, 27: 371–393.

Andersen, T. (1991). *The reflecting team.* New York: Norton.

Ayo, Y. (2010). Addressing issues of race and culture in supervision. In Burck, C. and Daniel, G. (Eds) *Mirrors and reflections: processes of systemic supervision.* London: Karnac.

Bateson, G. (1972). *Steps to an ecology of mind.* New York: Ballantine.

Bigner, J. and Wetchler, J. (2012) (Eds). *Handbook of LGBT-affirmative couple and family therapy.* New York: Routledge.

Bond, S. (2010). Putting a face to institutionalised racism. In Burck, C. and Daniel, G. (Eds) *Mirrors and reflections: processes of systemic supervision.* London: Karnac, pp. 249–266.

Bowen, M. (1972). Towards the differentiation of a self in one's own family of origin. In Framo, J. (Ed) *Family interaction: a dialogue between family reserachers and family therapists.* New York: Springer, pp. 111–173.

Boyd, E. (2010). Voice entitlement narratives in supervision. In Burck, C. and Daniel, G. (Eds) *Mirrors and reflections: processes of systemic supervision.* London: Karnac: 203–223.

Boyd-Franklin, N. (1989). *Black families in therapy.* New York: Guilford.

Bregman, O. and White, C. (2011) (Eds). *Bringing systems thinking to life.* New York: Routledge.

Burck, C. and Daniel, G. (2010). *Mirrors and reflections: processes of systemic supervision.* London: Karnac.

Burnham, J. (2005). Relational reflexivity: a tool for socially constructing therapeutic relationships. In Flaskas, C., Mason, B. and Perlesz, A. (2005) (Eds) *The space between.* London: Karnac: 1–18.

Burnham, J. (2012). Developments in Social GRRRAAACCEEESSS. In Krause, I-B. (Ed) *Mutual perspectives: culture and reflexivity in systemic psychotherapy.* London: Karnac.

Campbell, D. and Mason, B. (2002) (Eds). *Perspectives on supervision.* London: Karnac.

Carroll, L. (2007). New edition. *Alice through the looking glass.* London: Penguin.

Friedman, S. (1995) (Ed). *The reflecting team in action.* New York: Guilford.

Gibbs, G. (1988). *Learning by doing.* London: Further Education Unit.

Gorrell Barnes, G., Down, G. and McCann, D. (2000). *Systemic supervision.* London: JKP.

Haber, R. and Hawley, L. (2004). Family of origin as a supervisory consultative resource. *Family Process*, 43: 373–390.

Hedges, F. (2010). *Reflexivity in therapeutic practice.* Basingstoke: Palgrave Macmillan.

Hernández-Wolfe, P. and McDowell, T. (2014). Bridging complex identities with cultural equity and humility in systemic supervision. In Todd, T. and Storm, C. (Eds) *The complete systemic supervisor.* Chichester: Wiley & Sons, pp. 43–61.

Hoffman, L. (2002). *Family therapy: an intimate history.* New York: Norton.

Johns, C. (1995). Framing learning through reflection within Carper's fundamental ways of knowing in nursing. *Journal of Advanced Nursing,* 22: 226–234.

Krause, I-B. (2012) (Ed). *Mutual perspectives: culture and reflexivity in systemic psychotherapy.* London: Karnac.

Lee, R. and Nelson, T. (2014). *The contemporary relational supervisor.* New York: Routledge.

Lieberman, S. (1987). Going back to your own family. In Bentovim, A. Gorrell Barnes, G. and Cooklin, A. (Eds) *Family therapy: complementary frameworks of theory and practice.* London: Academic Press, pp. 205–220.

McGoldrick, M. (1982). Through the looking glass: supervision of a trainee's 'trigger' family. In Whiffen, R. and Byng-Hall, J. (Eds) *Family therapy supervision.* London: Academic Press.

McGoldrick, M., Giodano, J. and Garcia-Preto, N. (2005). *Ethnicity and family therapy.* New York: Guildford.

McGoldrick, M. and Hardy, K. (2008) (2nd edition) (Eds). *Re-visioning family therapy.* New York: Guilford.

McIntosh, P. (1998). White privilege: unpacking the invisible knapsack. In McGoldrick, M. (Ed) *Re-Visioning family therapy.* New York: Guilford: 238–249.

Maturana, H. and Varela, F. (1988). *The tree of knowledge: the biological roots of human understanding.* Boston: Shambala.

O'Hagan, K. (2001). *Cultural competence in the caring professions.* London: JKP.

Rivett, M., Tomsett, J., Lumsdon, P. and Holmes, P. (1997). Strangers in a familiar place. *Journal of Family Therapy,* 19: 43–57.

Rivett, M. and Woodcock, J. (2015). Étapes vers la connaissance systémique du Soi dans la formation des thérapeutes de la famille. In Ackermams, A. and Canevaro, A. (Eds) *la naissance d'un thérapeute familial.* Toulouse: Éditions: 279–302.

Rober, P. (1999). The therapist's inner conversation in family therapy practice: some ideas about the self of the therapist, therapeutic impasse, and the process of reflection. *Family Process,* 38: 209–228.

Schön, D. (1983). *The reflective practitioner.* London: Temple Smith.

Todd, T. and Storm, C. (2014). *The complete systemic supervisor.* Chichester: Wiley & Sons.

Vecchio, K. (2008). Dismantling white male privilege within family therapy. In McGoldrick, M. and Hardy, K. (2008) (2nd edition) (Eds). *Re-visioning family therapy.* New York: Guilford, pp. 250–260.

Weinstein, D. (2013). *The pathological family.* Ithaca: Cornell University Press.

Williams, B., Carpenter, J. and Timms, J. (2015). Family and systemic psychotherapists' experiences of personal therapeutic consultations as a tool for personal and professional development in training. *Journal of Family Therapy,* 37: 563–582.

Woodcock, J. and Rivett, M. (2007). Bringing the self into family therapy training: personal and professional consultations with trainee families. *Journal of Family Therapy,* 29: 351–354.

Yelloly, M. and Henkel, M. (1995). *Learning and teaching in social work.* London: JKP.

Epilogue
Destination or starting point?

A book can take you on a journey and since this book is about relationships, we think it is fitting to highlight that travelling on a journey is also a relational experience. Usually we share journeys with travelling companions. On this journey, a number of actors, hopefully a number of readers, and an array of family therapy teachers have accompanied us. Our intention has been to demonstrate the usefulness of ideas and techniques from the history of family therapy in the everyday practice of working with families. We hope that a range of professionals will be able to take away new skills and new ways of thinking about families from this book. The format we have adopted – text and film – has its disadvantages and inevitably we have been unable to explore or expand on everything that we might class as valuable. Despite these difficulties, the process of reading about a method, watching that method being used, reflecting upon it and then practising it, is the fundamental process of professional learning.

As writers, we are aware of where we have travelled and we think we have introduced readers to the important 'sites' on the family therapy map. Of course, we cannot predict where readers will visit, how the sites will be experienced or what future travel plans may emerge from reading this book. At the very least, we have described our own respect and deep gratitude to the originators within the field of family therapy. Their gifts to the practice of working with families are still so relevant in the contemporary world where pressures on families continue to grow; where state services seem to shrink year by year; where new interventions and 'third-sector' services seem to spring up constantly; and where the task of raising children, caring for older parents and building caring relationships, remain the challenge that they always have. In such a contemporary world the knowledge that we are fundamentally formed by connection and that we are embedded in a web of relationships continues to be a beacon of hope and a lantern of change.

Index

References to tables are denoted by the use of **bold**. References to figures are denoted by the use of *italics*.